The Reflective Practitioner

The Reflective Practitioner

HOW PROFESSIONALS THINK IN ACTION

Donald A. Schön

Basic Books, Inc., Publishers   New York

Library of Congress Cataloging in Publication Data

Schön, Donald A.
  The reflective practitioner.

  Includes bibliographical references and index.
  1. Professions. 2. Thought and thinking. 3. Self-
knowledge, Theory of. I. Title.
  HD8038.A1S35 1982   153.4   82–70855
  ISBN 0-465-06874-X (cloth)
  ISBN 0-465-06876-6 (paper)

Contents

Part III

CONCLUSION

Preface

This exploration of professional knowledge stems directly from my working life as an industrial consultant, technology manager, urban planner, policy analyst, and teacher in a professional school. Because of these experiences, the question of the relationship between the kinds of knowledge honored in academia and the kinds of competence valued in professional practice has emerged for me not only as an intellectual puzzle but as the object of a personal quest. I have become convinced that universities are not devoted to the production and distribution of fundamental knowledge in general. They are institutions committed, for the most part, to a *particular* epistemology, a view of knowledge that fosters selective inattention to practical competence and professional artistry.

This is not, of course, an unfamiliar point of view. Many people use the term "academic" in its pejorative sense. On the other hand, complaints about the elitism or obscurantism of the universities tend to be associated with a mystique of practical competence. When people use terms such as "art" and "intuition," they usually intend to terminate discussion rather than to open up inquiry. It is as though the practitioner says to his academic colleague, "While I do not accept *your* view of knowledge, I cannot describe my own." Sometimes, indeed, the practitioner appears to say, "My kind of knowledge is indescribable," or even, "I will not attempt to describe it lest I paralyze myself." These attitudes have contributed to a widening rift between the universities and the professions, research and practice, thought and action. They feed into the university's familiar dichotomy between the "hard" knowledge of science and scholarship and the "soft" knowledge of artistry and unvarnished opinion. There is nothing here to guide practitioners who wish to gain a better understanding of the practical uses and limits of research-based knowledge, or to help scholars who wish to take a new view of professional action.

We are in need of inquiry into the epistemology of practice. What is the kind of knowing in which competent practitioners engage? How is professional knowing like and unlike the kinds of knowledge presented in academic textbooks, scientific papers, and learned journals? In what sense, if any, is there intellectual rigor in professional practice?

In this book I offer an approach to epistemology of practice based on a close examination of what some practitioners—architects, psychotherapists, engineers, planners, and managers—actually do. I have collected a sample of vignettes of practice, concentrating on episodes in which a senior practitioner tries to help a junior one learn to do something. In my analysis of these cases, I begin with the assumption that competent practitioners usually know more than they can say. They exhibit a kind of knowing-in-practice, most of which is tacit. Nevertheless, starting with protocols of actual performance, it is possible to construct and test models of knowing. Indeed, practitioners themselves often reveal a capacity for reflection on their intuitive knowing in the midst of action and sometimes use this capacity to cope with the unique, uncertain, and conflicted situations of practice.

The heart of this study is an analysis of the distinctive structure of reflection-in-action. I shall argue that it is susceptible to a kind of rigor that is both like and unlike the rigor of scholarly research and controlled experiment. I shall also consider the question of its limits, some of which derive from myths about the relation of thought to action, while others are grounded in powerful features of the interpersonal and institutional contexts that we create for ourselves.

Finally, I shall suggest implications of the idea of reflective practice—implications for the professional's relation to his clients, for the organizational settings of practice, for the future interaction of research and practice, and for the place of the professions in the larger society. (The question of education for reflective practice, which I plan to treat more fully in a later book, I shall touch on very lightly here.)

The contributions I have found most helpful in this endeavor are those of people for whom research functions not as a distraction from practice but as a development of it. The late Raymond Hainer, for many years my closest friend and colleague, first made it possible for me to see the terrain I am now exploring. Chris Argyris, with whom I have worked closely for the last decade, has been a model of commitment to reflective practice. Jeanne Bamberger has introduced me to the joys and pains of close attention to the intuitive thinking revealed in the very particular phenomena of actual performance. And Martin Rein, with whom I taught several seminars on professional education, has shaped my ideas by giving me the benefit of criticisms derived from an inside view of my enterprise.

I am grateful to Yehudah Elkana, director of the Van Leer Institute in Jerusalem, who provided a hospitable environment for my writing in the spring of 1979. And I am especially in-debted to the Massachusetts Institute of Technology's Divi-sion for Study and Research in Education where I have found a climate more conducive to this work than any I believe I could have found elsewhere.

Donald A. Schön
Cambridge, Massachusetts
1982

Part I

PROFESSIONAL KNOWLEDGE AND REFLECTION-IN-ACTION

1

The Crisis
of Confidence in
Professional Knowledge

The professions have become essential to the very functioning of our society. We conduct society's principal business through professionals specially trained to carry out that business, whether it be making war and defending the nation, educating our children, diagnosing and curing disease, judging and punishing those who violate the law, settling disputes, managing industry and business, designing and constructing buildings, helping those who for one reason or another are unable to fend for themselves. Our principal formal institutions—schools, hospitals, government agencies, courts of law, armies—are arenas for the exercise of professional activity. We look to professionals for the definition and solution of our problems, and it is through them that we strive for social progress. In all of these functions we honor what Everett Hughes has called "the professions' claim to extraordinary knowledge in matters of great social importance";[1] and in return, we grant professionals extraordinary rights and privileges. Hence, professional careers are among the most coveted and remunerative, and there are few occupations that have failed to seek out professional status. As one author asked, are we seeing the professionalization of nearly everyone?[2]

But although we are wholly dependent on them, there are increasing signs of a crisis of confidence in the professions. Not only have we witnessed well-publicized scandals in which highly esteemed professionals have misused their autonomy— where doctors and lawyers, for example, have used their positions illegitimately for private gain—but we are also encountering visible failures of professional action. Professionally designed solutions to public problems have had unanticipated consequences, sometimes worse than the problems they were designed to solve. Newly invented technologies, professionally conceived and evaluated, have turned out to produce unintended side effects unacceptable to large segments of our society. A professionally conceived and managed war has been widely perceived as a national disaster. Professionals themselves have delivered widely disparate and conflicting recommendations concerning problems of national importance, including those to which professional activities have contributed.

As a result, there has been a disposition to blame the professions for their failures and a loss of faith in professional judgment. There have been strident public calls for external regulation of professional activity, efforts to create public organizations to protest and protect against professionally recommended policies, and appeals to the courts for recourse against professional incompetence. Even in the most hallowed professional schools of medicine and law, rebellious students have written popular exposés of the amoral, irrelevant, or coercive aspects of professional education.[3]

But the questioning of professionals' rights and freedoms—their license to determine who shall be allowed to practice, their mandate for social control, their autonomy—has been rooted in a deeper questioning of the professionals' claim to extraordinary knowledge in matters of human importance. This skepticism has taken several forms. In addition to the public loss of confidence noted above, there has been a virulent ideological attack on the professions, mostly from the Left. Some critics, like Ivan Illich, have engaged in a wholesale debunking of professional claims to special expertise.[4] Others have tried to show that professionals misappropriate specialized knowledge in their own interests and the interest of a power elite intent on preserving its dominance over the rest of the society.[5] Finally, and most significantly, professionals themselves have shown signs recently of a loss of confidence in their claims to extraordinary knowledge.

As short a time ago as 1963, *Daedalus,* the highly regarded journal of the American Academy of Arts and Sciences, published a volume on the professions that began, "Everywhere in American life, the professions are triumphant." The editors of *Daedalus* found evidence of triumph in the new visibility of the professions, the growing demand for their services, and their expansion in nearly all fields of practice:

We already devote an impressive percentage of the gross national product to the training of professionals . . . and the day is coming when the "knowledge industry" will occupy the same key role in the American economy that the railroad industry did a hundred years ago . . . At the midpoint of the fifteen year period (1955–1970) in which we are attempting to double the number of college professors—an awesome task which is made even more difficult by the simultaneous and equally grandiose expansion plans of all the other traditional professions, the spectacular proliferation of new professions and the increasing professionalization of business life—America has become more cognizant of the professions, and more dependent on their services, than at any previous time in our history. Thorsten Veblen's sixty-year-old dream of a professionally run society has never been closer to realization.[6]

The editors of *Daedalus* were by no means alone in their assessment of the situation. It was generally believed both that social needs for technical expertise were growing and that, as a cause and consequence of this growth, a professional knowledge industry had come into being. Richard Hofstadter wrote of the once self-sufficient "common man,"

he cannot even make his breakfast without using devices, more or less mysterious to him, which expertise has put at his disposal; and when he sits down to breakfast and looks at his morning newspaper he reads about a whole range of vital and intricate issues and acknowledges, if he is candid with himself, that he has not acquired competence to judge most of them.[7]

In his commencement address at Yale in 1962, John Kennedy had urged his young audience to "participate . . . in the solution of the problems that pour upon us, requiring the most sophisticated solutions to complex and obstinate issues."[8]

There were many references to a "second scientific revolution" which was producing a "knowledgeable society,"[9] an "active society," a "post-industrial society,"[10] organized around professional competence.

> The prodigious and increasing resources poured into research, the large and increasing numbers of trained people working on various natural and social "problems," and the expanding productivity resulting from this work is, at least in size, a new factor in social and . . . in political life. This "second scientific revolution" . . . reflects both a new appreciation of the role of scientific knowledge and a new merger of western organization and scientific skills.[11]

Professionals in the labor force had risen from 4 percent in 1900, to 8 percent in 1950, to 13 percent in 1966.[12] Daniel Bell predicted that professional and technical workers would reach 15 percent of the labor force by 1975 and might well rise to 25 percent by the year 2000.[13] "The specialist in his field must be supreme," as one commentator noted, "for who, other than another similarly qualified specialist, can challenge him?"[14] Even the critics of the professions conceded that it had become impossible to conceive of a modern nation without professions.[15]

In the meantime, as the professions geared up to meet the escalating demand for their services, they suffered from overload. In the *Daedalus* volume, the essay on medicine spoke of the overtaxed physician and of the task of coordinating the proliferating specialties which had arisen out of successful medical research and practice. The essay on science complained of the dangers to scientific professionalism inherent in the bureaucracies which had grown up around scientific research. The distinguished representative of the law stressed the difficulties in maintaining the independence of the bar, the "real problem . . . of making legal services available on a wider basis,"[16] and the problem of managing the "burgeoning mass of data to be assimilated."[17] The teacher, the military professional, even the politician, expressed similar sentiments. As Kenneth Lynn observed,

> It is notable how many of the contributors to this symposium emphasize the multiplicity of demands that are made on the contemporary clergyman, teacher, doctor and scientists.[18]

In nearly all articles, the note most sharply sounded was the problem of a success attributed, in Bernard Barber's words, to the fact that:

> the generalized knowledge and the community orientation characteristic of professional behavior are indispensable in our society as we now know it and as we want it to be. Indeed, our kind of society can now maintain its fundamental character only by enlarging the scope for professional behavior.[19]

The success of the professionals was thought to be due, in short, to the explosion of the "knowledge industry" whose output it was the function of the professional to apply with rigor, probity, and "community orientation" to the goals and problems of American life.

The only jarring voices in this hymn of confident approbation came from the representatives of divinity and city planning. James Gustafson spoke of "the clergyman's dilemma." The clergy, he observed,

> retains a loyalty to ancient traditions in thought, in institutional life and practice. Yet it cannot simply rest its case for contemporary validity in its faithfulness to the ancient and honorable paths of the fathers. The overused phrase "the problem of relevance" points to the reality of its dilemma . . . .[20]

And William Alonso spoke of his profession's "lagging understanding":

> In the past half-century our cities have outgrown our concepts and our tools, and I have tried to show how the lagging understanding of the changes in kind that go with changes in size has led us to try remedies which are unsuited to the ills of our urban areas . . . [21]

Yet in the period between 1963 and 1981, the expression of lagging understandings, unsuitable remedies, and professional dilemmas has become the norm, and the note of triumphant confidence in the knowledge industry is hardly to be heard at all. For in these years, both professional and layman have suffered through public events which have undermined belief in the competence of expertise and brought the legitimacy of the professions into serious question.

The nation had been enmeshed in a disastrous war which had caused it to seem at war with itself. The professional representatives of science, technology, and public policy had done very little to prevent or stop that war or to heal the rifts it produced. On the contrary, professionals seemed to have a vested interest in prolonging the conflict.

A series of announced national crises—the deteriorating cities, poverty, the pollution of the environment, the shortage of energy—seemed to have roots in the very practices of science, technology, and public policy that were being called upon to alleviate them.

Government-sponsored "wars" against such crises seemed not to produce the expected results; indeed, they often seemed to exacerbate the crises. The success of the space program seemed not to be replicable when the problems to be solved were the tangled socio-techno-politico-economic predicaments of public life. The concept of the "technological fix" came into bad odor. Indeed, some of the solutions advocated by professional experts were seen as having created problems as bad as or worse than those they had been designed to solve. Just as urban renewal had emerged in the early sixties as a destroyer of neighborhoods, its unexpected consequences attributed by critics like William Alonso to the weakness of its underlying theory, so in fields as diverse as housing, criminal justice, social services, welfare, and transportation, the most promising solutions, painstakingly worked out and advocated by the experts, came to be seen as problematic.[22] They were ineffective, they created new problems, they were derived from theories which had been shown to be fragile and incomplete. To some critics, the public predicaments of the society began to seem less like problems to be solved through expertise than like dilemmas whose resolutions could come about only through moral and political choice.[23]

Advocates for peace and for the civil rights of minorities joined forces and turned against the experts whom they saw as instruments of an all-powerful establishment. Around such issues as environmental pollution, consumer exploitation, the inequity and high cost of medical care, the perpetuation of social injustice, scientists and scientifically trained professionals found themselves in the unfamiliar role of villain.

Shortages became gluts. The 1970 census revealed that we had grossly overestimated the demand for teachers, at all levels of our education system. The shortage of scientists and engineers, so visible in the late 1950s, had evaporated by the mid-1960s. Even the much-discussed shortage of physicians began to seem, by the early 1970s, to be less a shortage than an unwillingness on the part of physicians to serve where they were most needed.

With the scandals of Medicare and Medicaid, with Watergate and its aftermath, the public image of the professions was further tarnished. Apparently professionals could not be counted on to police themselves, to live up to standards of probity which set them above the ethical level of the general public. Like everyone else, they seemed ready to put their special status to private use.

Cumulatively, these events not only undermined particular social programs, creating doubts about their underlying strategies of intervention and models of the world, but generated a pervasive sense of the complexity of the phenomena with which scientists and professionals in general were attempting to deal. The events of the mid-1960s and early 1970s eroded the confidence of the public, and of the professionals themselves, that there existed an armamentarium of theories and techniques sufficient to remove the troubles that beset society. Indeed, these troubles seemed, at least in part, attributable to the overweening pride of professional expertise.

In 1982, there is no profession which would celebrate itself in the triumphant tones of the 1963 *Daedalus* volume. In spite of the continuing eagerness of the young to embark on apparently secure and remunerative professional careers, the professions are in the midst of a crisis of confidence and legitimacy. In public outcry, in social criticism, and in the complaints of the professionals themselves, the long-standing professional claim to a monopoly of knowledge and social control is challenged—first, because professionals do not live up to the values and norms which they espouse, and second, because they are ineffective.

Professionals claim to contribute to social well-being, put their clients' needs ahead of their own, and hold themselves accountable to standards of competence and morality. But both popular and scholarly critics accuse the professions of serving themselves at the expense of their clients, ignoring their obligations to public service, and failing to police themselves effectively.[24] As one observer put it, "the more powerful the professions, the more serious the dangers of laxness in concern for public service and zealousness in promoting the practitioners' interests."[25] Surveys of client populations reveal a widespread belief that professionals overcharge for their services, discriminate against the poor and powerless in favor of the rich and powerful, and refuse to make themselves accountable to the public.[26] Among younger professionals and students, there are many who find the professions without real interest in the values they are supposed to promote: lawyers have no real interest in justice or compassion; physicians, in the equitable distribution of quality health care; scientists and engineers, in the beneficence and safety of their technologies.[27]

Evidence of professional ineffectiveness has been presented in scholarly and journalistic exposés of professionally managed disasters—the Vietnam War, the Bay of Pigs, the nuclear accident at Three Mile Island, the near-bankruptcy of New York City, to name only a few examples of this genre.[28] Critics have called attention to the technical expert's disposition to deploy his techniques, whatever the consequences. Charles Reich, for example, describes the Bureau of Reclamation as "a dam building machine which will keep building dams as long as there is running water in a stream in the United States . . . [without reference to] the values that dams destroy." He concludes that

professionals . . . can be counted on to do their job but not necessarily to define their job.[29]

And professionals have been loudly critical of their own failure to solve social problems, to keep from creating new problems, and to meet reasonable standards of competence in their service to their clients. In this vein, Warren Burger recently lashed out at the inadequate preparation and performance of trial lawyers in America, and David Rutstein was only among the first of many physicians to reflect publicly on the failure of the health-care system to keep pace with the enormous expansion of the nation's investment in medical research and technology.[30]

Some observers have also noted a trend toward deprofessionalization. Among such diverse professional groups as engineers, teachers, musicians, scientists, physicians, and statisticians, there has been a slackening of the labor market and a decline in economic status and working conditions, a pattern of institutional change which has been variously labelled "bureaucratization," "industrialization," or even "proletarianization" of the professions.[31] Professionals are unionizing in increasing numbers, apparently in recognition of their status as workers in a bureaucracy rather than as autonomous managers of their own careers.

The crisis of confidence in the professions, and perhaps also the decline in professional self-image, seems to be rooted in a growing skepticism about professional effectiveness in the larger sense, a skeptical reassessment of the professions' actual contribution to society's well-being through the delivery of competent services based on special knowledge. Clearly, this skepticism is bound up with the questions of professional self-interest, bureaucratization, and subordination to the interests of business or government. But it also hinges centrally on the question of professional knowledge. Is professional knowledge adequate to fulfill the espoused purposes of the professions? Is it sufficient to meet the societal demands which the professions have helped to create?

The crisis of confidence in the professions may not depend solely on the question of professional knowledge. On the other hand, even the muckrakers and radical critics, who emphasize professional self-interest and subordination to class-interest, envisage a purification and restructuring of the professions so that society may gain a fuller, more justly distributed access to the benefits of their special knowledge.[32] There remains, even for these critics, the question of the adequacy of professional knowledge to the needs and problems of society.

Let us consider, then, how the crisis of confidence in the professions has been interpreted by professionals who have given serious thought in their own fields to the adequacy of professional knowledge. On the whole, their assessment is that professional knowledge is mismatched to the changing character of the situations of practice—the complexity, uncertainty, instability, uniqueness, and value conflicts which are increasingly perceived as central to the world of professional practice.

In such fields as medicine, management, and engineering, for example, leading professionals speak of a new awareness of a complexity which resists the skills and techniques of traditional expertise. As physicians have turned their attention from traditional images of medical practice to the predicament of the larger health care system, they have come to see the larger system as a "tangled web" that traditional medical knowledge and skill cannot untangle. How can physicians influence a massively complex health care system which they do not understand and of which only a very small fraction is under their direct control?[33] The dean of a major school of management speaks of the inadequacy of established management theory and technique to deal with the increasingly critical task of "managing complexity."[34] The dean of a famous school of engineering observes that the nineteenth-century division of labor has become obsolete. Professionals are called upon to perform tasks for which they have not been educated, and "the niche no longer fits the education, or the education no longer fits the niche."[35]

Even if professional knowledge were to catch up with the new demands of professional practice, the improvement in professional performance would be transitory. The situations of practice are inherently unstable. Harvey Brooks, an eminent engineer and educator, argues that professions are now confronted with an "unprecedent requirement for adaptability":

> The dilemma of the professional today lies in the fact that both ends of the gap he is expected to bridge with his profession are changing so rapidly: the body of knowledge that he must use and the expectations of the society that he must serve. Both these changes have their origin in the same common factor— technological change . . . The problem cannot be usefully phrased in terms of too much technology. Rather it is whether we can generate technological change fast enough to meet the expectations and demands that technology itself has generated. And the four professions—medicine, engineering, business management and education—must bear the brunt of responsibility for generating and managing this change. This places on the professional a requirement for adaptability that is unprecedented.[36]

The role of the physician will be continually reshaped, over the next decades, by the reorganization and rationalization of medical care; the proliferating roles of enterprise will call for a redefinition of the businessman's role; and architects will have to function in radically new ways as a consequence of the introduction of new building technologies, new patterns of real estate and land development, and new techniques of information processing in design. As the tasks change, so will the demands for usable knowledge, and the patterns of task and knowledge are inherently unstable.[37]

The situations of practice are not problems to be solved but problematic situations characterized by uncertainty, disorder, and indeterminacy.[38] Russell Ackoff, one of the founders of the field of operations research, has recently announced to his colleagues that "the future of operations research is past"[39] because

> managers are not confronted with problems that are independent of each other, but with dynamic situations that consist of complex systems of changing problems that interact with each other. I call such situations *messes*. Problems are abstractions extracted from messes by analysis; they are to messes as atoms are to tables and charts . . . Managers do not solve problems: they manage messes.[40]

Ackoff argues that operations research has allowed itself to become identified with techniques, mathematical models, and algorithms, rather than with "the ability to formulate management problems, solve them, and implement and maintain their solutions in turbulent environments."[41] Problems are interconnected, environments are turbulent, and the future is indeterminate just in so far as managers can shape it by their actions. What is called for, under these conditions, is not only the analytic techniques which have been traditional in operations research, but the active, synthetic skill of "designing a desirable future and inventing ways of bringing it about."[42]

The situations of practice are characterized by unique events. Erik Erikson, the psychiatrist, has described each patient as "a universe of one,"[43] and an eminent physician has claimed that "85 percent of the problems a doctor sees in his office are not in the book."[44] Engineers encounter unique problems of design and are called upon to analyze failures of structures or materials under conditions which make it impossible to apply standard tests and measurements.[45] The unique case calls for an art of practice which "might be taught, if it were constant and known, but it is not constant."[46]

Practitioners are frequently embroiled in conflicts of values, goals, purposes, and interests. Teachers are faced with pressures for increased efficiency in the context of contracting budgets, demands that they rigorously "teach the basics," exhortations to encourage creativity, build citizenship, help students to examine their values. Workers in the fields of social welfare are also torn between a professional code which advocates attention to persons and bureaucratic pressure for increased efficiency in processing cases. School superintendants, industrial managers, and public administrators are asked to respond to the conflicting demands of the many different groups which hold a stake in their enterprises. Professionals engaged in research and development are not infrequently torn between a "professional" concern for technological elegance, consumer safety, or social well-being, and an institutional demand for short-term return on investment.

In some professions, awareness of uncertainty, complexity, instability, uniqueness, and value conflict has led to the emergence of professional pluralism. Competing views of professional practice—competing images of the professional role, the central values of the profession, the relevant knowledge and skills—have come into good currency. Leston Havens has written about the "babble of voices" which confuses practitioners in the field of psychotherapy.[47] Social workers have produced multiple, shifting images of the nature of their practice, as have architects and town planners.[48] Each view of professional practice represents a way of functioning in situations of indeterminacy and value conflict, but the multiplicity of conflicting views poses a predicament for the practitioner who must choose among multiple approaches to practice or devise his own way of combining them.

In sum, when leading professionals write or speak about their own crisis of confidence, they tend to focus on the mismatch of traditional patterns of practice and knowledge to features of the practice situation—complexity, uncertainty, instability, uniqueness, and value conflict—of whose importance they are becoming increasingly aware.

Surely this is a laudable exercise in self-criticism. Nevertheless, there is something puzzling about the translation of wavering confidence in professional expertise into these particular accounts of the troubles of the professions. If it is true, for example, that social reality has shifted out from under the nineteenth-century division of labor, creating new zones of complexity and uncertainty, it is also true that practitioners in such fields as management and industrial technology do sometimes find ways to make sense of complexity and reduce uncertainty to manageable risk.

If it is true that there is an irreducible element of art in professional practice, it is also true that gifted engineers, teachers, scientists, architects, and managers sometimes display artistry in their day-to-day practice. If the art is not invariant, known, and teachable, it appears nonetheless, at least for some individuals, to be learnable.

If it is true that professional practice has at least as much to do with finding the problem as with solving the problem found, it is also true that problem setting is a recognized professional activity. Some physicians reveal skills in finding the problems of particular patients in ways that go beyond the conventional boundaries of medical diagnosis. Some engineers, policy analysts, and operations researchers have become skilled at reducing "messes" to manageable plans. For some administrators, the need to "find the right problem" has become a conscious principle of action.

And if it is true, finally, that there are conflicting views of professional practice, it is also true that some practitioners do manage to make a thoughtful choice, or even a partial synthesis, from the babble of voices in their professions.

Why, then, should leading professionals and educators find these phenomena so disturbing? Surely they are not unaware of the artful ways in which some practitioners deal competently with the indeterminacies and value conflicts of practice. It seems, rather, that they are disturbed because they have no satisfactory way of describing or accounting for the artful competence which practitioners sometimes reveal in what they do. They find it unsettling to be unable to make sense of these processes in terms of the model of professional knowledge which they have largely taken for granted. Complexity, instability, and uncertainty are not removed or resolved by applying specialized knowledge to well-defined tasks. If anything, the effective use of specialized knowledge depends on a prior restructuring of situations that are complex and uncertain. An artful practice of the unique case appears anomalous when professional competence is modelled in terms of application of established techniques to recurrent events. Problem setting has no place in a body of professional knowledge concerned exclusively with problem solving. The task of choosing among competing paradigms of practice is not amenable to professional expertise.

The events which led from the "triumphant professions" of the early 1960s to the skepticism and unease of the 1970s and early 1980s have been at least as apparent to the professionals as to the general public. But the sense of confusion and unease which is discernable among leading professionals has an additional source. Professionals have been disturbed to find that they cannot account for processes they have come to see as central to professional competence. It is difficult for them to imagine how to describe and teach what might be meant by making sense of uncertainty, performing artistically, setting problems, and choosing among competing professional paradigms, when these processes seem mysterious in the light of the prevailing model of professional knowledge.

We are bound to an epistemology of practice which leaves us at a loss to explain, or even to describe, the competences to which we now give overriding importance.

From Technical
Rationality to
Reflection-in-Action

The Dominant Epistemology of Practice

According to the model of Technical Rationality—the view of professional knowledge which has most powerfully shaped both our thinking about the professions and the institutional relations of research, education, and practice—professional activity consists in instrumental problem solving made rigorous by the application of scientific theory and technique. Although all occupations are concerned, on this view, with the instrumental adjustment of means to ends, only the professions practice rigorously technical problem solving based on specialized scientific knowledge.

The model of Technical Rationality has exerted as great an influence on scholarly writing about the professions as on critical exposés of the role of the professions in the larger society. In the 1930s, for example, one of the earliest students of the professions asserted that

> it is not difficult to account in general for the emergence of the new professions. Large-scale organization has favored specialization. Specialized occupations have arisen around the new scientific knowledge.[1]

In a major book on the professions, published in 1970, Wilbert Moore embraced Alfred North Whitehead's distinction between a profession and an avocation. An avocation is "the antithesis to a profession" because it is "based upon customary activities and modified by the trial and error of individual practice."[2] In contrast, Moore said, a profession

> involves the application of general principles to specific problems, and it is a feature of modern societies that such general principles are abundant and growing.[3]

The same author argues further that professions are highly specialized occupations, and that

> the two primary bases for specialization within a profession are (1) the substantive field of knowledge that the specialist professes to command and (2) the technique of production or application of knowledge over which the specialist claims mastery.[4]

Finally, a recent critic of professional expertise sees the professional's claim to uniqueness as a " . . . preoccupation with a specialized skill premised on an underlying theory."[5]

The prototypes of professional expertise in this sense are the "learned professions" of medicine and law and, close behind these, business and engineering. These are, in Nathan Glazer's terms, the "major" or "near-major" professions.[6] They are distinct from such "minor" professions as social work, librarianship, education, divinity, and town planning. In the essay from which these terms are drawn, Glazer argues that the schools of the minor professions are hopelessly nonrigorous, dependent on representatives of academic disciplines, such as economics or political science, who are superior in status to the professions themselves. But what is of greatest interest from our point of view, Glazer's distinction between major and minor professions rests on a particularly well-articulated version of the model of Technical Rationality. The major professions are "disciplined by an unambiguous end—health, success in litigation, profit— which settles men's minds,"[7] and they operate in stable institutional contexts. Hence they are grounded in systematic, fundamental knowledge, of which scientific knowledge is the prototype,[8] or else they have "a high component of strictly technological knowledge based on science in the education which they provide."[9] In contrast, the minor professions suffer from shifting, ambiguous ends and from unstable institutional contexts of practice, and are *therefore* unable to develop a base of systematic, scientific professional knowledge. For Glazer, the development of a scientific knowledge base depends on fixed, unambiguous ends because professional practice is an instrumental activity. If applied science consists in cumulative, empirical knowledge about the means best suited to chosen ends, how can a profession ground itself in science when its ends are confused or unstable?

The systematic knowledge base of a profession is thought to have four essential properties. It is specialized, firmly bounded, scientific, and standardized. This last point is particularly important, because it bears on the paradigmatic relationship which holds, according to Technical Rationality, between a profession's knowledge base and its practice. In Wilbert Moore's words,

> If every professional problem were in all respects unique, solutions would be at best accidental, and therefore have nothing to do with expert knowledge. What we are suggesting, on the contrary, is that there are sufficient uniformities in problems and in devices for solving them to qualify the solvers as professionals . . . professionals apply very general principles, *standardized* knowledge, to concrete problems . . . [10]

This concept of "application" leads to a view of professional knowledge as a hierarchy in which "general principles" occupy the highest level and "concrete problem solving" the lowest. As Edgar Schein has put it,[11] there are three components to professional knowledge:

1. An *underlying discipline* or *basic science* component upon which the practice rests or from which it is developed.
2. An *applied science* or *"engineering"* component from which many of the day-to-day diagnostic procedures and problem-solutions are derived.
3. A *skills and attitudinal* component that concerns the actual performance of services to the client, using the underlying basic and applied knowledge.[12]

The application of basic science yields applied science. Applied science yields diagnostic and problem-solving techniques which are applied in turn to the actual delivery of services. The order of application is also an order of derivation and dependence. Applied science is said to "rest on" the foundation of basic science. And the more basic and general the knowledge, the higher the status of its producer.

When the representatives of aspiring professions consider

the problem of rising to full professional status, they often ask whether their knowledge base has the requisite properties and whether it is regularly applied to the everyday problems of practice. Thus, in an article entitled "The Librarian: From Occupation to Profession,"[13] the author states that

> the central gap is of course the failure to develop a general body of scientific knowledge bearing precisely on this problem, in the way that the medical profession with its auxiliary scientific fields has developed an immense body of knowledge with which to cure human diseases.

The sciences in which he proposes to ground his profession are "communications theory, the sociology or psychology of mass communications, or the psychology of learning as it applies to reading."[14] Unfortunately, however, he finds that

> most day-to-day professional work utilizes rather concrete rule-of-thumb local regulations and rules and major catalog systems . . . The problems of selection and organization are dealt with on a highly empiricist basis, concretely, with little reference to general scientific principles.[15]

And a social worker, considering the same sort of question, concludes that "social work is already a profession" because it has a basis in

> theory construction via systematic research. To generate valid theory that will provide a solid base for professional techniques requires the application of the scientific method to the service-related problems of the profession. Continued employment of the scientific method is nurtured by and in turn reinforces the element of *rationality* . . .[16]

It is by progressing along this route that social work seeks to "rise within the professional hierarchy so that it, too, might enjoy maximum prestige, authority, and monopoly which presently belong to a few top professions."[17]

If the model of Technical Rationality appeared only in such statements of intent, or in programmatic descriptions of professional knowledge, we might have some doubts about its dominance. But the model is also embedded in the institutional context of professional life. It is implicit in the institutionalized relations of research and practice, and in the normative curricula of professional education. Even when practitioners, educators, and researchers question the model of technical rationality, they are party to institutions that perpetuate it.

As one would expect from the hierarchical model of professional knowledge, research is institutionally separate from practice, connected to it by carefully defined relationships of exchange. Researchers are supposed to provide the basic and applied science from which to derive techniques for diagnosing and solving the problems of practice. Practitioners are supposed to furnish researchers with problems for study and with tests of the utility of research results. The researcher's role is distinct from, and usually considered superior to, the role of the practitioner.

> In the evolution of every profession there emerges the researcher-theoretician whose role is that of scientific investigation and theoretical systematization. In technological professions, a division of labor thereby evolves between the theory-oriented and the practice-oriented person. Witness the physician who prefers to attach himself to a medical research center rather than to enter private practice . . . [18]

In a similar vein, Nathan Glazer speaks of the sociologist, political scientist, or economist who, when he is invited to bring his discipline to the school of a minor profession, manifests a level of status disturbingly superior to that of the resident practitioners. And in schools of engineering, which have been transformed into schools of engineering science, the engineering scientist tends to place his superior status in the service of values different from those of the engineering profession.[19]

The hierarchical separation of research and practice is also reflected in the normative curriculum of the professional school. Here the order of the curriculum parallels the order in which the components of professional knowledge are "applied." The rule is: first, the relevant basic and applied science; then, the skills of application to real-world problems of practice. Edgar Schein's study of professional education led him to describe the dominant curricular pattern as follows:

> Most professional school curricula can be analyzed in terms of the form and timing of these three elements [of professional knowledge]. Usually the professional curriculum starts with a common science core followed by the applied science elements. The attitudinal and skill components are usually labelled "practicum" or "clinical work" and may be provided simultaneously with the applied science components or they may occur even later in the professional education, depending upon the availability of clients or the ease of simulating the realities that the professional will have to face.[20]

Schein's use of the term "skill" is of more than passing interest. From the point of view of the model of Technical Rationality institutionalized in the professional curriculum, real knowledge lies in the theories and techniques of basic and applied science. Hence, these disciplines should come first. "Skills" in the use of theory and technique to solve concrete problems should come later on, when the student has learned the relevant science—first, because he cannot learn skills of application until he has learned applicable knowledge; and secondly, because skills are an ambiguous, secondary kind of knowledge. There is something disturbing about calling them "knowledge" at all.

Again, medicine is the prototypical example. Ever since the Flexner Report, which revolutionized medical education in the early decades of this century, medical schools have devoted the first two years of study to the basic sciences—chemistry, physiology, pathology—as "the appropriate foundation for later clinical training."[21] Even the physical arrangement of the curriculum reflects the basic division among the elements of professional knowledge:

> The separation of the medical school curriculum into two disjunctive stages, the preclinical and the clinical, reflects the division between theory and practice. The division also appears in the location of training and in medical school facilities. The sciences of biochemistry, physiology, pathology and pharmacology are learned from classrooms and laboratories, that is, in formal academic settings. More practical training, in clinical arts such as internal medicine, obstetrics and pediatrics, takes place in hospital clinics, within actual institutions of delivery.[22]

And teaching roles tend to reflect the same division:

> Medical school faculties tend to be divided between the PhD's and MD's, between teachers of basic science and those in clinical programs.[23]

Even though the law might be thought to have a dubious basis in science, the introduction of the still-dominant pattern of legal education—by Christopher Columbus Langdell at Harvard University in the 1880s and 1890s—followed the normative curricular model. In his address before the Harvard Law School in 1886, Langdell argued that "first, law is a science, and secondly . . . all available materials of that science are contained in printed books."[24] Langdell claimed that legal education is better conducted in a law school than in a lawyer's office because legal study is based upon broad, scientifically determined principles which cut across state lines.

> For Langdell claimed law was a science . . . this meant that its principles could be developed from analysis of prior court decisions and could be used to predict subsequent ones. Just as Charles William Eliot was introducing the experimental laboratory into the study of natural sciences at Harvard, so it was Langdell's claim, with the study of previously decided cases.[25]

Even the famous "case method" was originally grounded in the belief that the teaching of scientific principles should precede the development of skills in their application.

In his recent review of the Harvard School of Business Administration, the school which first adapted Langdell's method to management education, Derek Bok, the current president of Harvard University, argues against case method. His argument reveals both his implicit belief in the normative curriculum of professional education and his adherence to the model of technical rationality.

Bok begins by noting that case teaching has certainly helped to keep professors "closely involved with the activities of real corporations" and has "forced them to work continuously at their teaching."[26] But he worries that

> although the case is an excellent device for teaching students to *apply* theory and technique, it does not provide an ideal way of communicating concepts and analytic methods in the first instance.[27]

Exclusive concentration on cases leaves students little time to "master analytic technique and conceptual material"—a limitation that has become more critical as "the corporate world grows more complex"—and it prevents faculty from engaging in "intensive work to develop better generalizations, theories and methods that can eventually be used to attack corporate problems in more effective ways."[28] What is especially interesting in this argument is its misreading of what many business case teachers would consider the heart of their teaching: carefully guided analysis of innumerable cases drawn from real-world business contexts in order to help students develop the generic problem-solving skills essential to effective management. Although some of the strongest advocates of case teaching admit that they cannot define these skills or relate them to general theory, they believe that the case method stands on its own unique merits.[29] President Bok has made a contrary assumption. He assumes that the business school faculty accepts both the mission to develop "better generalizations, theories and methods" and the normative idea of a curriculum which places general principles and methods before the skills of application. To faculty members who think they are engaged in a very different sort of educational enterprise, he argues from an unquestioned belief in a normative curriculum which derives from the model of Technical Rationality.

The Origins of Technical Rationality

It is striking that the dominant model of professional knowledge seems to its proponents to require very little justification. How comes it that in the second half of the twentieth century we find in our universities, embedded not only in men's minds but in the institutions themselves, a dominant view of professional knowledge as the application of scientific theory and technique to the instrumental problems of practice?

The answer to this question lies in the last three hundred years of the history of Western ideas and institutions. Technical Rationality is the heritage of Positivism, the powerful philosophical doctrine that grew up in the nineteenth century as an account of the rise of science and technology and as a social movement aimed at applying the achievements of science and technology to the well-being of mankind. Technical Rationality is the Positivist epistemology of practice. It became institutionalized in the modern university, founded in the late nineteenth century when Positivism was at its height, and in the professional schools which secured their place in the university in the early decades of the twentieth century.

Because excellent accounts of this story exist elsewhere,[30] I shall only touch on its main points here.

Since the Reformation, the history of the West has been shaped by the rise of science and technology and by the industrial movement which was both cause and consequence of the increasingly powerful scientific world-view. As the scientific world-view gained dominance, so did the idea that human progress would be achieved by harnessing science to create technology for the achievement of human ends. This Technological Program,[31] which was first vividly expressed in the writings of Bacon and Hobbes, became a major theme for the philosophers of the Enlightenment in the eighteenth century, and by the late nineteenth century had been firmly established as a pillar of conventional wisdom. By this time, too, the professions had come to be seen as vehicles for the application of the new sciences to the achievement of human progress. The engineers, closely tied to the development of industrial technology, became a model of technical practice for the other professions. Medicine, a learned profession with origins in the medieval universities, was refashioned in the new image of a science-based technique for the preservation of health. And statecraft came to be seen as a kind of social engineering. As the professions evolved and proliferated, they became, increasingly, the principal agents of the Technological Program.

As the scientific movement, industrialism, and the Technological Program became dominant in Western society, a philosophy emerged which sought both to give an account of the triumphs of science and technology and to purge mankind of the residues of religion, mysticism, and metaphysics which still prevented scientific thought and technological practice from wholly ruling over the affairs of men. It was in this spirit that, in the first half of the nineteenth century, Auguste Comte first expressed the three principal doctrines of Positivism. First, there was the conviction that empirical science was not just a form of knowledge but the only source of positive knowledge of the world. Second, there was the intention to cleanse men's minds of mysticism, superstition, and other forms of pseudo-knowledge. And finally, there was the program of extending scientific knowledge and technical control to human society, to make technology, as Comte said, "no longer exclusively geometrical, mechanical or chemical, but also and primarily political and moral."[32]

By late nineteenth century, Positivism had become a dominant philosophy. And in the early twentieth century, in the theories of the Vienna Circle, its epistemological program took on a beguiling clarity. Meaningful propositions were held to be of two kinds, either the analytic and essentially tautological propositions of logic and mathematics, or the empirical propositions which express knowledge of the world. The truth of the former was to be grounded in the fact that their negation implies a self-contradiction; the truth of the latter, in some relevant empirical observation. The only significant statements about the world were those based on empirical observation, and all disagreements about the world could be resolved, in principle, by reference to observable facts. Propositions which were neither analytically nor empirically testable were held to have no meaning at all. They were dismissed as emotive utterance, poetry, or mere nonsense.

As Positivists became increasingly sophisticated in their efforts to explain and justify the exclusivity of scientific knowledge, they recognized to what extent observational statements were theory-laden, and found it necessary to ground empirical knowledge in irreducible elements of sensory experience. They began to see laws of nature not as facts inherent in nature but as constructs created to explain observed phenomena, and science became for them a hypothetico-deductive system. In order to account for his observations, the scientist constructed hypotheses, abstract models of an unseen world which could be tested only indirectly through deductions susceptible to confirmation or disconfirmation by experiment. The heart of scientific inquiry consisted in the use of crucial experiments to choose among competing theories of explanation.

In the light of such Positivist doctrines as these, practice appeared as a puzzling anomaly. Practical knowledge exists, but it does not fit neatly into Positivist categories. We cannot readily treat it as a form of descriptive knowledge of the world, nor can we reduce it to the analytic schemas of logic and mathematics. Positivism solved the puzzle of practical knowledge in a way that had been foreshadowed by the Technological Program and by Comte's program for applying science to morality and politics. Practical knowledge was to be construed as knowledge of the relationship of means to ends. Given agreement about ends,[33] the question, "How ought I to act?" could be reduced to a merely instrumental question about the means best suited to achieve one's ends. Disagreement about means could be resolved by reference to facts concerning the possible means, their relevant consequences, and the methods for comparing them with respect to the chosen ends of action. Ultimately, the instrumental question could be resolved by recourse to experiment. And as men built up scientific understandings of cause and effect, causal relationships could be mapped onto instrumental ones. It would be possible to select the means appropriate to one's ends by applying the relevant scientific theory. The question, "How ought I to act?" could become a scientific one, and the best means could be selected by the use of science-based technique.

In the late nineteenth and early twentieth centuries, the professions of engineering and medicine achieved dramatic successes in reliably adjusting means to ends and became models of instrumental practice. The engineer's design and analysis of materials and artifacts, the physician's diagnosis and treatment of disease, became prototypes of the science-based, technical practice which was destined to supplant craft and artistry. For according to the Positivist epistemology of practice, craft and artistry had no lasting place in rigorous practical knowledge.

Universities came of age in the United States, assumed their now familiar structure and styles of operation, in the late nineteenth and early twentieth centuries when science and technology were on the rise and the intellectual hegemony of Positivism was beginning to be established. Although other traditions of thought were never wholly extinguished in American universities—indeed, in some places managed to preserve a kind of local dominance—nevertheless, in the United States more than in any other nation except Germany, the very heart of the university was given over to the scientific enterprise, to the ethos of the Technological Program, and to Positivism.

Indeed, it was from the Germanic tradition, carried to the United States after the Civil War by young American graduates of the German universities, that the new concept of the university as a multidisciplinary research institution took root in the United States, first in Johns Hopkins University, the founding of which was "perhaps the most decisive single event in the history of learning in the Western hemisphere."[34] And it was from the model of Johns Hopkins that other universities began to mold themselves around the German ideal and to manifest, as Edward Shils has written,

> a drift of opinion [toward] . . . the appreciation of knowledge, particularly knowledge of a scientific character. There was general agreement that knowledge could be accepted as knowledge only if it rested on empirical evidence, rigorously criticized and rationally analyzed . . . The knowledge which was appreciated was secular knowledge which continued the mission of sacred knowledge, complemented it, led to it, or replaced it; fundamental, systematically acquired knowledge was thought in some way to be a step toward redemption. This kind of knowledge held out the prospect of the transfiguration of life by improving man's control over the resources of nature and over the powers that weaken his body; it offered the prospect of better understanding of society which it was thought would lead to the improvement of society.[35]

With the coming of the new model of the university, the Positivist epistemology found expression in normative ideas about the proper division of labor between the university and the professions. As Thorsten Veblen argued in *The Higher Learning in America*, "The difference between the modern university and the lower and professional schools is broad and simple; not so much a difference of degree as of kind."[36] The universities have a higher mission to "fit men for a life of science and scholarship; and [they are] accordingly concerned with such discipline only as they will give efficiency in the pursuit of knowledge"; whereas the lower schools are occupied with "instilling such knowledge and habits as will make their pupils fit citizens of the world in whatever position in the fabric of workday life they may fall."[37] The proper relation between the higher and lower schools is one of separation and exchange. Quite simply, the professions are to give their practical problems to the university, and the university, the unique source of research, is to give back to the professions the new scientific knowledge which it will be their business to apply and test. Under no conditions are the technical men of the lower schools to be allowed into the university, for this would put them in a false position

> which unavoidably leads them to court a specious appearance of scholarship and so to invest their technological discipline with a degree of pedantry and sophistication; whereby it is hoped to give these schools and their work some scientific and scholarly prestige.[38]

Veblen's battle was, of course, quixotic. The evils against which he railed at the University of Chicago in 1916 were harbingers of a general trend. The survival-oriented interests of the professions reinforced the interest of university boards of governors in appropriating schools of useful knowledge. The professions did enter the new universities, in increasing numbers, until by 1963 Bernard Barber could write in *Daedalus* that "nearly all the well-established professions are located in the universities."[39]

But for this, the professionalizing occupations paid a price. They had to accept the Positivist epistemology of practice which was now built into the very tissue of the universities. And they had also to accept the fundamental division of labor on which Veblen had placed so great an emphasis. It was to be the business of university-based scientists and scholars to create the fundamental theory which professionals and technicians would apply to practice. The function of the professional school would be the transmission to its students of the generalized and systematic knowledge that is the basis of professional performance.[40]

But this division of labor reflected a hierarchy of kinds of knowledge which was also a ladder of status. Those who create new theory were thought to be higher in status than those who apply it, and the schools of "higher learning" were thought to be superior to the "lower."

Thus were planted the seeds of the Positivist curriculum, typical of professional schools in American universities, and the roots of the now-familiar split between research and practice.

Emerging Awareness of the Limits of Technical Rationality

Although it was in the early decades of the twentieth century that occupations professionalized and professional schools sought their places in the universities, it was World War II that gave a major new impetus both to the Technological Program and to the Positivist epistemology of practice.

In World War II, technologists drew upon scientific research as never before. Vannevar Bush created the first large-scale national research and development institute, the National Research and Development Corporation. The new discipline of operations research grew out of the American and British efforts to use applied mathematics for bomb tracking and submarine search. And the Manhattan project became the very symbol of the successful use of science-based technology for national ends. Its lesson seemed to be this: If a great social objective could be clearly defined, if a national commitment to it could be mustered, if unlimited resources could be poured into the necessary research and development, then any such objective could be achieved. The greatest beneficiary of this lesson was the institution of research and development itself. But as a side effect, there was also a reinforcement of the idea of scientific research as a basis for professional practice.

Following World War II, the United States government began an unparalleled increase in the rate of spending for research. As government spending for research increased, research institutions proliferated. Some were associated with the universities, others stood outside them. All were organized around the production of new scientific knowledge and were largely promoted on the basis of the proposition that the production of new scientific knowledge could be used to create wealth, achieve national goals, improve human life, and solve social problems. Nowhere was the rate of increase in research spending more dramatic, and nowhere were the results of that spending more visible, than in the field of medicine. The great centers of medical research and teaching were expanded, and new ones were created. The medical research center, with its medical school and its teaching hospital, became the institutional model to which other professions aspired. Here was a solid base of fundamental science, an equally solid body of applied clinical science, and a profession which had geared itself to implement the ever-changing products of research. Other professions, hoping to achieve some of medicine's effectiveness and prestige, sought to emulate its linkage of research and teaching institutions, its hierarchy of research and clinical roles, and its system for connecting basic and applied research to practice.

The prestige and apparent success of the medical and engineering models exerted a great attraction for the social sciences. In such fields as education, social work, planning, and policy making, social scientists attempted to do research, to apply it, and to educate practitioners, all according to their perceptions of the models of medicine and engineering. Indeed, the very language of social scientists, rich in references to measurement, controlled experiment, applied science, laboratories, and clinics, was striking in its reverence for these models.

In the mid-1950s, the Soviet launching of Sputnik gave a further impetus to national investment in science and technology. Sputnik shocked America into increased support for science, especially basic science, and created a new sense of urgency about the building of a society based on science. Suddenly we became acutely aware of a national shortage of professionals—scientists and engineers, but also physicians and teachers—who were seen as necessary to the development and application of scientific knowledge. It was the cumulative impact of these national responses to World War II and Sputnik which set the stage for the triumph of professionalism, the triumph celebrated in the *Daedalus* issue of 1963.

Between 1963 and 1982, however, both the general public and the professionals have become increasingly aware of the flaws and limitations of the professions. As I have pointed out in chapter 1, the professions have suffered a crisis of legitimacy rooted both in their perceived failure to live up to their own norms and in their perceived incapacity to help society achieve its objectives and solve its problems. Increasingly we have become aware of the importance to actual practice of phenomena—complexity, uncertainty, instability, uniqueness, and value-conflict—which do not fit the model of Technical Rationality. Now, in the light of the Positivist origins of Technical Rationality, we can more readily see why these phenomena are so troublesome.

From the perspective of Technical Rationality, professional practice is a process of problem *solving*. Problems of choice or decision are solved through the selection, from available means, of the one best suited to established ends. But with this emphasis on problem solving, we ignore problem *setting,* the process by which we define the decision to be made, the ends to be achieved, the means which may be chosen. In real-world practice, problems do not present themselves to the practitioner as givens. They must be constructed from the materials of problematic situations which are puzzling, troubling, and uncertain. In order to convert a problematic situation to a problem, a practitioner must do a certain kind of work. He must make sense of an uncertain situation that initially makes no sense. When professionals consider what road to build, for example, they deal usually with a complex and ill-defined situation in which geographic, topological, financial, economic, and political issues are all mixed up together. Once they have somehow decided what road to build and go on to consider how best to build it, they may have a problem they can solve by the application of available techniques; but when the road they have built leads unexpectedly to the destruction of a neighborhood, they may find themselves again in a situation of uncertainty.

It is this sort of situation that professionals are coming increasingly to see as central to their practice. They are coming to recognize that although problem setting is a necessary condition for technical problem solving, it is not itself a technical problem. When we set the problem, we select what we will treat as the "things" of the situation, we set the boundaries of our attention to it, and we impose upon it a coherence which allows us to say what is wrong and in what directions the situation needs to be changed. Problem setting is a process in which, interactively, we *name* the things to which we will attend and *frame* the context in which we will attend to them.

Even when a problem has been constructed, it may escape the categories of applied science because it presents itself as unique or unstable. In order to solve a problem by the application of existing theory or technique, a practitioner must be able to map those categories onto features of the practice situation. When a nutritionist finds a diet deficient in lysine, for example, dietary supplements known to contain lysine can be recommended. A physician who recognizes a case of measles can map it onto a system of techniques for diagnosis, treatment, and prognosis. But a unique case falls outside the categories of applied theory; an unstable situation slips out from under them. A physician cannot apply standard techniques to a case that is not in the books. And a nutritionist attempting a planned nutritional intervention in a rural Central American community may discover that the intervention fails because the situation has become something other than the one planned for.

Technical Rationality depends on agreement about ends. When ends are fixed and clear, then the decision to act can present itself as an instrumental problem. But when ends are confused and conflicting, there is as yet no "problem" to solve. A conflict of ends cannot be resolved by the use of techniques derived from applied research. It is rather through the non-technical process of framing the problematic situation that we may organize and clarify both the ends to be achieved and the possible means of achieving them.

Similarly, when there are conflicting paradigms of professional practice, such as we find in the pluralism of psychiatry, social work, or town planning, there is no clearly established context for the use of technique. There is contention over multiple ways of framing the practice role, each of which entrains a distinctive approach to problem setting and solving. And when practitioners do resolve conflicting role frames, it is through a kind of inquiry which falls outside the model of

Technical Rationality. Again, it is the work of naming and framing that creates the conditions necessary to the exercise of technical expertise.

We can readily understand, therefore, not only why uncertainty, uniqueness, instability, and value conflict are so troublesome to the Positivist epistemology of practice, but also why practitioners bound by this epistemology find themselves caught in a dilemma. Their definition of rigorous professional knowledge excludes phenomena they have learned to see as central to their practice. And artistic ways of coping with these phenomena do not qualify, for them, as rigorous professional knowledge.

This dilemma of "rigor or relevance" arises more acutely in some areas of practice than in others. In the varied topography of professional practice, there is a high, hard ground where practitioners can make effective use of research-based theory and technique, and there is a swampy lowland where situations are confusing "messes" incapable of technical solution. The difficulty is that the problems of the high ground, however great their technical interest, are often relatively unimportant to clients or to the larger society, while in the swamp are the problems of greatest human concern. Shall the practitioner stay on the high, hard ground where he can practice rigorously, as he understands rigor, but where he is constrained to deal with problems of relatively little social importance? Or shall he descend to the swamp where he can engage the most important and challenging problems if he is willing to forsake technical rigor?

In such "major" professions as medicine, engineering, or agronomy there are zones where practitioners can function as technical experts. But there are also zones where the major professions resemble the minor ones. Medical technologies such as kidney dialysis generate demands in excess of the nation's willingness to invest in medical care. Engineering that seems powerful and elegant when judged from a narrowly technical perspective may also carry unacceptable risks to environmental quality or human safety. Large-scale, industrialized agriculture destroys the peasant economies of the developing worlds. How should professionals take account of such issues as these?

There are those who choose the swampy lowlands. They deliberately involve themselves in messy but crucially important problems and, when asked to describe their methods of inquiry, they speak of experience, trial and error, intuition, and muddling through.

Other professionals opt for the high ground. Hungry for technical rigor, devoted to an image of solid professional competence, or fearful of entering a world in which they feel they do not know what they are doing, they choose to confine themselves to a narrowly technical practice.

The field of "formal modelling" offers an interesting context in which to observe the two responses.

During World War II, operations research grew out of the successful use of applied mathematics in submarine search and bomb tracking. After World War II, the development of the digital computer sparked widespread interest in formal, quantitative, computerized models which seemed to offer a new technique for converting "soft" problems into "hard" ones. A new breed of technical practitioner came into being. Systems analysts, management scientists, policy analysts, began to use formal modelling techniques on problems of inventory control, business policy, information retrieval, transportation planning, urban land use, the delivery of medical care, the criminal justice system, and the control of the economy. By the late 1960s, there was scarcely a described problem for which someone had not constructed a computerized model. But in recent years there has been a widening consensus, even among formal modellers, that the early hopes were greatly inflated. Formal models have been usefully employed to solve problems in such relatively undemanding areas as inventory control and logistics. They have generally failed to yield effective results in the more complex, less clearly defined problems of business management, housing policy, or criminal justice.

Formal modellers have responded to this unpleasant discovery in several different ways. Some have continued to ply their trade in the less demanding areas of the field. Some have abandoned their original training in order to address themselves to real-world problems. Others have decided to treat formal models as "probes" or "metaphors" useful only as sources of new perspectives on complex situations. But for the most part, the use of formal models has proceeded as though it had a life of its own. Driven by the evolving questions of theory and technique, formal modelling has become increasingly divergent from the real-world problems of practice. And practitioners who choose to remain on the high ground have continued to use formal models for complex problems, quite oblivious to the troubles incurred whenever a serious attempt is made to implement them.

Many practitioners have adopted this response to the dilemma of rigor or relevance, cutting the practice situation to fit professional knowledge. This they do in several ways. They may become selectively inattentive to data that fall outside their categories. Designers of management information systems may simply avoid noticing, for example, how their systems trigger games of control and evasion. They may use "junk categories" to explain away discrepant data, as technical analysts sometimes attribute the failure of their recommendations to "personality" or to "politics."[41] Or they may try to force the situation into a mold which lends itself to the use of available techniques. Thus an industrial engineer may simplify the actual arrangement of a manufacturing system in order to make it easier to analyze; or, more ominously, members of the helping professions may get rid of clients who resist professional help, relegating them to such categories as "problem tenant" or "rebellious child." All such strategies carry a danger of misreading situations, or manipulating them, to serve the practitioner's interest in maintaining his confidence in his standard models and techniques. When people are involved in the situation, the practitioner may preserve his sense of expertise at his clients' expense.

Some students of the professions have tried to take account of the limitations of technical expertise and have proposed new approaches to the predicament of professional knowledge. Among these are Edgar Schein and Nathan Glazer, whom I have already mentioned, and Herbert Simon, whose *The Sciences of the Artificial* has aroused a great deal of interest in professional circles. Each of these writers has identified a gap between professional knowledge and the demands of real-world practice. Their formulations of the gap are intriguingly different, yet they reveal an important underlying similarity.

To Schein, the gap lies in the fact that basic and applied sciences are "convergent," whereas practice is "divergent." He believes that some professions have already achieved, and that others will eventually achieve, "a high degree of consensus on the paradigms to be used in the analysis of phenomena and . . . what constitutes the relevant knowledge base for practice."[42] Nevertheless, Schein also believes that the problems of professional practice continue to have unique and unpredictable elements. One of the hallmarks of the professional, therefore, is his ability to "take a convergent knowledge base and convert it into professional services that are tailored to the *unique* requirements of the client system," a process which demands "divergent thinking skills."[43] About these, however, Schein has very little to say, and for good reason. If divergent skills could be described in terms of theory or technique, they would belong to one or another of the components of the hierarchy of professional knowledge. But if they are neither theory nor technique, and are still a kind of knowledge, how are they to be described? They must remain a mysterious, residual category.

For Glazer, the critical distinction is between kinds of professions. To professions like medicine and law Glazer attributes fixed and unambiguous ends, stable institutional contexts, and fixed contents of professional knowledge sufficient for rigorous practice. To professions such as divinity and social work he attributes ambiguous ends, shifting contexts of practice, and no fixed content of professional knowledge. Of these professions, he despairs. Thus the gap which Schein locates between "convergent" science and "divergent" practice, Glazer locates between major and minor professions.

It is Simon, however, who most clearly links the predicament of professional knowledge to the historical origins of the Positivist epistemology of practice. Simon believes that all professional practice is centrally concerned with what he calls "design," that is, with the process of "changing existing situations into preferred ones."[44] But design in this sense is precisely what the professional schools do not teach. The older schools have a knowledge of design that is "intellectually soft, intuitive, informal and cookbooky,"[45] and the newer ones, more absorbed into the general culture of the modern university, have become schools of natural science. Thus,

engineering schools have become schools of physics and mathematics; medical schools have become schools of biological science; business schools have become schools of finite mathematics.[46]

Both older and newer schools have "nearly abdicated responsibility for training in the core professional skill,"[47] in large part because such training would have to be grounded in a science of design which does not yet exist. Simon proposes to build a science of design by emulating and extending the optimization methods which have been developed in statistical decision theory and management science. An optimization problem is a well-formed problem of the following kind:

> A list of foods is provided, the command variables being quantities of the various foods that are to be included in the diet. The environmental parameters are the prices and nutritional contents (calories, vitamins, minerals, and so on) of each of the foods. The utility function is the cost (with a minus sign attached) of the diet, subject to the constraints, say, that it not contain more than 2000 calories per day, that it meet specified minimum needs for vitamins and minerals, and that rutabaga not be eaten more than once a week . . . The problem is to select the quantities of foods that will meet the nutritional requirements and side conditions at the given prices for the lowest cost.[48]

Here, ends have been converted to "constraints" and "utility functions"; means, to "command variables"; and laws, to "environmental parameters." Once problems are well formed in this way, they can be solved by a calculus of decision. As we have seen, however, well-formed instrumental problems are not given but must be constructed from messy problematic situations. Although Simon proposes to fill the gap between natural science and design practice with a science of design, his science can be applied only to well-formed problems already extracted from situations of practice.

Schein, Glazer, and Simon propose three different approaches to the limitations of Technical Rationality and the related dilemma of rigor or relevance. All three employ a common strategy, however. They try to fill the gap between the scientific basis of professional knowledge and the demands of real-world practice in such a way as to preserve the model of Technical Rationality. Schein does it by segregating convergent science from divergent practice, relegating divergence to a residual category called "divergent skill." Glazer does it by attributing convergence to the major professions, which he applauds, and divergence to the minor professions, which he dismisses. Simon does it by proposing a science of design which depends on having well-formed instrumental problems to begin with.

Yet the Positivist epistemology of practice, the model of professional knowledge to which these writers cling, has fallen into disrepute in its original home, the philosophy of science. As Richard Bernstein has written,

> There is not a single major thesis advanced by either nineteenth-century Positivists or the Vienna Circle that has not been devastatingly criticized when measured by the Positivists' own standards for philosophical argument. The original formulations of the analytic-synthetic dichotomy and the verifiability criterion of meaning have been abandoned. It has been effectively shown that the Positivists' understanding of the natural sciences and the formal disciplines is grossly oversimplified. Whatever one's final judgment about the current disputes in the post-empiricist philosophy and history of science . . . there is rational agreement about the inadequacy of the original Positivist understanding of science, knowledge and meaning.[49]

Among philosophers of science no one wants any longer to be called a Positivist, and there is a rebirth of interest in the ancient topics of craft, artistry, and myth—topics whose fate Positivism once claimed to have sealed. It seems clear, however, that the dilemma which afflicts the professions hinges not on science per se but on the Positivist view of science. From this perspective, we tend to see science, after the fact, as a body of established propositions derived from research. When we recognize their limited utility in practice, we experience the dilemma of rigor or relevance. But we may also consider science before the fact as a process in which scientists grapple with uncertainties and display arts of inquiry akin to the uncertainties and arts of practice.

Let us then reconsider the question of professional knowledge; let us stand the question on its head. If the model of Technical Rationality is incomplete, in that it fails to account for practical competence in "divergent" situations, so much the worse for the model. Let us search, instead, for an epistemology of practice implicit in the artistic, intuitive processes which some practitioners do bring to situations of uncertainty, instability, uniqueness, and value conflict.

Reflection-in-Action

When we go about the spontaneous, intuitive performance of the actions of everyday life, we show ourselves to be knowledgeable in a special way. Often we cannot say what it is that we know. When we try to describe it we find ourselves at a loss, or we produce descriptions that are obviously inappropriate. Our knowing is ordinarily tacit, implicit in our patterns of action and in our feel for the stuff with which we are dealing. It seems right to say that our knowing is *in* our action.

Similarly, the workaday life of the professional depends on tacit knowing-in-action. Every competent practitioner can recognize phenomena—families of symptoms associated with a particular disease, peculiarities of a certain kind of building site, irregularities of materials or structures—for which he cannot give a reasonably accurate or complete description. In his day-to-day practice he makes innumerable judgments of quality for which he cannot state adequate criteria, and he displays skills for which he cannot state the rules and procedures. Even when he makes conscious use of research-based theories and techniques, he is dependent on tacit recognitions, judgments, and skillful performances.

On the other hand, both ordinary people and professional practitioners often think about what they are doing, sometimes even while doing it. Stimulated by surprise, they turn thought back on action and on the knowing which is implicit in action. They may ask themselves, for example, "What features do I notice when I recognize this thing? What are the criteria by which I make this judgment? What procedures am I enacting when I perform this skill? How am I framing the problem that I am trying to solve?" Usually reflection on knowing-in-action goes together with reflection on the stuff at hand. There is some puzzling, or troubling, or interesting phenomenon with which the individual is trying to deal. As he tries to make sense of it, he also reflects on the understandings which have been implicit in his action, understandings which he surfaces, criticizes, restructures, and embodies in further action.

It is this entire process of reflection-in-action which is central to the "art" by which practitioners sometimes deal well with situations of uncertainty, instability, uniqueness, and value conflict.

Knowing-in-action. Once we put aside the model of Technical Rationality, which leads us to think of intelligent practice as an *application* of knowledge to instrumental decisions, there is nothing strange about the idea that a kind of knowing is inherent in intelligent action. Common sense admits the category of know-how, and it does not stretch common sense very much to say that the know-how is *in* the action—that a tightrope walker's know-how, for example, lies in, and is revealed by, the way he takes his trip across the wire, or that a big-league pitcher's know-how is in his way of pitching to a batter's weakness, changing his pace, or distributing his energies over the course of a game. There is nothing in common sense to make us say that know-how consists in rules or plans which we entertain in the mind prior to action. Although we sometimes think before acting, it is also true that in much of the spontaneous behavior of skillful practice we reveal a kind of knowing which does not stem from a prior intellectual operation.

As Gilbert Ryle has put it,

> What distinguishes sensible from silly operations is not their parentage but their procedure, and this holds no less for intellectual than for practical performances. "Intelligent" cannot be defined in terms of "intellectual" or "knowing *how*" in terms of "knowing *that*"; "thinking what I am doing" does not connote "both thinking what to do and doing it." When I do something intelligently . . . I am doing one thing and not two. My performance has a special procedure or manner, not special antecedents.[50]

And Andrew Harrison has recently put the same thought in this pithy phrase: when someone acts intelligently, he "acts his mind."[51]

Over the years, several writers on the epistemology of practice have been struck by the fact that skillful action often reveals a "knowing more than we can say." They have invented various names for this sort of knowing, and have drawn their examples from different domains of practice.

As early as 1938, in an essay called "Mind in Everyday Affairs," Chester Barnard distinguished "thinking processes" from "non-logical processes" which are not capable of being expressed in words or as reasoning, and which are only made known by a judgment, decision, or action.[52] Barnard's examples include judgments of distance in golf or ball-throwing, a high-school boy solving quadratic equations, and a practiced accountant who can take "a balance sheet of considerable complexity and within minutes or even seconds get a significant set of facts from it."[53] Such processes may be unconscious or they may occur so rapidly that "they could not be analyzed by the persons in whose brain they take place."[54] Of the high-school mathematician, Barnard says, memorably, "He could not write the text books which are registered in his mind."[55] Barnard believes that our bias toward thinking blinds us to the non-logical processes which are omnipresent in effective practice.

Michael Polanyi, who invented the phrase "tacit knowing," draws examples from the recognition of faces and the use of tools. If we know a person's face, we can recognize it among a thousand, indeed, among a million, though we usually cannot tell how we recognize a face we know. Similarly, we can recognize the moods of the human face without being able to tell, "except quite vaguely,"[56] by what signs we know them. When we learn to use a tool, or a probe or stick for feeling our way, our initial awareness of its impact on our hand is transformed "into a sense of its point touching the objects we are exploring."[57] In Polanyi's phrase, we attend "from" its impact on our hand "to" its effect on the things to which we are applying it. In this process, which is essential to the acquisition of a skill, the feelings of which we are initially aware become internalized in our tacit knowing.

Chris Alexander, in his *Notes Toward a Synthesis of Form*,[58] considers the knowing involved in design. He believes that we can often recognize and correct the "bad fit" of a form to its context, but that we usually cannot describe the rules by which we find a fit bad or recognize the corrected form to be good. Traditional artifacts evolve culturally through successive detections and corrections of bad fit until the resulting forms are good. Thus for generations the Slovakian peasants made beautiful shawls woven of yarns which had been dipped in homemade dyes. When aniline dyes were made available to them, "the glory of the shawls was spoiled."[59] The shawlmakers had no innate ability to make good shawls but "were simply able, as many of us are, to recognize bad shawls and their own mistakes. Over the generations . . . whenever a bad one was made, it was recognized as such, and therefore not repeated."[60] The introduction of aniline dyes disrupted the cultural process of design, for the shawlmakers could not produce wholly new designs of high quality; they could only recognize "bad fit" within a familiar pattern.

Ruminating on Alexander's example, Geoffrey Vickers points out that it is not only artistic judgments which are based on a sense of form which cannot be fully articulated:

> artists, so far from being alone in this, exhibit most clearly an oddity which is present in all such judgments. We can recognize and describe deviations from a norm very much more clearly than we can describe the norm itself.[61]

For Vickers, it is through such tacit norms that all of us make the judgments, the qualitative appreciations of situations, on which our practical competence depends.

Psycholinguists have noted that we speak in conformity with rules of phonology and syntax which most of us cannot describe.[62] Alfred Schultz and his intellectual descendants have analyzed the tacit, everyday know-how that we bring to social interactions such as the rituals of greeting, ending a meeting, or standing in a crowded elevator.[63] Birdwhistell has made comparable contributions to a description of the tacit knowledge embodied in our use and recognition of movement and gesture.[64] In these domains, too, we behave according to rules and procedures that we cannot usually describe and of which we are often unaware.

In examples like these, knowing has the following properties:

- There are actions, recognitions, and judgments which we know how to carry out spontaneously; we do not have to think about them prior to or during their performance.
- We are often unaware of having learned to do these things; we simply find ourselves doing them.
- In some cases, we were once aware of the understandings which were subsequently internalized in our feeling for the stuff of action. In other cases, we may never have been aware of them. In both cases, however, we are usually unable to describe the knowing which our action reveals.

It is in this sense that I speak of knowing-*in*-action, the characteristic mode of ordinary practical knowledge.

Reflecting-in-action. If common sense recognizes knowing-in-action, it also recognizes that we sometimes think about what we are doing. Phrases like "thinking on your feet," "keeping your wits about you," and "learning by doing" suggest not only that we can think about doing but that we can think about doing something while doing it. Some of the most interesting examples of this process occur in the midst of a performance.

Big-league baseball pitchers speak, for example, of the experience of "finding the groove":

Only a few pitchers can control the whole game with pure physical ability. The rest have to learn to adjust once they're out there. If they can't, they're dead ducks.

[You get] a special feel for the ball, a kind of command that lets you repeat the exact same thing you did before that proved successful.

Finding your groove has to do with studying those winning habits and trying to repeat them every time you perform.[65]

I do not wholly understand what it means to "find the groove." It is clear, however, that the pitchers are talking about a particular kind of reflection. What is "learning to adjust once you're out there"? Presumably it involves noticing how you have been pitching to the batters and how well it has been working, and on the basis of these thoughts and observations, changing the way you have been doing it. When you get a "feel for the ball" that lets you "repeat the exact same thing you did before that proved successful," you are noticing, at the very least, that you have been doing something right, and your "feeling" allows you to do that something again. When you "study those winning habits," you are thinking about the know-how that has enabled you to win. The pitchers seem to be talking about a kind of reflection on their patterns of action, on the situations in which they are performing, and on the know-how implicit in their performance. They are reflecting *on* action and, in some cases, reflecting *in* action.

When good jazz musicians improvise together, they also manifest a "feel for" their material and they make on-the-spot adjustments to the sounds they hear. Listening to one another and to themselves, they feel where the music is going and adjust their playing accordingly. They can do this, first of all, because their collective effort at musical invention makes use of a schema—a metric, melodic, and harmonic schema familiar to all the participants—which gives a predictable order to the piece. In addition, each of the musicians has at the ready a repertoire of musical figures which he can deliver at appropriate moments. Improvisation consists in varying, combining, and recombining a set of figures within the schema which bounds and gives coherence to the performance. As the musicians feel the direction of the music that is developing out of their interwoven contributions, they make new sense of it and adjust their performance to the new sense they have made.

They are reflecting-in-action on the music they are collectively making and on their individual contributions to it, thinking what they are doing and, in the process, evolving their way of doing it. Of course, we need not suppose that they reflect-in-action in the medium of words. More likely, they reflect through a "feel for the music" which is not unlike the pitcher's "feel for the ball."

Much reflection-in-action hinges on the experience of surprise. When intuitive, spontaneous performance yields nothing more than the results expected for it, then we tend not to think about it. But when intuitive performance leads to surprises, pleasing and promising or unwanted, we may respond by reflecting-in-action. Like the baseball pitcher, we may reflect on our "winning habits"; or like the jazz musician, on our sense of the music we have been making; or like the designer, on the misfit we have unintentionally created. In such processes, reflection tends to focus interactively on the outcomes of action, the action itself, and the intuitive knowing implicit in the action.

Let us consider an example which reveals these processes in some detail.

In an article entitled "If you want to get ahead, get a theory," Inhelder and Karmiloff-Smith[66] describe a rather unusual experiment concerning "children's processes of discovery in action."[67] They asked their subjects to balance wooden blocks on a metal bar. Some of the blocks were plain wooden blocks, but others were conspicuously or inconspicuously weighted at one end. The authors attended to the spontaneous processes by which the children tried to learn about the properties of the blocks, balance them on the bar, and regulate their actions after success or failure.

They found that virtually all children aged six to seven began the task in the same way:

all blocks were systematically first tried at their geometric center.[68]

And they found that slightly older children would not only place all blocks at their geometric center but that

> when asked to add small blocks of varying shapes and sizes to blocks already in balance, they added up to ten blocks precariously one on top of the other at the geometric center rather than distributing them at the extremities.[69]

They explain this persistent and virtually universal behavior by attributing to the children what they call a "theory-in-action": a "geometric center theory" of balancing, or, as one child put it, a theory that "things always balance in the middle."

Of course, when the children tried to balance the counterweighted blocks at their geometric centers, they failed. How did they respond to failure? Some children made what the authors called an "action-response."

> They now placed the very same blocks more and more systematically at the geometric center, with only very slight corrections around this point. They showed considerable surprise at not being able to balance the blocks a second time ("Heh, what's gone wrong with this one, it worked before") . . . Action sequences then became reduced to: Place carefully at geometric center, correct very slightly around this center, abandon all attempts, declaring the object "impossible" to balance.[70]

Other children, generally between the ages of seven and eight, responded in a very different way. When the counterweighted blocks failed to balance at their geometric centers, these children began to de-center them. They did this first with conspicuously counterweighted blocks. Then

> gradually, and often almost reluctantly, the 7 to 8 year olds began to make corrections also on the inconspicuous weight blocks

. . . At this point, we observed many pauses during action sequences on the inconspicuous weight items.[71]

Later still,

As the children were now really beginning to question the generality of their geometric center theory, a negative response at the geometric center sufficed to have the child rapidly make corrections toward the point of balance.[72]

And finally,

children paused *before* each item, roughly assessed the weight distribution of the block by lifting it ("you have to be careful, sometimes it's just as heavy on each side, sometimes it's heavier on one side"), inferred the probable point of balance and then placed the object immediately very close to it, without making any attempts at first balancing at the geometric center.[73]

The children now behaved as though they had come to hold a theory-in-action that blocks balance, not at their geometric centers, but at their centers of gravity.

This second pattern of response to error, the authors call "theory-response." Children work their way toward it through a series of stages. When they are first confronted with a number of events which refute their geometric center theories-in-action, they stop and think. Then, starting with the conspicuous-weight blocks, they begin to make corrections away from the geometric center. Finally, when they have really abandoned their earlier theories-in-action, they weigh all the blocks in their hands so as to infer the probable point of balance. As they shift their theories of balancing from geometric center to center of gravity, they also shift from a "success orientation" to a "theory orientation." Positive and negative results come to be taken not as signs of success or failure in action but as information relevant to a theory of balancing.

It is interesting to note that as the authors observe and describe this process, they are compelled to invent a language. They describe theories-in-action which the children themselves cannot describe.

> Indeed, although the (younger) child's action sequences bear eloquent witness to a theory-in-action implicit in his behavior, this should not be taken as a capacity to conceptualize explicitly on what he is doing and why.[74]

Knowing-in-action which the child may represent to himself in terms of a "feel for the blocks," the observers redescribe in terms of "theories." I shall say that they convert the child's know*ing*-in-action to know*ledge*-in-action.

A conversion of this kind seems to be inevitable in any attempt to talk about reflection-in-action. One must use words to describe a kind of knowing, and a change of knowing, which are probably not originally represented in words at all. Thus, from their observations of the children's behavior, the authors make verbal descriptions of the children's intuitive understandings. These are the authors' theories about the children's knowing-in-action. Like all such theories, they are deliberate, idiosyncratic constructions, and they can be put to experimental test:

> just as the child was constructing a theory-in-action in his endeavor to balance the blocks, so we, too, were making on-the-spot hypotheses about the child's theories and providing opportunities for negative and positive responses in order to verify our own theories![75]

Reflecting-in-practice The block-balancing experiment is a beautiful example of reflection-in-action, but it is very far removed from our usual images of professional practice. If we are to relate the idea of reflection-in-action to professional practice, we must consider what a practice is and how it is like and unlike the kinds of action we have been discussing.

The word "practice" is ambiguous. When we speak of a lawyer's practice, we mean the kinds of things he does, the kinds of clients he has, the range of cases he is called upon to handle. When we speak of someone practicing the piano, however, we mean the repetitive or experimental activity by which he tries to increase his proficiency on the instrument. In the first sense, "practice" refers to performance in a range of professional situations. In the second, it refers to preparation for performance. But professional practice also includes an element of repetition. A professional practitioner is a specialist who encounters certain types of situations again and again. This is suggested by the way in which professionals use the word "case"—or project, account, commission, or deal, depending on the profession. All such terms denote the units which make up a practice, and they denote types of family-resembling examples. Thus a physician may encounter many different "cases of measles"; a lawyer, many different "cases of libel." As a practitioner experiences many variations of a small number of types of cases, he is able to "practice" his practice. He develops a repertoire of expectations, images, and techniques. He learns what to look for and how to respond to what he finds. As long as his practice is stable, in the sense that it brings him the same types of cases, he becomes less and less subject to surprise. His knowing-in-practice tends to become increasingly tacit, spontaneous, and automatic, thereby conferring upon him and his clients the benefits of specialization.

On the other hand, professional specialization can have negative effects. In the individual, a high degree of specialization can lead to a parochial narrowness of vision. When a profession divides into subspecialties, it can break apart an earlier wholeness of experience and understanding. Thus people sometimes yearn for the general practitioner of earlier days, who is thought to have concerned himself with the "whole patient," and they sometimes accuse contemporary specialists of treating particular illnesses in isolation from the rest of the patient's life experience. Further, as a practice becomes more repetitive and routine, and as knowing-in-practice becomes increasingly tacit and spontaneous, the practitioner may miss important opportunities to think about what he is doing. He may find that, like the younger children in the block-balancing experiment, he is drawn into patterns of error which he cannot correct. And if he learns, as often happens, to be selectively inattentive to phenomena that do not fit the categories of his knowing-in-action, then he may suffer from boredom or "burn-out" and afflict his clients with the consequences of his narrowness and rigidity. When this happens, the practitioner has "over-learned" what he knows.

A practitioner's reflection can serve as a corrective to over-learning. Through reflection, he can surface and criticize the tacit understandings that have grown up around the repetitive experiences of a specialized practice, and can make new sense of the situations of uncertainty or uniqueness which he may allow himself to experience.

Practitioners do reflect *on* their knowing-in-practice. Sometimes, in the relative tranquility of a postmortem, they think back on a project they have undertaken, a situation they have lived through, and they explore the understandings they have brought to their handling of the case. They may do this in a mood of idle speculation, or in a deliberate effort to prepare themselves for future cases.

But they may also reflect on practice while they are in the

midst of it. Here they reflect-in-action, but the meaning of this term needs now to be considered in terms of the complexity of knowing-in-practice.

A practitioner's reflection-in-action may not be very rapid. It is bounded by the "action-present," the zone of time in which action can still make a difference to the situation. The action-present may stretch over minutes, hours, days, or even weeks or months, depending on the pace of activity and the situational boundaries that are characteristic of the practice. Within the give-and-take of courtroom behavior, for example, a lawyer's reflection-in-action may take place in seconds; but when the context is that of an antitrust case that drags on over years, reflection-in-action may proceed in leisurely fashion over the course of several months. An orchestra conductor may think of a single performance as a unit of practice, but in another sense a whole season is his unit. The pace and duration of episodes of reflection-in-action vary with the pace and duration of the situations of practice.

When a practitioner reflects in and on his practice, the possible objects of his reflection are as varied as the kinds of phenomena before him and the systems of knowing-in-practice which he brings to them. He may reflect on the tacit norms and appreciations which underlie a judgment, or on the strategies and theories implicit in a pattern of behavior. He may reflect on the feeling for a situation which has led him to adopt a particular course of action, on the way in which he has framed the problem he is trying to solve, or on the role he has constructed for himself within a larger institutional context.

Reflection-in-action, in these several modes, is central to the art through which practitioners sometimes cope with the troublesome "divergent" situations of practice.

When the phenomenon at hand eludes the ordinary categories of knowledge-in-practice, presenting itself as unique or unstable, the practitioner may surface and criticize his initial understanding of the phenomenon, construct a new description of it, and test the new description by an on-the-spot experiment. Sometimes he arrives at a new theory of the phenomenon by articulating a feeling he has about it.

When he finds himself stuck in a problematic situation which he cannot readily convert to a manageable problem, he may construct a new way of setting the problem—a new frame which, in what I shall call a "frame experiment," he tries to impose on the situation.

When he is confronted with demands that seem incompatible or inconsistent, he may respond by reflecting on the appreciations which he and others have brought to the situation. Conscious of a dilemma, he may attribute it to the way in which he has set his problem, or even to the way in which he has framed his role. He may then find a way of integrating, or choosing among, the values at stake in the situation.

The following are brief examples of the kinds of reflection-in-action which I shall illustrate and discuss at greater length later on.

An investment banker, speaking of the process by which he makes his judgments of investment risk, observes that he really cannot describe everything that goes into his judgments. The ordinary rules of thumb allow him to calculate "only 20 to 30 percent of the risk in investment." In terms of the rules of thumb, a company's operating numbers may be excellent. Still, if the management's explanation of the situation does not fit the numbers, or if there is something odd in the behavior of the people, that is a subject for worry which must be considered afresh in each new situation. He recalls a situation in which he spent a day with one of the largest banks in Latin America. Several new business proposals were made to him, and the bank's operating numbers seemed satisfactory. Still, he had a gnawing feeling that something was wrong. When he thought about it, it seemed that he was responding to the fact that he had been treated with a degree of deference out of all proportion to his actual position in the international world of banking. What could have led these bankers to treat him so inappropriately? When he left the bank at the end of the day, he said to his colleague, "No new business with that outfit! Let the existing obligations come in, but nothing new!" Some months later, the bank went through the biggest bankruptcy ever in Latin America—and all the time there had been nothing wrong with the numbers.

An ophthalmologist says that a great many of his patients bring problems that are not in the book. In 80 or 85 percent of the cases, the patient's complaints and symptoms do not fall into familiar categories of diagnosis and treatment. A good physician searches for new ways of making sense of such cases, and invents experiments by which to test his new hypotheses. In a particularly important family of situations, the patient suffers simultaneously from two or more diseases. While each of these, individually, lends itself to familiar patterns of thought and action, their combination may constitute a unique case that resists ordinary approaches to treatment.

The ophthalmologist recalls one patient who had inflammation of the eye (uveitis) combined with glaucoma. The treatment for glaucoma aggravated the inflammation, and the treatment for uveitis aggravated the glaucoma. When the patient came in, he was already under treatment at a level insufficient for cure but sufficient to irritate the complementary disease.

The ophthalmologist decided to remove all treatment and wait to see what would emerge. The result was that the patient's uveitis, a parasitic infection, remained in much reduced form. On the other hand, the glaucoma disappeared altogether, thus proving to have been an artifact of the treatment. The opthalmologist then began to "titrate" the patient. Working with very small quantities of drugs, he aimed not at total cure but at a reduction of symptoms which would allow the patient to go back to work. (Seven lives depended on his 5000 ocular cells!) The prognosis was not good, for uveitis moves in cycles and leaves scars behind which impede vision. But for the time being, the patient was able to work.

In his mid-thirties, sometime between the composition of his early work *The Cossacks* and his later *War and Peace,* Lev Nikolayevitch Tolstoy became interested in education. He started a school for peasant children on his estate at Yasnaya Polanya, he visited Europe to learn the latest educational methods, and he published an educational journal, also called *Yasnaya Polanya.* Before he was done (his new novel eventually replaced his interest in education), he had built some seventy schools, had created an informal teacher-training program, and had written an exemplary piece of educational evaluation.

For the most part, the methods of the European schools filled him with disgust, yet he was entranced by Rousseau's writings on education. His own school anticipated John Dewey's later approach to learning by doing, and bore the stamp of his conviction that good teaching required "not a method but an art." In an essay, "On Teaching the Rudiments," he describes his notion of art in the teaching of reading:

> Every individual must, in order to acquire the art of reading in the shortest possible time, be taught quite apart from any other, and therefore there must be a separate method for each. That which forms an insuperable difficulty to one does not in the least keep back another, and vice versa. One pupil has a good memory, and it is easier for him to memorize the syllables than to comprehend the vowellessness of the consonants; another reflects calmly and will comprehend a most rational sound method; another has

a fine instinct, and he grasps the law of word combinations by reading whole words at a time.

The best teacher will be he who has at his tongue's end the explanation of what it is that is bothering the pupil. These explanations give the teacher the knowledge of the greatest possible number of methods, the ability of inventing new methods and, above all, not a blind adherence to one method but the conviction that all methods are one-sided, and that the best method would be the one which would answer best to all the possible difficulties incurred by a pupil, that is, not a method but an art and talent.

. . . Every teacher must . . . by regarding every imperfection in the pupil's comprehension, not as a defect of the pupil, but as a defect of his own instruction, endeavor to develop in himself the ability of discovering new methods . . . [76]

An artful teacher sees a child's difficulty in learning to read not as a defect in the child but as a defect "of his own instruction." So he must find a way of explaining what is bothering the pupil. He must do a piece of experimental research, then and there, in the classroom. And because the child's difficulties may be unique, the teacher cannot assume that his repertoire of explanations will suffice, even though they are "at the tongue's end." He must be ready to invent new methods and must "endeavor to develop in himself the ability of discovering them."

Over the last two years, researchers at the Massachusetts Institute of Technology have undertaken a program of in-service education for teachers, a program organized around the idea of on-the-spot reflection and experiment, very much as in Tolstoy's art of teaching. In this Teacher Project,[77] the researchers have encouraged a small group of teachers to explore their own intuitive thinking about apparently simple tasks in such domains as mathematics, physics, music, and the perceived behavior of the moon. The teachers have made some important discoveries. They have allowed themselves to become confused about subjects they are supposed to "know"; and as they have tried to work their way out of their confusions, they have also begun to think differently about learning and teaching.

Early in the project, a critical event occured. The teachers were asked to observe and react to a videotape of two boys engaged in playing a simple game. The boys sat at a table, separated from one another by an opaque screen. In front of one boy, blocks of various colors, shapes, and sizes were arranged in a pattern. In front of the other, similar blocks were lying on the table in no particular order. The first boy was to tell the second one how to reproduce the pattern. After the first few instructions, however, it became clear that the second boy had gone astray. In fact, the two boys had lost touch with one another, though neither of them knew it.

In their initial reactions to the videotape, the teachers spoke of a "communications problem." They said that the instruction giver had "well-developed verbal skills" and that the receiver was "unable to follow directions." Then one of the researchers pointed out that, although the blocks contained no green squares—all squares were orange and only triangles were green—she had heard the first boy tell the second to "take a green square." When the teachers watched the videotape again, they were astonished. That small mistake had set off a chain of false moves. The second boy had put a green thing, a triangle, where the first boy's pattern had an orange square, and from then on all the instructions became problematic. Under the circumstances, the second boy seemed to have displayed considerable ingenuity in his attempts to reconcile the instructions with the pattern before him.

At this point, the teachers reversed their picture of the situation. They could see why the second boy behaved as he did. He no longer seemed stupid; he had, indeed, "followed instructions." As one teacher put it, they were now "giving him reason." They saw reasons for his behavior; and his errors, which they had previously seen as an inability to follow directions, they now found reasonable.

Later on in the project, as the teachers increasingly challenged themselves to discover the meanings of a child's puzzling behavior, they often spoke of "giving him reason."

In examples such as these, something falls outside the range of ordinary expectations. The banker has a feeling that something is wrong, though he cannot at first say what it is. The physician sees an odd combination of diseases never before described in a medical text. Tolstoy thinks of each of his pupils as an individual with ways of learning and imperfections peculiar to himself. The teachers are astonished by the sense behind a student's mistake. In each instance, the practitioner allows himself to experience surprise, puzzlement, or confusion in a situation which he finds uncertain or unique. He reflects on the phenomena before him, and on the prior understandings which have been implicit in his behavior. He carries out an experiment which serves to generate both a new understanding of the phenomena and a change in the situation.

When someone reflects-in-action, he becomes a researcher in the practice context. He is not dependent on the categories of established theory and technique, but constructs a new theory of the unique case. His inquiry is not limited to a deliberation about means which depends on a prior agreement about ends. He does not keep means and ends separate, but defines them interactively as he frames a problematic situation. He does not separate thinking from doing, ratiocinating his way to a decision which he must later convert to action. Because his experimenting is a kind of action, implementation is built into his inquiry. Thus reflection-in-action can proceed, even in situations of uncertainty or uniqueness, because it is not bound by the dichotomies of Technical Rationality.

Although reflection-in-action is an extraordinary process, it is not a rare event. Indeed, for some reflective practitioners it is the core of practice. Nevertheless, because professionalism is still mainly identified with technical expertise, reflection-in-action is not generally accepted—even by those who do it—as a legitimate form of professional knowing.

Many practitioners, locked into a view of themselves as technical experts, find nothing in the world of practice to occasion reflection. They have become too skillful at techniques of selective inattention, junk categories, and situational control, techniques which they use to preserve the constancy of their knowledge-in-practice. For them, uncertainty is a threat; its admission is a sign of weakness. Others, more inclined toward and adept at reflection-in-action, nevertheless feel profoundly uneasy because they cannot say what they know how to do, cannot justify its quality or rigor.

For these reasons, the study of reflection-in-action is critically important. The dilemma of rigor or relevance may be dissolved if we can develop an epistemology of practice which places technical problem solving within a broader context of reflective inquiry, shows how reflection-in-action may be rigorous in its own right, and links the art of practice in uncertainty and uniqueness to the scientist's art of research. We may thereby increase the legitimacy of reflection-in-action and encourage its broader, deeper, and more rigorous use.

Part II

PROFESSIONAL CONTEXTS FOR REFLECTION-IN-ACTION

Introduction

In the six chapters of part II, we will explore examples of professional practice in the light of the following questions:

- In practice of various kinds, what form does reflection-in-action take? What are the differences, and what features of the process are similar?
- Reflection-in-action may be directed to strategies, theories, frames, or role frames. How do these processes interact with one another, and how does technical problem solving relate to them?
- Is there a kind of rigor peculiar to reflection-in-action and, if so, how is it like and unlike rigorous technical problem solving?

What sets the limits of our ability to reflect-in-action? How do individual and institutional constraints interact with one another? And in what directions should we look to increase the scope and depth of reflection-in-action?

In selecting cases of professional practice for exploration, I have been guided by several considerations. I have looked for a mix of "hard" and "soft" professions. I have chosen some cases that exemplify reflection-in-action and others that exhibit the limits to it. I have taken some examples from actual practice and some from records of professional education. In the latter case, although the context is at one remove from actual practice, there is the advantage that individuals tend to make their reflection-in-action public.

I will begin, in chapters 3 and 4, with examples of reflection-in-action drawn from two very different professional practices, architecture and psychotherapy, and in chapter 5 I will compare the two examples. I shall describe there what I take to be the general form of the process and some of the main criteria of rigor appropriate to it.

In chapter 6 I will explore examples of the arts of engineering design and scientific research, in which I see further variations on the theme of reflection-in-action, and I will describe the practice of an engineer who reflects-in-action on the socio-political context of technical problem solving.

In chapter 7 I will show how the evolution of town planning has influenced the context of practice, and how a practitioner's system of knowledge-in-practice hinges on his way of framing his role. In this case, where a practitioner reflects on his strategies of action but not on his framing of situation and role, we will explore certain limits to the scope of reflection.

The field of management, which I will discuss in chapter

8, has been powerfully influenced by management science and, at the same time, by the persistent view of management as an art. I will consider the art of management as a form of reflection-in-action.

Finally, in the conclusion to part II, I will review similarities and differences in reflection-in-action across the professions and criticize some familiar beliefs about the dangers of reflection and the limits to it.

Design as a
Reflective Conversation
with the Situation

The Design Professions

The family of design professions, of which architecture is the best known, includes urban design (the design of urban places), regional planning (concerned with the structure and ecology of whole regions), and the type of town planning that produces plans for the physical structures of cities. For many years, these fields have been changing and in changing relationship to one another. Architecture, once the mother profession, now occupies a somewhat ambiguous position within the larger family.

In engineering there is also a family of design professions.

Product designers concern themselves with the structure and appearance of industrial products. Industrial engineers design the mechanisms and layouts of production processes. And engineering specialists of various sorts design such large-scale products as ships, aircraft, dams, and roads.

In the last twenty years or so, the concept of design has broadened. We have begun to see cultural evolution as an informal, collective, generational process of design, as in Chris Alexander's story of the Slovakian peasant shawls. Herbert Simon and others have suggested that all occupations engaged in converting actual to preferred situations are concerned with design. Increasingly there has been a tendency to think of policies, institutions, and behavior itself, as objects of design.

It is questionable how far in this direction we ought to go. We risk ignoring or underestimating significant differences in media, contexts, goals, and bodies of knowledge specific to the professions. But we may also discover, at a deeper level, a generic design process which underlies these differences.

In this chapter I shall focus on design in the field of architecture, which I have had a particularly good opportunity to study. But architecture is worthy of study for other, less idiosyncratic reasons. It is perhaps the oldest recognized design profession and, as such, functions as prototype for design in other professions. If there is a fundamental process underlying the differences among design professions, it is in architecture that we are most likely to find it.

The search is complicated, however, by the fact that the boundaries of architecture are continually shifting, and even among practices clearly labelled "architecture" there are many variations. The field of architecture proper has been constricted by the emergence of newer professions such as planning, construction engineering, and landscape design. Within architecture itself, following the long reign of the Beaux Arts tradition in the late nineteenth and early twentieth centuries, practitioners have tended to align themselves with a bewildering array of contending schools, each of which has laid claim to architecture.

Some of these schools have consciously returned to historical precedents, such as the Italian hill towns or the Gothic cathedrals. Others have formed around the stylistic innovations and methods of great men such as Le Corbusier, Wright, Kahn, Aalto, and Mies van der Rohe. Some deplore the intrusions of contemporary technologies and commercial forms, while others celebrate the artifacts of contemporary American culture. Some have aspired to simplicity and purity of design or to the craftsmanlike use of materials, while others exploit the technological possibilities of industrial building technology or the rich cultural store of American vernacular. Some have reacted against the formalism of the dominant styles, treating design as a social process which should respond to the needs and preferences of the people who live and work in buildings.

For a student of the field—and perhaps even more for a student *in* the field—the multiplicity of voices is confusing. How should we regard the controversies among the contending schools? Should we take them as competing definitions of the field, which entail very different concepts of professional knowledge and practice? Or as stylistic variations of a design process that is essentially the same for all schools?

In the following pages, I shall draw from a particular example a description of designing which underlies the differences among schools and suggests a generic process shared by the various design professions. I shall consider designing as a conversation with the materials of a situation.

A designer makes things. Sometimes he makes the final product; more often, he makes a representation—a plan, program, or image—of an artifact to be constructed by others. He works in particular situations, uses particular materials, and employs a distinctive medium and language. Typically, his making process is complex. There are more variables—kinds of possible moves, norms, and interrelationships of these—than can be represented in a finite model. Because of this complexity, the designer's moves tend, happily or unhappily, to produce consequences other than those intended. When this happens, the designer may take account of the unintended changes he has made in the situation by forming new appreciations and understandings and by making new moves. He shapes the situation, in accordance with his initial appreciation of it, the situation "talks back," and he responds to the situation's back-talk.

In a good process of design, this conversation with the situation is reflective. In answer to the situation's back-talk, the designer reflects-in-action on the construction of the problem, the strategies of action, or the model of the phenomena, which have been implicit in his moves.

An Example of Reflective Designing

In the remainder of this chapter, I shall use a particular example of architectural designing to explore the reflective conversation which underlies the variety of schools of architecture.

I have drawn a case from a design studio,[1] a type of professional education, traditional in schools of architecture, in which students undertake a design project under the supervision of a master designer. In the case I have selected, the studio master, Quist, reviews the work of one of his students, Petra.[2]

This review takes place early in the semester. Its setting is the loft-like studio space in which each of the twenty students has arranged his own drawing tables, papers, books, pictures, and models. This is the space in which students spend much of their working lives, at times talking together, but mostly engaged in private, parallel pursuit of the common design task. At the beginning of the semester, Quist gave all of the students a "program"—a set of design specifications, in this case, for the design of an elementary school, and a graphic description of the site on which the school is to be built.

In the course of the semester, each student is to develop his own version of the design, recording his results in preliminary sketches, working drawings, and models. At the end of the semester, there will be a "crit" at which the students present their designs to Quist and to a group of outside critics (the "jury"). At intervals throughout the semester Quist holds design reviews with each student, and it is just such a review which Quist, in our protocol, conducts with Petra.

Here it is Quist who reflects on Petra's initial designing. For several weeks Petra has worked on the early phases of her design, and she has prepared some drawings. Quist examines these drawings, while Petra describes how she is stuck—how she has set problems that she cannot solve.

After a while, Quist places a sheet of tracing paper over Petra's sketches and begins to draw over her drawing. As he draws, he talks. He says, for example,

> The kindergarten might go over here . . . then you might carry the gallery level through—and look down into here . . .

But as Quist says these things he also draws, placing the kindergarten "here" in the drawing, making the line that "carries the gallery level through." His words do not describe what is already there on the paper but parallel the process by which he makes what is there. Drawing and talking are parallel ways of designing, and together make up what I will call the *language of designing*.

Design as a Reflective Conversation with the Situation

The verbal and non-verbal dimensions are closely connected. Quist's lines are unclear in their reference except insofar as he says what they mean. His words are obscure except insofar as Petra can connect them with the lines of the drawing. His talk is full of dychtic utterances—"here," "this," "that"—which Petra can interpret only by observing his movements. In our interpretation of the protocol, we must reconstruct Quist's pointing and drawing, referring to the sketches which accompany the transcript and, on occasion, making new sketches which clarify Quist's meanings.

Whether Quist and Petra speak in words or drawings, their utterances refer to spatial images which they try to make congruent with one another. As they become more confident that they have achieved congruence of meaning, their dialogue tends to become elliptical and inscrutable to outsiders.

The language of designing is a language for doing architecture, a language game[3] which Quist models for Petra, displaying for her the competences he would like her to acquire. But Quist's discourse is also punctuated by parentheses in which he talks about designing. He says, for example,

You should begin with a discipline, even if it is arbitrary . . .

and again,

The principle is that you work simultaneously from the unit and from the total and then go in cycles . . .

These are examples of a *language about designing,* a metalanguage by means of which Quist describes some features of the process he is demonstrating and with which he introduces Petra, however cursorily, to reflection on the action of designing.

In the protocol which follows, both kinds of language are intertwined.

The protocol This design review lasts for about twenty minutes, and may be divided into several phases. In the first of these, Petra presents her preliminary sketches and describes the problems she has encountered. Quist then focuses on one of these problems. He reframes it in his own terms and proceeds to demonstrate the working out of a design solution. There follows a brief interval of reflection on the demonstration to date. Quist then sets out the next steps Petra will have to undertake, including one (the calibration of the grid) which leads him to try to get her to look differently at the representation of slopes. There is, finally, a coda of reflection on all that has gone before.

Petra's presentation. Petra: I am having trouble getting past the diagrammatic phase—I've written down the problems on this list.
I've tried to butt the shape of the building into the contours of the land there—but the shape doesn't fit into the slope.
[She has a model with a slightly exaggerated slope; they discuss this.]
I chose the site because it would relate to the field there but the approach is here. So I decided the gym must be here—so [showing rough layout] I have the layout like this.

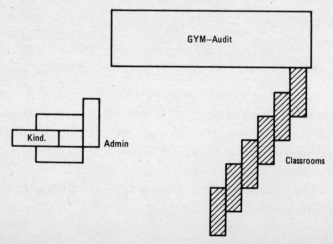

Quist: What other big problems?

Petra: I had six of these classroom units, but they were
too small in scale to do
much with. So I changed
them to this much more
significant layout (the L
shapes). It relates one to
two, three to four, and
five to six grades, which is
more what I wanted to do
educationally   anyway.
What I have here is a
space in here which is
more of a home base. I'll
have an outside/outside
which can be used and an
outside/inside which can
be used—then that opens
into your resource library/
language thing.

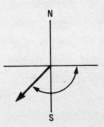

Q: This is to scale?

P: Yes.

Q: Okay, say we have introduced scale.
But in the new setup, what about north-south?

[He draws his orientation diagram]

[Showing preferred orientation:]

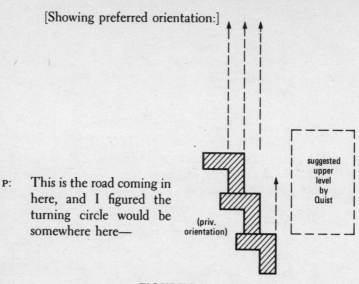

P: This is the road coming in here, and I figured the turning circle would be somewhere here—

FIGURE 3.1

Petra has taken the contours of the land seriously, accepting the norm that building shape and land contours must fit one another. In her sketches she has tried the experiment of "butting" the shape of her building into the contours of the slope, but the experiment has failed; hence the problem.

Petra has also experimented with the size and arrangement of her classroom units. She has found that classrooms must reach a threshold of scale in order to be "significant" enough for design. By regrouping the six smaller classroom units into three large L-shaped ones, she has tried for "more significant scale." But in doing so, she has also put next to one another the spaces which contain the people who ought most to encounter one another, and she has created a "home base," which sounds like a good place to be, a private outer space which can be used by the kids, and an inner space which has to do, perhaps, with the circulation of the school.

> *Quist's reframing of the problem.* Q: Now this would allow you one private orientation from here and it would generate geometry in this direction. It would be a parallel . . .
> P: Yes, I'd thought of twenty feet . . .
> Q: You should begin with a discipline, even if it is arbitrary, because the site is so screwy—you can always break it open later.

The main problem, in Quist's view, is not that of fitting the shape of the building to the slope; the site is too "screwy" for that. Instead, coherence must be given to the site in the form of a geometry—a "discipline"—which can be imposed upon it. In the remainder of this phase of the protocol, Quist plays out the consequences of such a move.

Quist's demonstration will now center on the new problem of coordinating the constructed geometry with the "screwy" contours of the slope. But the geometry can be "broken open" again. I think this means that you can dissolve the original discipline in order to try another one, and that you can later make knowing violations of the initial geometry. In Quist's metaphor, the geometry is a sort of armor which can be broken open in places, once it has been constructed. He will speak often of the need to "soften" a consistent discipline by consciously departing from it.

> *Quist's demonstration.* Q: Now in this direction, that being the gully and that the hill, that could then be the bridge, which might generate an upper level which could drop down two ways.

[One way from the classrooms] We get a total differential potential here from one end of classroom to far end of the other. There is 15 feet max, right?—so we could have as much as 5-foot inter-

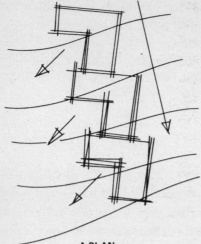

A PLAN

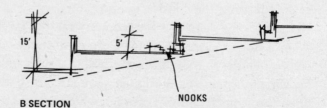

15′　　　5′

NOOKS

B SECTION

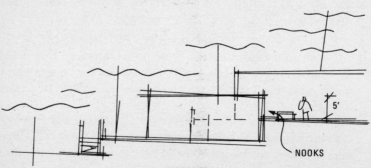

5′

NOOKS

C SECTION

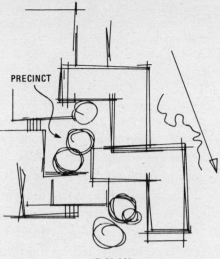

PRECINCT

D PLAN

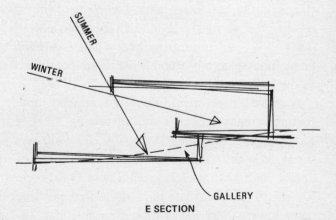

SUMMER

WINTER

GALLERY

E SECTION

vals, which for a kid is maximum height, right? The section through here could be one of nooks in here and the differentiation between this unit and this would be at two levels.

The sketches in figure 3.1 will help to make clear what is going on in this passage. Quist now proceeds to play out the imposition of the two-dimensional geometry of the L-shaped classrooms upon the "screwy" three-dimensional contours of the slope. The L-shaped classrooms are carved into the slope, as in sketch A. The "differentiation potential," as shown in the sectional sketch B, is from the near end of the classroom lying highest on the slope to the far end of the classroom which is lowest on the slope. The "15 feet max" is given by the total drop in the slope over the distance represented by the three classrooms. The slope is now divided into three levels, one for each of the classrooms, as in B. C shows the "interval" from the ground on one level to the roof of the classroom which stands on the next lower level. The roofs of the classroom will rise five feet above the ground at the next level up, and since five feet is "maximum height for a kid," kids will be able to be in "nooks," as in sketch C, which are approximately as high as the tallest kid.

A drawing experiment has been conducted, and its outcome partially confirms Quist's way of setting the L-shaped classrooms upon the incoherent slope. Classrooms now flow down the slope in three stages, creating protected spaces "maximum height for a kid" at each level. These Quist sees as "nooks," something he could not have done had the level difference come to very much less or more than five feet. To say that the section "could be one of nooks" is to invest these spaces with a special kind of value made possible by the level differences, and it is this which partially confirms Quist's earlier move.

Q: 'Now you would give preference to that as a precinct which opens out into here and into here and then, of course, we'd have a wall—on the inside there could be a wall or steps to relate in downward. Well, that either happens here or here, and you'll have to investigate which way it should or can go. If it happens this way, the gallery is northwards—but I think the gallery might be a kind of garden—a sort of soft back area to these.

The kindergarten might go over here—which might indicate that the administration over here—just sort of like what you have here—then this works slightly with the contours—

The "nooks" open out into "precincts" whose treatment is a new problem. Retaining walls are required at each level, as in D, but they also mark the different levels. Walls or steps now function as punctuation, marking boundaries and relationships. Quist invites Petra to consider the gallery as a "soft back area," as in sketch D, which would go well with the "hard" classrooms. It can also be "a kind of garden."

The resulting array—L-shaped classrooms, gallery, kindergarten, and administration—now "works slightly" with the contours of the slope. With this, Quist harks back to his reframing of Petra's original problem. When she couldn't butt the shape of the buildings into the screwy slope, Quist imposed on it a geometry of parallels suggested by the L-shaped classrooms. Now the resulting configuration "works slightly" with them. The fit is not very strong, but it is enough.

Q: Then you might carry the gallery level through—and look down into here—which is nice.
Let the land generate some sub-ideas here, which could be very nice. Maybe the cafeteria needn't be such a formal function—maybe it could come into here to get summer sun here and winter here.

P: Now this gallery is more a general pass-through that anyone can use.

Q: It's a general pass-through that anyone has the liberty to pass through, but it is not a corridor. It marks a level difference from here to here—it might have steps or ramp up to it.

P: My concern is that the circulation through this way—the gallery is generating something awfully cute, but how to pass through here [the library space]?

[More examples of Quist answering questions before they are asked]

Q: So don't think of the auditorium as a hard-edged block there.

Quist draws the extension of the gallery as he voices its possibility, imagining the experience of a person who would be following such a path, and he finds the result "nice," once more creating a confirmation of the string of moves made to date.

Petra has not "let" the cafeteria diverge from its regular geometric shape. He invites her to "soften it" by taking advantage of the site's north-south orientation which will cause the sun to fall on the slope at different angles in summer and winter, as in sketch E. Similarly, he invites her to "soften" the auditorium by relating it to nearby spaces.

Intermediate reflection. P: Where I was hung up was with the original shape; this here makes much more sense.

Q: Much more sense—so that what you have in gross terms is this [he points to his gallery]. It is an artifice—the sort of thing Aalto would invent just to give it some order. He's done that on occasion. So in a very minor way, that is the major thing. This repetitive thing in an organized way—there is this which is not repetitive. It is very nice and just the right scale. It also has a sort of verbal order that you could explain to someone.

The gallery, which had begun in Petra's mind as a minor element of the design, a "general pass-through," has now become "in a minor way . . . the major thing." Quist's reframing and reworking of the problem have led to a reappreciation of the situation, which he now evaluates in terms of norms drawn from several domains—form, scale, and verbal explainability.

> *Next steps.* Q: Now you have to think about the size of this middle area. You should have the administration over here.
>
> P: Well, that does sort of solve the problems I had with the administration blocking access to the gym.
>
> Q: No good, horrible—it just ruins the whole idea—but if you move it over there, it is in a better location and opens up the space.

The size of the middle area (not its detailed design) can come up now that they have solved the big problem of adapting the geometry of the classrooms to the screwy slope. In the middle area, they are again concerned with the location of major programmatic elements in relation to one another. And with his criticism of the position of the administration, Quist implies that everything he has so far done—the construction of a basic geometry, the imposition of that geometry upon the slope, the creation of the gallery—constitutes an internally coherent whole, all moves having been made with fidelity to the implications set up by earlier moves.

> Q: Now the calibration of this becomes important. You just have to draw and draw and try out different grids.
>
> P: Well, there seemed to be a strange correlation between the two.
>
> Q: No—look at it sideways. It looks much steeper in sections. You see, sections always seem much steeper in reality. Try

driving up a ten-degree road—you think you would never make it [draws his slope. diagram]

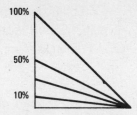

Coda. P: Yes, this was the main thing to get down—how that basic unit—I was thinking in much closer terms coming through the thing.

Q: [Cuts her off] Yeah, and the other thing is the subjection to a common set of geometry. You'll see that that will be a common problem which will come up with everyone, either too much constraint or not enough. How to do that, that is the problem of this problem.

P: It's amazing—intuitively you look at the shape and you know it's wrong, but it's very hard to get down to the reason . . .

Q: Yeah, well, that is what you are here for. So—I'd worry about the basic geometry on the site. I wouldn't concentrate on the roof.

Q: The principle is that you work simultaneously from the unit and from the total and then go in cycles—back and forth, back and forth—which is what you've done a couple of times stutteringly. You have some ideas of the whole which is the grid thing, but you don't know its dimensions. You've done something about this by eliminating that idea, which I think is a good decision. You keep going on—you are going to make it.

Quist returns to his earlier theme ("You should begin with a discipline, even if it is arbitrary"), but now develops it. The basic geometry should bind the designer, but under a norm of moderation. And in fact Quist has continually urged Petra to "soften" her "hard" geometric forms and to depart on occasion from the basic geometry—but only after it has been established.

Quist has been able to give Petra reasons for her intuitions. Now he makes a basic design principle explicit: attention must oscillate between the "whole" and the "unit," the global and the local. Under the metaphor of designing as speaking, Quist contrasts her "stuttering" with his own smooth delivery.

Analysis of the Protocol

Quist's designing takes the form of a reflective conversation with the situation.

At the beginning of the review, Petra is stuck:

I've tried to butt the shape of the building into the contours of the land there—but the shape doesn't fit into the slope.

Quist criticizes her framing of the problem, pointing out that she has tried to fit the shapes of the buildings into the contours of a "screwy" slope which offers no basis for coherence. Instead, he resets her problem:

You should begin with a discipline, even if it is arbitrary . . . you can always break it open later.

Petra should make the screwy site coherent by imposing on it a discipline of her own, a "what if" to be adopted in order to discover its consequences. If these are unsatisfactory, she can always "break it open later."

From "you should begin with a discipline" to "this works

slightly with the contours," Quist plays out the consequences of the new discipline by carving the geometry into the slope. In the medium of sketch and spatial-action language, he represents buildings on the site through moves which are also experiments. Each move has consequences described and evaluated in terms drawn from one or more design domains. Each has implications binding on later moves. And each creates new problems to be described and solved. Quist designs by spinning out a web of moves, consequences, implications, appreciations, and further moves.

Once the smaller classroom units have been made into L-shaped aggregates, they are "more satisfactory in scale," "put grade one next to grade two," and imply ("generate") a "geometry of parallels in this direction." Given these changes, Quist invents a new move: "that being the gully and that the hill, that could then be the bridge." The bridge also generates something new, an upper level which "could drop down two ways."

Each move is a local experiment which contributes to the global experiment of reframing the problem. Some moves are resisted (the shapes cannot be made to fit the contours), while others generate new phenomena. As Quist reflects on the unexpected consequences and implications of his moves, he listens to the situation's back talk, forming new appreciations which guide his further moves. Most significantly, he becomes aware that the gallery he has created, the "soft back area" to the L-shaped classrooms, has become "in a minor way . . . the major thing." Seizing on the gallery's potential, he "extends it here so as to look down into here." Later, he carefully avoids placing the administration building on the site in a way that would spoil "the whole idea."

Thus the global experiment in reframing the problem is also

a reflective conversation with the situation in which Quist comes to appreciate and then to develop the implications of a new whole idea. The reframing of the problem is justified by the discovery that the new geometry "works slightly with the contours," yields pleasant nooks, views, and soft back areas, and evokes in the situation the potential for a new coherence. Out of his reframing of Petra's problem, Quist derives a problem he can solve and a coherent organization of materials from which he can make something that he likes.

Three dimensions of this process are particularly noteworthy: the domains of language in which the designer describes and appreciates the consequences of his moves, the implications he discovers and follows, and his changing stance toward the situation with which he converses.

Design domains. Quist makes his moves in a language of designing which combines drawing and speaking. In this language, words have different roles. When Quist speaks of a cafeteria that could "come down into here to get summer sun here," "an upper level [which could] drop down two ways," "steps to relate in downward," he uses spatial action language. He attributes actions to elements of the design as though they were creating form and organizing space. At the same time, he anticipates the experienced felt-path[4] of a user of the building who could *find* that the upper level drops down or that the steps relate in downwards. Quist also uses words to name elements of the design ("steps," a "wall," an "administration"), to describe the consequences and implications of moves and to reappreciate the situation.

Elements of the language of designing can be grouped into clusters, of which I have identified twelve (figure 3.2). These design domains contain the names of elements, features, relations, and actions, and of norms used to evaluate problems,

FIGURE 3.2
Normative Design Domains

Domains	Definitions	Examples
Program/Use	Functions of buildings or building components; uses of buildings or site; specifications for use	"gym," "auditorium," "classroom"; "5′, which is maximum height for a kid"; "no city will plow a road that steep"
Siting	Features elements, relations of the building site	"land contour," "slope," "hill," "gully"
Building Elements	Buildings or components of buildings	"gym," "kindergarten," "ramp," "wall," "roof," "steps"
Organization of Space	Kinds of spaces and relations of spaces to one another	"a general pass-through," "outside/outside," "layout"
Form	1) Shape of building or component 2) Geometry 3) Markings of organization of space 4) Experienced felt-path of movement through spaces	"hard-edged block," "a geometry of parallels," "marks a level difference from here to here," "carry the gallery through and look down into here, which is nice"
Structure/Technology	Structures, technologies, and processes used in building	"a construction module for these (classrooms)"
Scale	Magnitudes of building and elements in relation to one another	"a 20′ parallel," "too small in scale to do much with," "just the right scale"
Cost	Dollar cost of construction	(none in this protocol)
Building Character	Kind of building, as sign of style or mode of building	("warehouse," "hangar," "beach cottage"—but not in this protocol)
Precedent	Reference to other kinds of buildings, styles, or architectural modes	"an artifice . . . the sort of thing Aalto would invent"
Representation	Languages and notations by which elements of other domains are represented	"look at it in section," "1/16 scale model"
Explanation	Context of interaction between designer and others	"the sort of verbal order you could explain to someone"

consequences, and implications. As he designs, Quist draws on a repertoire of design domains to fulfill a variety of constructive, descriptive, and normative functions.

In the domain of program/use, for example, such terms as "classroom," "administration," and "kindergarten" name buildings according to their uses. Phrases like "maximum height for a kid" and "how to pass through . . . the library space" describe the experience of using the buildings.

In the siting domain, Petra uses "contours of the land" to describe her problem, and Quist uses "hill," "gully," and "slope" to construct some of the early steps by which he carves the geometry into the slope.

In the domain of organization of space, Petra speaks of the "outside/outside" created by her L-shaped classrooms, and Quist characterizes the gallery as "a general pass-through that anyone has the liberty to pass through, but . . . not a corridor."

The domain of form has four meanings, distinct but interrelated. First there are the geometrical shapes of buildings, like Petra's "hard-edged block." There is also the sense of global geometry, as in "the geometry of parallels generated by the L-shaped classrooms." There is form as a visible sign of the organization of space, as in Quist's observation that the gallery marks level differences in the slope. And finally, there are frequent references to the felt-paths of those who will travel through the organized space, apprehending the figures, qualities, and relations which arise in the experience of movement from place to place.

In their appreciations of the situation they are shaping, Quist and Petra employ feelingful or associative terms such as "home base," "nook," "garden," and "soft back area." "A kind of garden" is not literally a garden, and the "soft back area" is not literally soft, but the metaphors of "garden" and "soft" are used to convey particular values of experience.

Often moves are found to have consequences and implications that cut across design domains. The retaining walls are necessary to the structural soundness of the buildings carved into the slope, but they also mark off formal differences in the levels of the slope. The gallery, which Petra finds "awfully cute," also creates problems of circulation. When design terms are ambiguous in this way, they may create confusion, but they also call attention to multiple consequences. Terms like "stair," "ramp," and "wall" refer both to particular building elements and to formal functions such as "marking" and "relating in." "Gallery" refers both to an organization of space and to a particular precedent ("the sort of thing Aalto would invent"). Aspiring members of the linguistic community of design learn to detect multiple reference, distinguish particular meanings in context, and use multiple reference as an aid to vision across design domains.

The designer's repertoire of domains has a structure of priorities for attending to features of situations. In our protocol, there are many references to organization of space, especially to the location of major building elements such as the gym, turning circle, bridge, and kindergarten. There are several references to scale, building elements, program/use, and the several senses of form. But there are only single references in each of the domains of precedent, structure/technology, and explanation. The domains of cost and building character do not appear in the protocol at all. The relative frequency of reference to design domains reveals Quist's priorities for attention at this early stage of the process.

Implications. When Petra says,

> This is the road coming in here, and I figured the turning circle would be somewhere here . . .

and when Quist later remarks that

> the kindergarten might go over here—which might indicate that
> the administration [goes] over here

they are noting the implications of earlier moves for later ones,
on the basis of a system of norms that governs the relative
placement of major building elements. This system includes
norms for access (the administration building's central accessi-
bility to all other units), circulation (ease and clarity of movement from one unit to another), and use ("opening up the
space"). Thus a decision to locate a road or a kindergarten
"here" has implications for the location of a turning circle or
an administration "there." In this sense, there is a literal logic
of design, a pattern of "if . . . then" propositions that relates
the cumulative sequence of prior moves to the choices now
confronting the designer.

Because of the contextual relatedness of norms drawn from
the domains of site, program, geometry, felt-path, structure,
and the like, the designer's moves yield systems of implications.
These constitute a discipline. *If* Petra chooses to "locate the
site here because it would relate to the field there . . . [and]
the approach is here," *then* "the gym must be here." As Quist
says, however, a discipline can always be broken open later. The
implications of prior moves must generally be honored but may
be violated on occasion if they are violated in a knowledgeable
way.

The web of moves has many branchings, which complicates
the problem of discovering and honoring implications. Given
the layering of the classrooms on the slope, for example, there
could be "a wall or steps to relate in downwards" which might
"happen here or here." These are choice-points. As he reflects-
in-action on the situation created by his earlier moves, the de-

signer must consider not only the present choice but the tree of further choices to which it leads, each of which has different meanings in relation to the systems of implications set up by earlier moves. Quist's virtuosity lies in his ability to string out design webs of great complexity. But even he cannot hold in mind an indefinitely expanding web. At some point, he must move from a "what if?" to a decision which then becomes a design node with binding implications for further moves. Thus there is a continually evolving system of implications within which the designer reflects-in-action.

The testing of local moves is partly linked to, and partly independent of, this system of implications. Quist discovers that the three classroom levels carved into the slope yield a "total differentiation potential of fifteen feet maximum" which would permit "as much as five-foot intervals" and he subsequently notices that these spaces, seen in section, could be made into "nooks." Here he affirms a local move because he finds that it has produced a situation out of which he can make something that he likes. In this he makes use of his knowledge of the relations between slopes of various grades and their uses. But he finds further support for the dimensions of the geometry he has carved into the slope when he discovers that the resulting configuration "works slightly with the contours." His method of carving the geometry of the classrooms into the slope is affirmed in one way when he sees it as a local experiment and in another way when he sees it as part of a global experiment.

Moves also lead to the apprehension of new problems such as the treatment of the "precincts" which flow out from the nooks, and they lead to new potentials for the creation of desirable artifacts such as the softening of the hard-edged shape of the cafeteria by allowing it to "come down into here to get summer sun here and winter sun here." In the designer's conversation with the materials of his design, he can never make a move which has only the effects intended for it. His materials are continually talking back to him, causing him to apprehend unanticipated problems and potentials. As he appreciates such new and unexpected phenomena, he also evaluates the moves that have created them.

Thus the designer evaluates his moves in a threefold way: in terms of the desirability of their consequences judged in categories drawn from the normative design domains, in terms of their conformity to or violation of implications set up by earlier moves, and in terms of his appreciation of the new problems or potentials they have created.

Shifts in stance. As Quist spins out his web of moves, his stance toward the design situation undergoes a series of changes.

Sometimes he speaks of what "can" or "might" happen, and sometimes of what "should" or "must" happen. He shifts from a recognition of possibility and freedom of choice to an acceptance of the imperatives which follow from choice. He urges Petra to step into the problem freely, imposing her own constructs upon it. Without this freedom, there can be no "what if?" But he also calls attention to the discipline of implications generated by her moves. The geometry of the L-shaped classrooms must be followed. Degrees of slope imply constraints on possible uses of the site. Implications for access to sun, circulation, boundary marking, nook-ness, street plowing, consistency of scale, access to gym or administration, fate of trees, are at stake in a relatively uncomplicated series of moves. As Quist draws out these implications, he demonstrates fidelity to the "musts" by which the freely chosen "what ifs?" are to be judged.

He also demonstrates how the whole is at stake in every partial move. Once a whole idea has been created, a bad placement of the administration can ruin it. Hence the designer must oscillate between the unit and the total, and—as Quist points out in one of his infrequent meta-comments—he must oscillate between involvement and detachment. Quist becomes at times so involved in the local development of forms that the design appears to be making itself. But he also steps back from the projected experience of passage through the space in order to take note of the larger relationships on which the qualities of the whole idea will depend.

Finally, as he cycles through iterations of moves and appreciations of the outcomes of moves, Quist shifts from tentative adoption of a strategy to eventual commitment. This shift enables him to achieve economy of design, simplifying the evolving web of moves to make his thought-experiment manageable.

The Underlying Process of Reflection-in-Action

Petra's problem solving has led her to a dead end. Quist reflects critically on the main problem she has set, reframes it, and proceeds to work out the consequences of the new geometry he has imposed on the screwy site. The ensuing inquiry is a global experiment, a reflection-in-action on the restructured problem. Quist spins out a web of moves, subjecting each cluster of moves to multiple evaluations drawn from his repertoire of design domains. As he does so, he shifts from embracing freedom of choice to acceptance of implications, from involvement in the local units to a distanced consideration of the resulting whole, and from a stance of tentative exploration to one of commitment. He discovers in the situation's back-talk a whole new idea which generates a system of implications for further moves. His global experiment is also a reflective conversation with the situation.

It is not difficult to see how a design process of this form might underlie differences of language and style associated with the various schools of architecture. Designers might differ, for example, with respect to the priorities they assign to design domains at various stages of the process. They might focus less on the global geometry of buildings, as Quist does, than on the site or on the properties and potentials of materials. They might let the design depend more heavily on the formal implications of construction modules. Their governing images might be framed in terms of building character, and they might allow particular precedents to influence more frankly the order they impose on the site. But whatever their differences of language, priorities, images, styles, and precedents, they are likely to find themselves, like Quist, in a situation of complexity and uncertainty which demands the imposition of an order. From whatever sources they draw such an initial discipline, they will treat its imposition on the site as a global experiment whose results will be only dimly apparent in the early stages of the process. They will need to discover its consequences and implications. And though they may differ from Quist in their way of appreciating these, they will, like him, engage in a conversation with the situation they are shaping. Although their repertoire of meanings may be different from Quist's, they are likely to find new and unexpected meanings in the changes they produce and to redirect their moves in response to such discoveries. And if they are good designers, they will reflect-in-action on the situation's back-talk, shifting stance as they do so from "what if?" to recognition of implications, from involvement in the unit to consideration of the total, and from exploration to commitment.

This underlying process might emerge with greater clarity if Quist's demonstration were not so masterful. In his unfailing virtuosity, he gives no hint of detecting and correcting errors in his own performance. He zeroes in immediately on fundamental schemes and decisions which quickly acquire the status of commitments. He compresses and perhaps masks the process by which designers learn from iterations of moves which lead them to reappreciate, reinvent, and redraw. But this may be because he has developed a very good understanding of and feeling for what he calls "the problem of this problem." If he can zero in so quickly on a choice of initial geometry which he knows how to make work with the screwy slope, it is perhaps because he has seen and tried many approaches to situations like this one. Like a chess master who develops a feeling for the constraints and potentials of certain configurations of pieces on the board, Quist seems to have developed a feeling for the kind of conversation which this design situation sets in motion. He does not need to play out all of the trees of moves which might follow from his initial reframing of the problem. It is this which permits him so confidently at the outset to describe the site as screwy and to dismiss it as a starting point for design coherence. From this source, perhaps, comes the confidence, the directness, and the simplicity of his demonstration. But Quist reflects very little on his own reflection-in-action, and it would be easy for a student or observer to miss the fundamental structure of inquiry which underlies his virtuoso performance.

4

Psychotherapy:
The Patient as
a Universe of One

The Context of Psychotherapeutic Practice

At the turn of the century, psychiatry held a rather obscure and tenuous position among the medical specialties. Psychiatrists concerned themselves for the most part with the treatment of the insane. They had little to do with the psychological troubles of ordinary people, who might turn in their distress to religion, to the popular philosophy of moral uplift, or to a variety of sects and cults of the mind. Psychiatry made a very faint claim to a basis in scientific knowledge.

By the end of World War II, however, psychiatry had become a powerful force in American society, had extended its reach beyond the asylum and had made serious inroads into provinces that once belonged to religion or popular philosophy. Indeed, psychiatry itself had become a new popular philosophy, at least for the affluent middle classes—so much that Dr. Norman Zinberg, writing in the *Daedalus* volume on the professions in the early 1960s, could complain that psychiatry's popular appeal had created excessive expectations for it and made the psychiatrist an object of suspicion to his medical colleagues.[1]

Although this transformation had been due in no small measure to the phenomenal rise in American life of one kind of psychiatry, psychoanalysis, the whole field had become, in Leston Havens's term, a babble of many voices. At first, psychiatrists who identified themselves with medicine sought to protect themselves against the incursions of non-physicians such as clinical psychologists. After World War II, however, the field spilled over the boundaries of medicine and a plethora of psychotherapies began to make their claims. Within psychiatry proper, Havens has described four main schools: objective-descriptive psychiatry, psychoanalysis, interpersonal psychiatry, and existential psychiatry.[2] In the larger therapeutic universe, there are also various sorts of group therapy, family therapy, operant conditioning, Rogerian therapy, Gestalt therapy, short-term therapy, and transactional analysis, to name only a few of the more prominent voices.

The fragmentation of the field provoked several kinds of response. Psychoanalysts tried to preserve their special status. Psychiatrists who wanted to keep close to medical science were attracted by advances in psychopharmacology. Representatives of different schools of therapy debated and competed more or less openly with one another. Some professional schools chose to specialize in a particular approach to therapy, while others offered a supermarket of approaches among which students were expected to choose.

At the same time, there were important changes under way in the larger societal context of therapeutic practice. Mental hospitals came under severe public criticism as "snakepits" and "dumping grounds," and sociologists offered damaging accounts of the techniques of labelling and social control by which psychiatrists fostered the social role of the mentally ill. These critical trends provided ammunition for the Mental Health Act of 1964, which set out a legislative basis for depopulating mental hospitals and de-institutionalizing the care of the mentally ill. Many community mental health centers alligned themselves with the growing interest in preventive services. In the full flush of the 1960s, some psychiatrists openly turned against their profession and devoted themselves to community organization.

In the period between 1965 and 1981, the questioning of therapeutic effectiveness has taken legislative form. Congress has demanded proof of effectiveness as a condition for third-party payments to practitioners. The de-institutionalization of the mental hospitals has continued, spurred on by public concerns over the cost of hospital care. Psychoanalysis appears to have lost some of its hold on the field, as clinical psychology has become stronger and new professionals, such as social workers, have moved into therapeutic roles. The babble of contending schools of therapy continues, apparently without damage to popular acceptance of psychotherapy, which has grown from a treatment for the seriously ill or a luxury for the well-to-do, to more or less standard fare for people in all walks of life.

Among the representatives of the competing schools of therapy, many continue to defend their exclusive claims and leave to the student or the client the difficult task of choosing among them. But there have been other approaches to the predicament posed by therapeutic pluralism. Havens has tried to describe what therapists of various schools actually do, by treating the schools as sources of therapeutic techniques appropriate to different sorts of patients and problems. Other writers have tried to describe fundamental processes of inquiry shared by therapists of various schools. Some practitioners, for example, share a disposition to regard the patient as a unique case—in Erik Erikson's words, "a universe of one." These practitioners, however much they may differ from one another in language and technique, share an approach to therapy that distinguishes them from those who regard patients as examples of standard diagnostic categories. The practitioners of the unique case are of special interest from the point of view of the study of reflection-in-action.

In the following pages, I will describe and analyze an interaction between a psychiatric resident and his supervisor. I have again selected an incident from professional education where a practitioner's reflection-in-action is more likely to be made public than it is in ordinary practice. I have chosen a practitioner who takes a psychoanalytical point of view, while recognizing that a protocol drawn from the work of Carl Rogers, Fritz Perls, or Salvador Minuchin might have produced a very different set of materials for analysis. It seems to me, nevertheless, that therapists, who are in other respects very different from one another must still frame the problem of the particular patient, construct and test interpretations of his behavior, and design interventions aimed at helping him. The supervisor, in the case that follows, goes about his business in a manner peculiar to his underlying model of therapy, but the generality of his tasks links his inquiry to other therapies of the unique case.

The Supervisory Session

The therapist is a third-year resident in psychiatry. His current supervisor, a psychoanalyst, is one of some sixty supervisors with whom he has met in the course of his three-year training program. The resident sees his current supervisor for one half-hour every week, averaging one supervisory session for every seven or eight sessions with the patient. Because the resident has been troubled by his relations with this supervisor, he has agreed to tape-record the session and then to discuss the resulting protocol,[3] hoping to learn from reflection on the record of the meeting.

He begins by informing the supervisor that his patient, a young woman, has returned to therapy after a hiatus of several months.

> R: She had decided that she wasn't getting anywhere in therapy, and I agreed somewhat that the same issues were coming up again and again—and primarily that issue of her getting stuck in the relationship with the man she had been seeing four or five years at that time, and advances on her part were matched by his withdrawal, and vice versa.

The Supervisor asks,

> In what way did she get stuck with you, I mean, in terms of the same way she got stuck in the relationship?
>
> R: Well, she tended to feel that any insights led to very little change, and we both noticed that even though she saw the pattern of her relationship outside of the therapy, it didn't do much good in her life . . . and it was difficult for her to really get emotionally involved in the therapy itself, that she was . . . quite guarded about talking about her past sadnesses and disappointments about them.

The Supervisor asks whether that was also a problem in her relationship with her boyfriend.

> R: Yes, she tended to restrict the feelings that she had in that relationship, especially the affectionate ones . . . and the sad ones.

Summarizing, the Supervisor observes,

> So here she rather quickly brings into the relationship that she's having difficulty and can't express her feelings . . . she's stuck, that she feels somewhat—maybe lowered self-esteem because she's stuck.

Then he asks,

> Did you at any time tell her that it's not surprising that what she experienced in her other relationships is experienced with you, and that here you have the advantage of looking at how she gets stuck and trying to work it out together . . . ?

The Resident answers with a rather perfunctory affirmative:

> Yeah, that was part of the work . . .

He goes on to describe the conditions of his patient's re-entry into therapy, the negotiation of fees and times of appointments, and begins to reflect on these early sessions:

> [What] has remained really paramount in her mind is wanting something, someone to rely on . . . sort of a constant object. Maybe in a way I've sort of served as that just by being available. She, during the first several sessions, repeated a lot of the pattern in the therapy that she had originally come in with in terms of feeling . . . very stuck . . .
>
> S: (interrupts) What does she mean when she says stuck? What's your experience?

This question stimulates the Resident to produce a long example, which the Supervisor probes with further questions.

R: Well . . . there's very much a pattern of her coming in and telling me about a fight she has had . . . often around some kind of misunderstanding. For instance, about the third session, she was saying that they went up to their old haunt . . . During the visit up there, he asked her whether or not a certain woman had called her. And this woman was a mutual friend, mostly a friend of his . . . And the patient thought that this woman had been spending some time with her boy friend. In fact, she knew that they had been together . . .

S: (interrupts) What do you mean, "been together"?

R: That they had just visited together . . . She had some suspicions. . . . And she said that they fought the rest of the time, mainly over the suspicions she had. Which has been one of their themes. That he goes out with other women and that she can't stand that. And he's not willing to stop. And she's not willing to lay down what she will and will not accept. And so she feels hurt and angry and suspicious when he's with any other woman. Meanwhile, he doesn't like it at all when she goes out with other men.

S: Does she go out with other men?

R: She doesn't, no . . . but that particular night, they fought the whole night. He took her to a restaurant and she said, "He knows I don't like lobster." He ordered her meal, which was lobster.

S: What do you mean, he ordered her meal? You mean she was sitting there and doesn't say anything?

R: Yeah, I mean he takes control in many situations.

S: Did you ask her, I mean, how does that happen? If you don't like lobster, did you manage while sitting at the table to order something else yourself?

R: Well, in the past, she said that if she argues with him, there'll be a fight. And it is very painful. Either she has to go along with him . . . and there isn't a fight. Or she argues and objects, and there is a fight. And she feels she loses either way. If there's a fight, she invariably loses the fight.

s: How does she lose the fight?

R: Well, it seems that mostly it's because she feels terrible when the fight's over. That he attacks her in the fight with many ways he thinks she is inadequate . . . She feels worse. And then the other part of it is she's not willing to risk a total severing of the relationship. There have been a number of times now, when she's told him she'll never call him again. And she doesn't want him to call her. And usually after a month, she'll relent . . .

The Supervisor asks then,

Well, what's your understanding of why it's this way? Do you have some sense of what the conflicts are?

The Resident responds with new anecdotes, but the Supervisor continues to press for an explanation.

s: You know, I don't get a sense of what you feel from seeing her. How would you characterize her problems in your own mind, psychodynamically? . . . We don't know a lot about her, but what does the material suggest?

R: Well, at this point there are a couple of suspicions.

s: All right, hypotheses.

R: One is that she has a lot of trouble getting emotionally involved, especially with men . . .

s: What's it do to her?

R: I can only suspect that she's very fearful of what it's going to mean in terms of her own autonomy, in terms of her own ability to make decisions and choices. And in terms of her identity. When she gets very close, in this particular relationship especially, she loses a sense of herself. She has to define herself by the other person.

s: Why does she do that? Do you think because she has some basic problems with who's who? Or is it at some other level?

R: Well, I think she has enough ego capacity that when she's not deeply involved, that she does have a sense of herself . . . But when she gets very close and very dependent on someone, which is her longing very much, the boundaries break down . . .

The Supervisor now offers a hypothesis of his own:

s: You may be right . . . you know her better than I do, we'd have to wait and see. My own sense of it is that she's very disturbed at her own aggression. That she can't assert herself. And yet she can't even mail a letter for herself. You know, she becomes dependent, and when you say, "Well, why do you do it that way . . . end up eating lobster when you don't like it?" she says, "Well, what can I do?" And then she says "If it leads to an argument, then I feel very guilty." And she's guilty, and part of her guilt is accepting as reality all of the criticisms that her boyfriend levels at her . . .

He urges the Resident to use this hypothesis in the therapy:

I would try to get her curious about it. Say, "Look, you seem able to assert yourself and you get what you want [which the Resident, trying to qualify the Supervisor's hypothesis, had just argued was the case in the patient's school and work] but in this particular area you do seem to be stunted." But I think that her fear of being aggressive and asserting herself is at least in part based on her fear of separation which is . . . that she's going to be left . . . and that she can't somehow take care of herself.

The Resident plunges at this point into new material drawn from the patient's history: her relationship with an alcoholic father, her anger at her mother for driving the father away, her recognition that her present relationship is very similar to the relationship with her father, her early marriage which was "subordinate, in a way, but unexciting." This leads him to a new interpretation:

r: This is the other theme, that she feels a little dead. She feels lifeless, without conflict. Something has to be going on out there between her and someone else in a conflictual way.

s: Yeah, I'm not . . . It may be that she feels dead. I don't know
      yet . . .

The Supervisor refrains from joining the Resident's excursion
into the patient's history and avoids committing himself to the
new hypothesis. Instead, he returns to the present story of the
patient's relationship with her boyfriend (illuminated, perhaps,
by comparison with her "unexciting" marriage), and offers a
new interpretation of his own:

> The man who's nice doesn't interest her. In order for the man
> to be exciting, they have to be a bit of a bastard.

This leads the Resident to speculate that indeed the patient
may have left therapy the first time because he was "too much
of a nice guy." When she wanted to return, he had become
more "hardnosed," demanding that she pay more money—
perhaps, as the Supervisor then says, "becoming the bastard
who she likes and expects you to be,"

> or that you might turn into him sometimes, or that you might be
> struggling and ineffective. And I would look for signs of one or
> the other developing in the relationship. But you see, you have
> to ask yourself, "Is this all a way in which she can't be satisfied
> because she feels so guilty about it?"

The Supervisor then returns to his earlier line of thought:

> She constantly keeps herself frustrated . . . well, anyone who con-
> stantly keeps themselves frustrated, you have to wonder whether
> they are in love with frustration in some way . . . or that because
> they're guilty about getting something for themselves that they
> have to constantly put roadblocks in the way. I don't know if the
> two are mutually exclusive but I think she's someone who really
> . . .

R: I think they go together somewhat.
S: Yeah, yeah, yeah.
R: I mean, if she feels guilty, she wants punishment.
S: Yeah.
R: Not only does she not want pleasure.

The Supervisor opens up a new line of inquiry.

S: What does she want punishment for? For her agressive angry thoughts, her sexual wishes? You'd have to look and see whether these arguments interfere with their sexual life . . .
R: At times they stimulate it, too.
S: I see.
R: At times, they both get mutually stimulated.
S: If she is punished, then she can enjoy, or if she enjoys, then she needs to be punished, or something. I would see this as a woman who really feels quite guilty.
R: Um.
S: About what, we have to decide . . . and really has without knowing it constantly thwarted her ability to be satisfied, and that's where she's stuck.

The Resident offers a proposal:

I posit her guilt might be her identification with her mother. She's angry at her mother for driving her father away. How much does she feel that she's responsible?

But the Supervisor cautions against leaping beyond the evidence:

Yeah, well, we don't know . . . It's too early to know all of these things.

and he suggests that they now review the patient's history:

Well, it might be helpful at this point to go over the history, to get some sense of the context.

As the Resident continues to speculate on the patient's feelings of guilt, the Supervisor counters,

I think if we can get some sense of this woman's frustration, and of the way in which she continues to frustrate herself . . .

And in his parting comment, he redirects the Resident's attention to his relationship with the patient:

R: She made a comment something like, "Is that the theory now?"

S: Yet, yeah . . . she will find ways of distancing you, just like she does her boyfriend.

Therapeutic Knowledge-in-Practice

Erik Erikson has described the psychotherapist's task as one of listening to the patient's complaint, eliciting its history, and making, testing, and delivering interpretations of the patient's data. The main questions of therapy have to do with the reliability of interpretation:

In what way can the psychological clinician make his own perceptions and thought reliable, in the face of the patient's purely verbal and social expression, and in the absence of non-verbal supportive instruments?[4]

For Erikson, this is not a matter of objective knowledge but of "disciplined subjectivity."[5] It derives from a reciprocal obligation in which the patient must verbalize everything and the analyst, in order to discover the patient's unconscious and refrain from imposing unconscious assumptions of his own, must listen in a special way, waiting for the gradual emergence of the themes which signal the patient's message. The material ought not to be subsumed under existing categories. The patient is "a 'series of one' who must be understood in terms of the unique experiences of his life."[6] The analyst must "set aside all preconceptions, listening afresh and testing the explanations as they arise."[7]

Emergent interpretations are to be tested first for their plausibility and then for their utility in intervention. Erikson observes that the clinician

> has no right to test his reconstructions until his trial formulations have combined into a comprehensive interpretation which feels right to him, and which promises, when appropriately verbalized, to feel right to the patient.[8]

Then, and only then,

> the clinician usually finds himself compelled to speak, in order to help the patient in verbalizing his affects and images in a more communicative manner, and to communicate his own impressions.[9]

The correctness of an interpretation does not always lie in the patient's "immediate assent," but rather

> in the way in which the communication between patient and therapist "keeps moving," leading to new and surprising insights and to the patient's greater assumption of responsibility for himself.[10]

In the testing of interpretations and, indeed, in the entire interpretive inquiry, Erikson gives a special place to the phenomenon of transference. The patient has "an interest in repeating the past in the present" which leads him to transfer "messages from other life situations" to the therapeutic one.[11] This interest may prevent the patient from cooperating with the associative procedure. The analyst's interpretation may free the patient to cooperate, but only if the analyst detects and interprets the countertransferences which would prevent him from listening in the recommended way. What is most important about the transference is that through it, the patient brings into therapy meanings, unconscious motivations, and strategies of behavior which can be surfaced and examined, harnessing to the work of therapeutic inquiry his interest in repeating the past in the present.

In the protocol we have examined, the Supervisor lives out the main lines of Erikson's description of therapeutic practice. As he listens to the Resident's reconstruction of his patient's material, he builds and tests interpretations. Because he encounters the patient only through the Resident's stories, he does not exhibit the analyst's special way of listening nor enter into the reciprocal obligation with the patient. But he advises the Resident how to do these things and, especially, how to make use of the phenomenon of the transference.

At the very beginning of the session, when the Resident describes his patient as stuck in her relationship with her boyfriend and "getting nowhere in therapy," the Supervisor asks,

In what way did she get stuck with you, I mean, in terms of the same way she got stuck in the relationship?

With this slight change in the question, the Supervisor restructures the puzzle. Centering attention on the connection between "stuck in the relationship" and "stuck with you," he anchors the inquiry in the patient's transference, where the relationship between patient and therapist can serve as a window on the patient's life outside therapy. So restructured, the question lends itself to a method of investigation which the Supervisor knows how to pursue. It motivates and guides his further questioning and inference.

Accordingly, he turns immediately to the Resident's experience of what the patient means when she says she is stuck. He intends to elicit data about the patient's meanings, and these are forthcoming. But he does not listen passively to the Resident's reports of his patient's stories. He probes them actively. Following the story of the patient's fight with her boyfriend, for example, he asks, "What do you mean, 'been together'?" "Does she go out with other men?" "What do you mean, he ordered her meal?" "How does she lose the fight?" These questions suggest an origin in the Supervisor's image of the sorts of stories which would throw light on the way in which the patient is stuck. The incident of the boyfriend ordering the patient's meal contributes to an emerging picture of the patient's passivity and dependence. The Supervisor's "How come?" leads the Resident to describe the patient's dilemma: she feels she loses whether she goes along with her boyfriend's demands or resists them. The Supervisor's "How does she lose the fight?" induces the Resident to describe the patient's fears of feeling terrible after such fights, her anxiety that she will be abandoned, her feelings of inadequacy about herself.

Such questions suggest a repertoire of meanings and psychodynamic patterns accessible to the Supervisor, but apparently not to the Resident. The Supervisor uses his repertoire to pursue the development of stories until he finds them ready for interpretation. When they reach this stage of development, he stops probing and shifts, rather abruptly, to a search for explanations:

> Well, what's your understanding of why it's this way? Do you have some sense of what the conflicts are?

With this, he not only asks for an explanation but indicates the domain in which to look for it. The story of the patient's fight with her boyfriend has revealed a dilemma rooted in conflicts the patient cannot resolve.

When the Resident responds by telling more stories about the patient's earlier life, the Supervisor brings him back to the search for interpretation:

> You know, I don't get a sense of what you feel from seeing her. How would you characterize her problems in your own mind, psychodynamically?

Now the Resident attempts an explanation, an account of the patient's trouble in getting emotionally involved, "especially with men." This the Supervisor brushes aside. He has an explanation of his own:

> My own sense of it is that she's very disturbed at her own aggression. That she can't assert herself.

As he develops this alternative, the Supervisor demonstrates a particular way of drawing interpretations from the data of the stories:

> And yet she can't even mail a letter for herself. You know, she becomes dependent, and when you say, "Well, why do you do it that way, end up eating lobster when you don't even like it?" she says, "Well, what can I do?" And then she says, "If it leads to an argument, then I feel very guilty." And she's guilty, and part

of her guilt is accepting as reality all of the criticisms that her boy-friend levels at her.

This passage moves gradually through a chain of inferences. From the fact that the patient allows her boyfriend to mail her letters and order her meals, it follows that she is unable to assert herself. She becomes dependent. Given her depen-dence, an argument with her boyfriend causes her to feel guilty. (The Resident's "feeling terrible" has become "feeling guilty.")

The Supervisor has now linked her dependency to her feel-ings of inadequacy and guilt, and these, to her tendency to ac-cept all of her boyfriend's criticisms as reality. In this con-densed explanation, the Supervisor pulls scattered bits of information together, grounding each partial interpretation in a piece of evidence drawn from the Resident's account of his patient's stories. In contrast, the Resident leaps to such inter-pretations as "the shaky boundaries of the self," "the feeling of deadness," and the "feeling of responsibility for the father's leaving," without basing them on the patient's material and without the benefit of a careful progression of questioning and testing. To each of the Resident's interpretive leaps, the Super-visor responds, "I don't know yet . . . we have to wait and see."

The Supervisor's gradual construction of an interpretation proceeds with his observation that "the man who's nice doesn't interest her." This leads to "for the man to be exciting, they have to be a bit of a bastard," and then to "she constantly keeps herself frustrated." But constant self-frustration demands an explanation. The Supervisor suggests two alternatives:

well, anyone who constantly keeps herself frustrated, you have to wonder whether they are in love with frustration in some way . . . or that because they're guilty about getting something for themselves that they have to constantly put roadblocks in the way.

Both of these explanations can go together, says the Resident, and the Supervisor agrees. "If she feels guilty, she wants punishment." Guilt can lead her to seek punishment which she then finds gratifying. But punishment for what? Again there are two possibilities, "agressive, angry thoughts" or "sexual wishes." In order to decide between these alternatives, the Supervisor conducts an experiment. He asks whether the punishing fights interfere with the patient's sex life with her boyfriend. On being informed that they sometimes stimulate it, he infers that punishment responds to sexual wishes, and he offers a new synthesis:

> If she is punished, then she can enjoy, or if she enjoys, then she needs to be punished, or something. I would see this as a woman who really feels quite guilty . . . about what, we have to decide . . . and really has without knowing it constantly thwarted her ability to be satisfied, and that's where she's stuck.

The repeated "really" suggests a coming-to-rest, as though the Supervisor were now satisfied that his initial question has been answered. He has constructed an interpretation which explains how she is stuck in the relationship with her boyfriend, and he proceeds to show how this interpretation also explains how she is stuck in therapy. He does this by inviting the Resident to reflect on the ways in which he finds himself becoming the person his patient wants and needs him to be:

> You begin to review being the bastard who she likes and expects you to be, in her own view, to struggle with and to be excited by, but not to be satisfied by . . . or that you might turn into him sometimes, or that you might be struggling and ineffective. And I would

look for signs of one or the other developing in the relationship. But you see, you have to ask yourself, "Is this all a way in which she can't be satisfied because she feels so guilty about it?"

This interpretation, which connects the two senses in which the patient is stuck, also suggests a strategy of intervention. The Resident should observe how he is being drawn into the patient's transference. Rather than colluding in his process, he should suggest to her

that what she experiences in her relationships is experienced with you, and that here you have the advantage of looking at how she gets stuck and trying to work it out together.

The Resident should get the patient interested in the puzzle of her self-frustration:

I would try to get her curious about it. Say, "Look, you seem able to assert yourself and get what you want, but in this particular area you do seem to be stunted."

These interventions would test the utility of the interpretation whose plausibility the Supervisor has established through a chain of interpretive inference. It would do so by involving the patient in an inquiry similar to the one the Supervisor and Resident have just undertaken. The new interpretation will be affirmed if the patient finds it compelling. But the hypothesis testing is also a therapeutic intervention. As therapist and patient "look at how she gets stuck and try to work it out together," they will discover how she has recreated in therapy the most troubling features of her life outside of therapy.

In spite of his suggested strategy of intervention, the Supervisor holds his interpretation loosely. When the Resident leaps to an explanation of the patient's guilt, the Supervisor cautions,

"Well, we don't know yet. It's too early to know all of these things." Instead, he returns to the general observation with which his earlier chain of inference began:

> I think if we can get some sense of this woman's frustration, and of the way in which she continues to frustrate herself . . .

Having constructed and tested a solution to the puzzle, the Supervisor means to keep it open to further inquiry. The Resident should use the tentative solution to guide his work with the patient, but he should keep the puzzle alive.

Throughout the entire dialogue with the Resident, the Supervisor has been demonstrating a reflective conversation with the patient's material. He has reframed the problem of the patient in such a way as to locate it squarely in the transference: the puzzle is to explain how the patient is stuck in the therapy as she is stuck in her relationship with her boyfriend. In the subsequent puzzle solving, two streams of data must be integrated. A sense must be found which links the patient's stories of her life experience with the Resident's experience of the patient in therapy. The two kinds of data are accumulated gradually and the Supervisor probes and develops them until the precipitate of an interpretation seems ready to form. The interpretive process proceeds step by step. Beginning with generalized observations only one step removed from the language of the stories, the Supervisor builds a chain of inferences in which each link is grounded in themes drawn from the patient's experience. He joins these together in an explanation which connects the patient's recurrent dilemma to a generalized account of inner conflicts. This explanation leads the Supervisor to a further question (punishment for what?) which generates alternative hypotheses. In order to discriminate between these, he conducts a crucial experiment in the form of a question. With the answer in hand, he proposes an interpretive synthesis which explains the material of the patient's stories, and he extends it to account for the patient's continual self-frustration in therapy. At this point, when he has given a plausible account of the two ways in which the patient is stuck, he proposes an intervention designed to test his account. The Resident should try to get the patient interested in her continual self-frustration, engaging her in a conscious use of the transference to gain insight into her life outside of therapy.

What does the Resident make of this demonstration? After listening to the tape recording of this session, he complains that the Supervisor was not telling him what he wanted to hear. Then, upon reflection, he adds that he was not asking for what he wanted to know. He doubts that the Supervisor is an effective role model for him. He wants more help than he is getting, but feels angry when he asks for it. He senses that the Supervisor has formed a negative judgment about him which has never been expressed, and he seeks to explain his troubles with the Supervisor in terms of conflicting approaches to psychotherapy: "He is more psychoanalytic, while I deal more with conscious phenomena." Yet he displays in the protocol an eagerness to join, indeed, to compete with, the Supervisor's psychoanalytic inquiry.

It is clear, both from the protocol and from private interviews, that the Resident discerns in the Supervisor's performance a knowing-in-practice that he values, but he is frustrated in his attempts to grasp it. What eludes him is the system of understandings which lies behind the Supervisor's inquiry. When the Supervisor demonstrates what he takes as a story sufficient for interpretation, when he focuses on certain details while leaving others in the background, he appears to be guided by a repertoire of story types, interpretive explanations, and psychodynamic patterns. He uses these but does not describe them. He does not try to tell the Resident what leads him to select certain details for attention or to accept a story as adequate for interpretation. Similarly, he does not say why he brushes aside the Resident's proferred interpretations, why he says repeatedly, "we don't know enough, we'd have to wait and see . . . " He does not reveal the thoughts and feelings which guide him in his shifts from one phase of inquiry to the next. He reflects-in-action but he does not reflect on his reflection-in-action.

The Resident does not know whether the Supervisor would be unwilling, or perhaps unable, to make more of his knowing-in-practice explicit. The Resident has not asked for this, and the Supervisor has not offered it. As the Resident says, rather wistfully,

> I am not explicit about what I want from the Supervisor and he is not explicit about what he gives, and so it just happens.

Nor has the Supervisor tried to discover what the Resident makes of his demonstration. His approach to instruction consists in demonstrating and advocating a kind of therapeutic reflection-in-action, but it is also an approach of mystery and mastery.[12] He demonstrates his mastery of the material, but he keeps the sources of his performance mysterious.

The Resident has a complementary approach to learning. It is one of mystery and passivity. He witholds his feelings of dissatisfaction and frustration, and he follows the Supervisor's lead, seeking to join in interpretive moves whose sources remain mysterious to him. He does not question the hidden sources of the Supervisor's performance, and he does not ask for what he wants to learn.

It is very striking that the two therapists do not make their own interaction into an object of mutual reflection. In one of his interviews, the Resident discovers this point. Excitedly, he shows how his relationship with the Supervisor resembles the patient's relationship to her therapist, especially in the matter of control and cooperation. Like his patient, the Resident feels stuck in his relationship to the person who is supposed to help him, wanting more from him than he feels he is getting, yet angry at himself for wanting more. But these issues do not come up for discussion in the clinical supervision itself. Had they done so, the boundaries of reflection might have been stretched to include the meaning of the Supervisor's demonstration, the Supervisor might have begun to reflect on his own reflection-in-action, and the Resident might have begun to gain access to the mysterious sources of the Supervisor's performance.

5

The Structure of
Reflection-in-Action

Introduction

In the two previous chapters, I have discussed examples of
practice in two professions usually considered very different
from one another.

The differences between architecture and psychotherapy are
so very striking that at first glance there seems to be very little
point in searching for resemblances. To begin with, the goals
of the two professions have almost nothing to do with one another. The one aims at designing good buildings on a site; the
other, at curing mental illness or helping people to cope with
the problems they encounter in their lives. One uses the media
of sketchpad, delineations, scale models; the other, talk. The
architect works in his studio; the therapist, in a clinic or office.
And the two professions draw on very different bodies of professional knowledge.

But in the two cases there are also similarities. To be sure, these are partly a function of my methods of selection and study, but they are also, in part, a function of the practices themselves.

In both examples, the practitioner approaches the practice problem as a unique case. He does not act as though he had no relevant prior experiences; on the contrary. But he attends to the peculiarities of the situation at hand. Quist pays attention to the special problem of this screwy site and the Supervisor, to the special problem of this frustrated patient. Neither one behaves as though he were looking for cues to a standard solution. Rather, each seeks to discover the particular features of his problematic situation, and from their gradual discovery, designs an intervention.

In neither example is the problem given. Or rather, the student presents a problem that the teacher criticizes and rejects. The student has gotten stuck and does not know how to go further. The teacher, who attributes the student's predicament to his way of framing the problem, tries to make new sense of the problematic situation he is encountering at secondhand. The situation is complex and uncertain, and there is a problem in finding the problem.

These points of similarity create the conditions for reflection-in-action. Because each practitioner treats his case as unique, he cannot deal with it by applying standard theories or techniques. In the half hour or so that he spends with the student, he must construct an understanding of the situation as he finds it. And because he finds the situation problematic, he must reframe it.

The cases are similar in the further sense that in both architecture and psychiatry there are many competing views of the nature of the practice. There is controversy not only about the best way of solving specific problems, but about what problems are worth solving and what role the practitioner should play in their solution. I propose that by attending to the practitioner's reflection-in-action in both cases it is possible to discover a fundamental structure of professional inquiry which underlies the many varieties of design or therapy advocated by the contending schools of practice.

Finally, in each case the practitioner gives an artistic performance. He responds to the complexity, which confuses the student, in what seems like a simple, spontaneous way. His artistry is evident in his selective management of large amounts of information, his ability to spin out long lines of invention and inference, and his capacity to hold several ways of looking at things at once without disrupting the flow of inquiry.

It is the art of these practitioners that I shall compare and discuss in the following pages. Their art seems to me to be, in considerable measure, a kind of reflection-in-action. In spite of the very great differences between their two cases, Quist and the Supervisor engage in a process whose underlying structure is the same: a reflective conversation with a unique and uncertain situation.

The main lines of this process can be readily drawn. Indeed, they are not very far below the surface of the examples as I have described them.

In each case, the student has set and tried to solve a problem and has been unable to solve the problem as set. Petra cannot butt the shapes of the building into the contours of the slope; neither can the Resident unravel the puzzle of the patient by analyzing her relationships with others. In each case the teacher responds by surfacing and criticizing the student's framing of the problem. He does this implicitly, leaving his criticism of the old problem to be inferred from his way of restructuring it. Petra must infer that the site is incoherent and cannot give an order to the design. The Resident must infer that he cannot make sense of the patient's stalemated relation to her boyfriend without looking at it in relation to her stalemate with himself.

As the practitioner reframes the student's problem, he suggests a direction for reshaping the situation. Petra is urged to impose a geometry onto the slope, a geometry seen as generated by the L-shaped classrooms. The Resident is invited to join the two streams of experience drawn from the patient's life in and out of therapy. The practitioner asks the student to step into the situation, to make himself part of it—in Quist's case, by imposing his own order onto the site; in the Supervisor's, by treating his own relations with the patient as a microcosm of the patient's life outside of therapy.

The practitioner then takes the reframed problem and conducts an experiment to discover what consequences and implications can be made to follow from it. Quist's global, frame-testing experiment begins with "You must impose a discipline" and ends with "which works slightly with the contours." The Supervisor's begins with "How is she stuck . . . ?" and ends with, "This is really a woman who feels quite guilty . . . and that's how she's stuck."

In order to see what can be made to follow from his reframing of the situation, each practitioner tries to adapt the situation to the frame. This he does through a web of moves, discovered consequences, implications, appreciations, and further moves. Within the larger web, individual moves yield phenomena to be understood, problems to be solved, or opportunities to be exploited. Quist discovers spaces that can be made into nooks. The Supervisor finds a procedure for answering the question, "Punishment for what?" These are local experiments nested within larger ones.

But the practitioner's moves also produce unintended changes which give the situations new meanings. The situation talks back, the practitioner listens, and as he appreciates what he hears, he reframes the situation once again. When Quist discovers that his moves have produced a gallery which is "in a minor way . . . the major thing," he becomes aware of a new whole idea, which sets criteria for the further designing. When the Supervisor discerns in the patient's stories the pattern which he describes as "continual self-frustration," he sets a re-structured problem of interpretation which guides his further inquiry.

In this reflective conversation, the practitioner's effort to solve the reframed problem yields new discoveries which call for new reflection-in-action. The process spirals through stages of appreciation, action, and reappreciation. The unique and uncertain situation comes to be understood through the attempt to change it, and changed through the attempt to understand it.

Such is the skeleton of the process. It suggests several further questions.

1. The practitioner conducts an experiment in reframing the problematic situation. But how is such an experiment to be evaluated? The practitioner judges his problem-solving effectiveness in terms of an objective function, but how ought he to judge the problem setting which establishes the objective function?

2. When the practitioner takes seriously the uniqueness of the present situation, how does he make use of the experience he has accumulated in his earlier practice? When he cannot apply familiar categories of theory or technique, how does he bring prior knowledge to bear on the invention of new frames, theories, and strategies of action?

3. Reflection-in-action is a kind of experimenting. But practice situations are notoriously resistant to controlled experiment. How does the practitioner escape or compensate for the prac-

tical limits to controlled experiment? In what sense, if any, is there rigor in on-the-spot experiment?

4. Technical problem solving involves a characteristic stance toward inquiry, as suggested by terms such as objectivity, control, and distance. These terms have limited application to the processes demonstrated by Quist and the Supervisor. Nevertheless, *their* stance toward inquiry is critical to the quality of their reflection-in-action. How should we describe it?

Questions such as these point to a further elaboration of reflection-in-action as an epistemology of practice. One might try to answer them by appeal to a structure of inquiry, but I do not know what such a structure might be or how it might be discovered, if not by reflection on the actual practice of experienced, competent practitioners who reflect-in-action. Accordingly, I shall approach these questions by looking for answers to them implicit in Quist's designing and in the Supervisor's interpretive inquiry.

Evaluating Experiments in Problem Setting

Quist and the Supervisor act as though they were judging their reframing of the students' problems in terms of these questions:

Can I solve the problem I have set?
Do I like what I get when I solve this problem?
Have I made the situation coherent?
Have I made it congruent with my fundamental values and theories?
Have I kept inquiry moving?

Although a problem-setting experiment cannot be judged in terms of its effectiveness, the practitioner tries nevertheless to set a problem he can solve. If Quist and the Supervisor failed to do this, they would be stuck as their students are stuck. Hence they step into the situation with a framing of the problem for which they feel they can find a solution. Quist chooses a geometry of parallels which can be made to work slightly with the contours of the slope; at the same time, he sets a threshold standard of fit which enables him to say that "slightly" is enough. The Supervisor frames the patient's problem in terms of the transference which lends itself both to a strategy of inquiry and a strategy of intervention. Neither practitioner can know, at the moment of reframing, what the solution to the problem will be, nor can he be sure that the new problem will be soluble at all. But the frame he has imposed on the situation is one that lends itself to a method of inquiry in which he has confidence.

When the practitioner tries to solve the problem he has set, he seeks both to understand the situation and to change it. Quist's moves test the new geometry's suitability to the slope and at the same time they carve the L-shaped classrooms into the slope, producing a new configuration of buildings on the site. The Supervisor, operating at one remove from the patient, sees the therapeutic situation through the Resident's reports. As he elicits new stories and probes them, he tests his evolving understanding and at the same time draws out new phenomena which alter his experience of the situation.

The practitioner's moves produce some unintended effects. Quist discovers that as he carves the classrooms into the slope, he makes intervals of five feet. He finds that the gallery can be "extended to look down into here" and that it contrasts with the classrooms. The Supervisor's line of questioning elicits the surprising and puzzling story of the patient's fight with her boyfriend. The practitioner evaluates his problem-setting experiment by determining whether he likes these unintended changes, or likes what he can make of them. Quist observes that five feet is maximum height for a kid, so that the five-foot intervals can be made into nooks. The extension of the gallery is "nice" and makes a "soft back area" to the hard-edged classrooms. The Supervisor sees in the story of the fight the signs of the patient's passivity and dependence which he will pursue in his further questioning.

In these instances, the practitioner affirms his reframing of the problem, because he values the unintended changes he has made and discovered. Quist values nooks, nice views, and a softening of hard-edged forms. The Supervisor values self-assertion, independence, and the ability to free oneself from dead ends; the story, which reveals the absence of these qualities in the patient, gives him a direction in which to seek interpretative understanding. The evaluation of the frame experiment is grounded in the practitioner's appreciative system.

Through the unintended effects of action, the situation talks back. The practitioner, reflecting on this back-talk, may find new meanings in the situation which lead him to a new reframing. Thus he judges a problem-setting by the quality and direction of the reflective conversation to which it leads. This judgment rests, at least in part, on his perception of potentials for coherence and congruence which he can realize through his further inquiry.

Quist interweaves local experiments with one another, honoring in each new experiment the implications generated by earlier moves. He finds that the spaces created by carving the L-shaped classrooms into the slope open out into "precincts" which must be given precedence. He observes that a middle area has been created whose treatment must be consistent with the overall geometry. By the time the new configuration has been found to work slightly with the contours and the gallery has emerged as the focus of the design, there is, at the level of the global geometry of the buildings on the site, a whole idea so powerful for Quist that he calls Petra's placement of the administration "horrible" because it would spoil that idea.

The Supervisor builds gradually from his perception of the patient's dilemma toward an interpretive synthesis congruent with his fundamental values and theories. He reaches for partial interpretations which stay close to the data of the thematic stories he has elicited from the Resident. He guides his search for explanations by reference to the psychoanalytic themes of "inner conflict" and "guilt." By the time he has fully surfaced his interpretive synthesis, he has imbued it with the capacity to account for the earlier, partial interpretations and has made it congruent with psychoanalytic theory.

Thus the practitioner evaluates his experiment in reframing the problematic situation not only by his ability to solve the new problem he has set but by his appreciations of the unintended effects of action, and especially by his ability, in conversation with the situation, to make an artifact that is coherent and an idea that is understandable. But the achievement of coherence does not put an end to inquiry. On the contrary, the practitioner also evaluates his reframing by its ability, in Erikson's phrase, to keep inquiry moving. Quist concludes his review by describing new questions which flow from the design—the size of the middle area, the dimensions of the grid, the treatment of the trees. And the Supervisor, fearful of premature closure, rounds off his interpretive journey with the exhortation, "If only we can get an idea of the way this woman keeps herself frustrated. . . ." A successful reframing of the problematic situation leads to a continuation of the reflective conversation.

Bringing Past Experience to Bear on a Unique Situation

Quist recognizes many familiar things in Petra's situation, and he places them within familiar, named categories such as "parallels," "classrooms," "slope," and "wall." Similarly, the Supervisor recognizes and names examples of "self-assertion," "dependence," and "guilt." But when it comes to the situation as a whole, each practitioner does not subsume it under a familiar category but treats it as a unique entity for which he must invent a uniquely appropriate description.

The Supervisor's initial description of the patient's problem opens up a line of inquiry into the unique experience of this woman. He may have seen other patients who were continually self-frustrating or guilty, but he does not diagnose this patient as a case of guilt as a physician might diagnose someone as a case of mumps or chicken pox. Rather, he attends to her particular way of being guilty and to the role guilt plays in her inability to satisfy herself. The notions of guilt and self-frustration guide his attempts to discover what is *different* about this patient's experience.

Quist has very likely seen other screwy sites, but his initial description of this one does not place it within a design category that calls for a standard solution. Rather, it sets in motion an inquiry into the peculiar features of *these* slopes which respond in very special ways to the imposition of a geometry of parallels, creating a particular set of problems and a particular coherence.

It is in relation to the unique features of his problematic situation that each practitioner undertakes the problem-setting experiment we have just discussed. But just this is puzzling. How can an inquirer use what he already knows in a situation which he takes to be unique?

He cannot apply a rule drawn from past experience, like the rule Quist gives for uses appropriate to slopes of various grades; for he would then ignore the uniqueness of the situation, treating it as an instance of a class of familiar things. Nor does he invent a new description out of whole cloth, without any reference to what he already knows. It is clear that Quist and the Supervisor use a great deal of their experience and knowledge, and it is far from clear what might be meant by the spontaneous generation of a description.

What I want to propose is this: The practitioner has built up a *repertoire* of examples, images, understandings, and actions. Quist's repertoire ranges across the design domains. It includes sites he has seen, buildings he has known, design problems he has encountered, and solutions he has devised for them. The Supervisor's repertoire includes patients he has seen or read about, types of stories he has heard and psychodynamic patterns associated with them, interventions he has tried, and patients' responses to them. A practitioner's repertoire includes the whole of his experience insofar as it is accessible to him for understanding and action.

When a practitioner makes sense of a situation he perceives to be unique, he *sees* it *as* something already present in his repertoire.[1] To see *this* site as *that* one is not to subsume the first under a familiar category or rule. It is, rather, to see the unfamiliar, unique situation as both similar to and different from the familiar one, without at first being able to say similar or different with respect to what. The familiar situation functions as a precedent, or a metaphor, or—in Thomas Kuhn's phrase—an exemplar for the unfamiliar one.[2] Kuhn's description of the functioning of exemplars in scientific problem solving is apposite here:

> confronted with a problem, [one] seeks to see it as like one or more
> of the exemplary problems he has encountered before . . . his basic
> criterion is a perception of similarity that is both logically and psy-
> chologically prior to any of the numerous criteria by which that
> same identification might have been made . . . Under appropriate
> circumstance . . . there is a means of processing data into similarity
> sets which does not depend on a prior answer to the question, simi-
> lar with respect to what?[3]

Seeing *this* situation as *that* one, one may also *do* in this situation *as* in that one. When a beginning physics student sees
a pendulum problem as a familiar inclined plane problem, he
can set up the new problem and solve it, using procedures both
similar to and different from those he has used before. Just as
he sees the new problem as a variation on the old one, so his
new problem-solving behavior is a variation on the old. Just as
he is unable at first to articulate the relevant similarities and
differences of the problems, so he is unable at first to articulate
the similarities and differences of his problem-solving procedures. Indeed, the whole process of *seeing-as* and *doing-as* may
proceed without conscious articulation.

On the other hand, the inquirer may reflect on the similarities and differences he has perceived or enacted. He may do
this by consciously comparing the two situations, or by describing *this* situation in the light of a tacit reference to the other.
When Quist immediately calls Petra's site "screwy" and says
that she must impose a discipline on it, which she can always
break open later, I believe he is seeing her situation as one or
more others with which he is familiar and carrying over to her
problem variations of strategies he has employed before. And
when the Supervisor asks how the woman is stuck in her relation with her boyfriend as she is stuck in her relation to the
therapist, I believe he is doing very much the same sort of
thing. In both cases, the later descriptions of the situation are

reflections on and elaborations of the first, unarticulated perceptions of similarity and difference.

It would be a mistake to attribute to the inquirer at the beginning of such a process the articulated description which he achieves later on—to say, for example, that Quist must have known unconsciously at the beginning just how this site is screwy and just how the geometry of parallels can be successfully imposed on it. To do so would be to engage in instant historical revisionism. The perception of similarity and difference implicit in Quist's initial description of the situation is, as Kuhn says, both logically and psychologically prior to his later articulation of it.

It is our capacity to see unfamiliar situations as familiar ones, and to do in the former as we have done in the latter, that enables us to bring our past experience to bear on the unique case. It is our capacity to *see-as* and *do-as* that allows us to have a feel for problems that do not fit existing rules.

The artistry of a practitioner like Quist hinges on the range and variety of the repertoire that he brings to unfamiliar situations. Because he is able to *see* these *as* elements of his repertoire, he is able to make sense of their uniqueness and need not reduce them to instances of standard categories.

Moreover, each new experience of reflection-in-action enriches his repertoire. Petra's case may function as an exemplar for new situations. Reflection-in-action in a unique case may be generalized to other cases, not by giving rise to general principles, but by contributing to the practitioner's repertoire of exemplary themes from which, in the subsequent cases of his practice, he may compose new variations.

Rigor in On-the-Spot Experiment

Seeing-as is not enough, however. When a practitioner sees a new situation as some element of his repertoire, he gets a new way of seeing it and a new possibility for action in it, but the adequacy and utility of his new view must still be discovered in action. Reflection-in-action necessarily involves experiment.

Indeed, as we have seen, Quist and the Supervisor conduct reflective conversations with their situations which are experiments in reframing. From their repertoires of examples, images, descriptions, they have derived (by seeing-as) a way of framing the present, unique situation. They try, then, to shape the situation to the frame; and they evaluate the entire process by criteria I have described earlier in this chapter—whether they can solve the problem they have set; whether they value what they get when they solve it (or what they can make of what they get); whether they achieve in the situation a coherence of artifact and idea, a congruence with their fundamental theories and values; whether they can keep inquiry moving. Nested within the larger problem-setting experiment, there are also local experiments of various sorts.

But in what sense is this really experimenting?

The question arises because there is another sense of experiment which is central to the model of professional knowledge as technical rationality, one which Quist and the Supervisor, in their inquiries, do not seem to exemplify at all. In this sense, experimenting is an activity by which a researcher confirms or refutes a hypothesis. Its logic is roughly as follows.[4]

The researcher wants to account for a puzzling phenomenon, Q. He entertains several hypotheses about Q, each of which explains it. That is, from each hypothesis, if true, Q would follow. Suppose, for example, that the question were one of discovering how mosquitoes find their way to their warm-blooded targets.[5] A researcher might entertain three hypotheses: that they are attracted to the target by distinctive smells, by temperature, or by humidity. Then the explanatory relation might look like this: "If the target is humid, and mosquitoes are attracted to humidity," then "mosquitoes are attracted to the target (other conditions being equal)."

But how does the researcher determine which of the hypotheses is correct? John Stuart Mill's description of the logic of experimental method still seems to me to be the most useful. He identified three fundamental methods of experiment. Given phenomenon Q and competing hypotheses A, B and C,

- The Method of Agreement consists in showing that when A (or B or C) is present, Q is also present. For example, when the target exceeds a certain threshold of humidity, then mosquitoes are attracted to it.
- The Method of Difference consists in showing that when A (or B or C) is absent, then Q is also absent. For example, when the target is *not* humid, then mosquitoes are not attracted to it.
- The Method of Concomitant Variations consists in showing that variations in A (or B or C) are accompanied by comparable variations in Q. For example, when the target's humidity varies, the degree of mosquitoes' attraction to it also varies.

Some version of the Method of Difference is essential to valid experimental inference. For when A and Q are co-present, there may be some other factor—C, for example—which is also co-present and is the cause of Q. For example, if the distinctive smells always accompany humidity when mosquitoes are attracted to a target such as a human hand, how can the experimenter distinguish the effects of smell from the effects of humidity? In order to make such a discrimination, he must be able to produce a situation in which he can selectively control the presence, or absence, or variation of the several variables named by the competing hypotheses. For example, researchers have devised an artificial target in which they can produce and vary independently the intensity of smell, temperature, or humidity. They have been able to show that, in the absence of smell, a combination of temperature and humidity will attract mosquitoes; whereas the distinctive smells of human skin, in the absence of temperature and humidity in the required ranges, will fail to do so.

The method of experimental hypothesis testing follows a process of elimination. The experimenter tries to produce conditions that disconfirm each of the competing hypotheses, by showing that the conditions that would follow from each hypothesis are not the observed ones. As Karl Popper has put it,[6] the experimenter conducts a competition among hypotheses, rather like a horse race. The hypothesis that most successfully resists refutation is the one that he accepts. Popper also points out, however, that hypotheses must always be accepted tentatively. For another hypothesis might be found which resists refutation more successfully still. For example, there might be some other factor, as yet undiscovered, which is present along with humidity and temperature and in the absence of which mosquitoes are no longer attracted to the target.

In order to stage such a competition of hypotheses, employing Mill's Methods of Agreement and Difference (or Concomitant Variations), the experimenter must be able to achieve selective variation of the factors named by the competing hypotheses. He must be able to vary the degree of humidity, for example, while keeping temperature and smell constant. And he must also be able to isolate the experimental situation from confounding changes in the environment—a human smell wafted into the apparatus, for example. These are central functions of the research laboratory. If laboratory experiment is not feasible or desirable, the experimenter may have recourse to records of large numbers of naturally occurring variations of the phenomena in which he is interested. To these records he can apply the Method of Concomitant Variations, through statistical analysis of naturally occurring correlations of variables. In this case, he simulates, or provides a substitute for, the technique of laboratory experiment.

In association with this model of controlled experiment, there is also the requirement for a particular kind of stance toward inquiry. The experimenter is expected to adhere to norms of control, objectivity, and distance. By controlling the experimental process, he is to achieve objectivity, seeing to it that other inquirers who employ the same methods will achieve the same results. And to this end, he is expected to preserve his distance from experimental phenomena, keeping his biases and interests from affecting the object of study.

Under conditions of everyday professional practice the norms of controlled experiment are achievable only in a very limited way. The practitioner is usually unable to shield his experiments from the effects of confounding changes in the environment. The practice situation often changes rapidly, and may change out from under the experiment. Variables are often locked into one another, so that the inquirer cannot separate them. The practice situation is often uncertain, in the sense that one doesn't know what the variables are. And the very act of experimenting is often risky.

Hence, according to the model of Technical Rationality, emphasis is placed on the separation of research from practice. On this view, practice should be based on scientific theory achievable only through controlled experiment, which cannot be conducted rigorously in practice. So to researchers and the research setting falls the development of basic and applied science, while to practitioners and the practice setting falls the use of scientific theories to achieve the instrumental goals of practice.

On this view, reflection-in-action is not really experiment.

In what, then, does the experimenting of Quist and the Supervisor consist? What is the logic of experimental inference which they employ? In what sense, if any, is their experimenting rigorous?

Let us step back to consider what experimenting means. I want to show that hypothesis-testing experiment is only one of several kinds of experiment, each of which has its own logic and its own criteria of success and failure. Because in practice these several kinds of experiment are mixed up together, experiment in practice is of a different order than experiment in the context of research.

In the most generic sense, to experiment is to act in order to see what the action leads to. The most fundamental experimental question is, "What if?"

When action is undertaken only to see what follows, without accompanying predictions or expectations, I shall call it *exploratory experiment*. This is much of what an infant does when he explores the world around him, what an artist does when he juxtaposes colors to see what effect they make, and what a newcomer does when he wanders around a strange neighborhood. It is also what a scientist often does when he first encounters and probes a strange substance to see how it will respond. Exploratory experiment is essential to the sort of science that does not appear in the scientific journals, because it has been screened out of the scientists' accounts of experimental results (perhaps because it does not conform to the norms of controlled experiment). Exploratory experiment is the probing, playful activity by which we get a feel for things. It succeeds when it leads to the discovery of something there.

There is another way in which we sometimes do things in

order to see what happens: we take action in order to produce an intended change. A carpenter who wants to make a structure stable tries fastening a board across the angle of a corner. A chess player advances his pawn in order to protect his queen. A parent gives his child a quarter to keep the child from crying. I shall call these *move-testing experiments.* Any deliberate action undertaken with an end in mind is, in this sense, an experiment. In the simplest case, where there are no unintended outcomes and one either gets the intended consequences or does not, I shall say that the move is *affirmed* when it produces what is intended for it and is *negated* when it does not. In more complicated cases, however, moves produce effects beyond those intended. One can get very good things without intending them, and very bad things may accompany the achievement of intended results. Here the test of the affirmation of a move is not only Do you get what you intend? but Do you like what you get? In chess, when you accidentally checkmate your opponent, the move is good and you do not take it back because its results are unexpected? On the other hand, giving a child a quarter may not only get him to stop crying, but also teach him to make money by crying—and the unintended effect is not so good. In these cases a better description of the logic of move-testing experiments is this: Do you like what you get from the action, taking its consequences as a whole? If you do, then the move is affirmed. If you do not, it is negated.

A third kind of experimenting, *hypothesis testing,* I have already described. Hypothesis-testing experiment succeeds when it effects an intended discrimination among competing hypotheses. If, for a given hypothesis, its predicted consequences fit what is observed, and the predictions derived from alternative hypotheses conflict with observation, then we can say that the first hypothesis has been *confirmed* and the others, *disconfirmed*—or, in Popper's more accurate formulation, the first hypothesis has demonstrated a greater competitive resistance to refutation.

In practice, the hypothesis subjected to experiment may be one that has been implicit in the pattern of one's moves, like the geometric center and center of gravity theories of the block-balancing experiments. In the on-the-spot experimenting characteristic of reflection-in-action, the *logic* of hypothesis testing is essentially the same as it is in the research context. If a carpenter asks himself, What makes this structure stable? and begins to experiment to find out—trying now one device, now another—he is basically in the same business as the research scientist. He puts forward hypotheses and, within the limits of the constraining features of the practice context, tries to discriminate among them—taking as disconfirmation of a hypothesis the failure to get the consequences predicted from it. The logic of his experimental inference is the same as the researcher's.

What is it, then, that is distinctive about the experimenting that goes on in practice?

The practice context is different from the research context in several important ways, all of which have to do with the relationship between changing things and understanding them. The practitioner has an interest in transforming the situation from what it is to something he likes better. He also has an interest in understanding the situation, but it is in the service of his interest in change.

When the practitioner reflects-in-action in a case he perceives as unique, paying attention to phenomena and surfacing his intuitive understanding of them, his experimenting is at once exploratory, move testing, and hypothesis testing. The three functions are fulfilled by the very same actions. And from this fact follows the distinctive character of experimenting in practice.

Let us consider, in this light, the reflection-in-action of Quist and the Supervisor.

When Quist imposes his geometry of parallels onto the screwy slope, he undertakes a global sequence of moves whose intent is to transform the situation into one that fits the geometry. His move-testing experiment succeeds because he solves the problem he has set and because, in addition, he likes what he can make of what he gets.

The Supervisor's situation, the experienced situation, is the one he perceives through the Resident's reports. In his framing of the problem of the situation, he focusses on the need to connect two streams of experience—the patient's experience in therapy and outside it—and in solving the problem, he connects them.

In both cases, the global moves are affirmed.

The practitioners' moves also function as exploratory probes of their situations. Their moves stimulate the situation's back-talk, which causes them to appreciate things in the situation that go beyond their initial perceptions of the problem. Quist perceives a new whole idea, created unexpectedly by the gallery's appearance as centerpiece of the design. For the Supervisor, there is the surprising story of the patient's fight with her boyfriend, which signals the patient's passivity and dependence and sets the course of his inquiry toward a new interpretive synthesis. In both cases, the exploratory experiment consists in the practitioner's conversation with the situation, in the back-talk which he elicits and appreciates.

In both cases, further, the practitioner's reframing of the problem of the situation carries with it a hypothesis about the situation. He surfaces the model of the phenomena associated with his student's framing of the problem, which he rejects. He proposes a new problem and with it, a new model of the phenomena, which he proceeds to treat as a hypothesis to be tested.

In Quist's case, the hypothesis is that this slope and this geometry of parallels can be made to fit one another. In the Supervisor's case, it is that the patient's transference will reveal how she is stuck in her therapy as she is stuck in her relationship with her boyfriend.

When we compare the practitioner's hypothesis-testing experiment to the method of controlled experiment, however, there are several notable differences.

The practitioner makes his hypothesis come true. He acts as though his hypothesis were in the imperative mood.[7] He says, in effect, "Let it be the case that X . . .", and shapes the situation so that X becomes true. Quist *carves* his geometry into the slope. The Supervisor channels his inquiry toward stories which illustrate the patient's transference and probes them to elicit themes suitable for explanation in terms of the transference. The practitioner's hypothesis testing consists of moves that change the phenomena to make the hypothesis fit.

The practitioner violates the canon of controlled experiment, which calls for objectivity and distance. In controlled experiment, the inquirer is supposed to refrain from imposing his biases and interests on the situation under study. He is supposed to avoid what, in the context of human beings, is popularly called the "Hawthorne Effect." [8] It is true that in laboratory experiment, experimenters are also expected to manipulate the experimental phenomena (as the researchers manipulate the mosquitoes' attraction to their artificial target). But *their* experiment has to do with a *type* of naturally occurring phenomenon which they study through the artificial situation of the laboratory. They manipulate the artificial situation, but leave the naturally occurring phenomena alone. Moreover, the canon of experimental method prohibits them from influencing the experimental situation to make it conform to their hypotheses; on the contrary, they are expected to strive for disconfirmation.

In the inquiries of Quist and the Supervisor, the unique situation at hand *is* the domain of inquiry. As the inquirers influence it, they influence the totality of their object of study. And they seek to exert influence in such a way as to confirm, not refute, their hypotheses.

Nevertheless, their situations are not wholly manipulable. They may resist the inquirers' attempts to shape them and in so doing, may yield unintended effects. Quist might have found that his slope could not be made to conform to his geometry of parallels, and might then have gone back to try other geometries. As it is, he sets the criterion of fit so that "slightly" is enough. The Supervisor might have found no evidence of transference of the patient's life pattern to the therapeutic relationship—although he does everything he can to set up the situation so that he will find such evidence. Thus the practitioners' hypothesis-testing experiments are not wholly self-fulfilling.

Their hypothesis-testing experiment is a game with the situation. They seek to make the situation conform to their hypothesis but remain open to the possibility that it will not. Thus their hypothesis-testing activity is neither self-fulfilling prophecy, which insures against the apprehension of disconfirming data, nor is it the neutral hypothesis testing of the method of controlled experiment, which calls for the experimenter to avoid influencing the object of study and to embrace disconfirming data. The practice situation is neither clay to be molded at will nor an independent, self-sufficient object of study from which the inquirer keeps his distance.

The inquirer's relation to this situation is *transactional.* [9] He shapes the situation, but in conversation with it, so that his own models and appreciations are also shaped by the situation. The phenomena that he seeks to understand are partly of his own making; he is *in* the situation that he seeks to understand.

This is another way of saying that the action by which he tests his hypothesis is also a move by which he tries to effect a desired change in the situation, and a probe by which he explores it. He understands the situation by trying to change it, and considers the resulting changes not as a defect of experimental method but as the essence of its success.

This fact has an important bearing on the practitioner's answer to the question, When should I stop experimenting?

In the context of controlled experiment, given Popper's dictum, the experimenter might keep on experimenting indefinitely—as long as he is able to invent new, plausible hypotheses which might resist refutation more effectively than those he has already tried. But in practice situations like Quist's and the Supervisor's—where experimental action is also a move and a probe, where the inquirer's interest in changing the situation takes precedence over his interest in understanding it—hypothesis testing is bounded by appreciations. It is initiated by the perception of something troubling or promising, and it is terminated by the production of changes one finds on the whole satisfactory, or by the discovery of new features which give the situation new meaning and change the nature of the questions to be explored. Such events bring hypothesis testing to a close even when the inquirer has not exhausted his store of plausible alternative hypotheses.

In Quist's case, he has made the geometry of parallels work slightly with the contours of the slope. But other geometries might also have been made to do so. Why does he stop here? Because he has produced changes he has found satisfactory, has made of unintended outcomes something that he likes, and has produced an unintended artifact which creates a new whole idea.

In the Supervisor's case, other interpretive syntheses might have accounted for the patient's tendency to keep herself continually frustrated. Her search for punishment might have been stimulated not only by angry thoughts or sexual wishes but by other factors. Why does the Supervisor not seek and test alternatives to these hypotheses? Because he has constructed an interpretive synthesis which accounts for and ties together the several stories he has elicited. He has made something coherent, congruent with his overarching theory, and susceptible to test by intervention.

It is true that the larger inquiry continues beyond these findings, its further directions set by them. But the experimenter need discriminate among contending hypotheses only to the point where his moves are affirmed or yield new appreciations of the situation. Thus hypothesis-testing experiment has a more limited function in practice than in research. And because of this, constraints on controlled experiment in the practice situation are less disruptive of inquiry than they would otherwise be.

On the other hand, the practice context places demands on hypothesis testing which are not present in the context of research. The hypothesis must lend itself to embodiment in a move. Quist has no interest in a hypothesis about the site which he cannot immediately translate into design. The Supervisor has no interest in hypotheses about the patient which are not immediately translatable into interpretive inquiry which can be tested in the intervention.

These distinctive features of experimenting in practice carry with them distinctive norms for rigor. The inquirer who reflects-in-action plays a game with the situation in which he is bound by considerations relevant to the three levels of experiment—exploration, move testing, and hypothesis testing. His primary interest is in changing the situation. But if he ignores its resistances to change, he falls into mere self-fulfilling prophecy. He experiments rigorously when he strives to make the situation conform to his view of it, while at the same time he remains open to the evidence of his failure to do so. He must learn by reflection on the situation's resistance that his hypothesis is inadequate, and in what way, or that his framing of the problem is inadequate, and in what way. Moreover, he plays his game in relation to a moving target, changing the phenomena as he experiments. Whether he ought to reflect-in-action, and how he ought to experiment, will depend on the changes produced by his earlier moves. The full range of changes, those that match or fail to match his expectations together with those that fall outside the scope of his intentions, are encompassed in this schema:

Consequences in relation to intention	Desirability of all perceived consequences, intended or unintended
1. Surprise	Undesirable
2. Surprise	Desirable or neutral
3. No surprise	Desirable or neutral
4. No surprise	Undesirable

The first is a typical case for reflection-in-action. The move fails to produce its intended result, and its consequences, intended and unintended, are considered undesirable. The move is negated and the theory associated with it is refuted. The inquirer then responds to the negation of the move by reflecting on its underlying theory.

Consider, as an example of this process, Petra's early report of her experiments with classroom units.

I had six of these classroom units, but they were too small in scale to do much with.

So I changed them to this much more signifi-cant layout (the L-shapes). It relates one to two, three to four, and five to six, which is more what I wanted to do educationally anyway. What I have is a space in here which is more of a home base.

Here we have a sequence of two experiments. In the first, Petra's implicit theory of action might be described as something like

If you want a satisfactory arrangement of the classrooms, make it like this.

But she finds the arrangement unsatisfactory and attributes that outcome to the fact that the units were "too small in scale to do much with." She says, in effect,

I had the view that something satisfactory could be made with units of that size, but I was wrong.

She then invents a new arrangement, and finds it (as she seems to have expected) "much more significant." She also becomes aware of additional, apparently unintended benefits: the new arrangement puts proximate grades next to one another and it yields a partially protected space which she calls a "home base."

The two experiments are chained together in a learning sequence. Petra's first move fails to produce the results intended for it and yields a situation which she finds on the whole unsatisfactory. She responds by surfacing the theory which she believes had led to her false expectation (here, a theory of the scale appropriate to classroom units), making a theory response to error. She criticizes and restructures her theory, and tests her new theory by producing the more aggregated L-shaped units. She gets the result she intended; hence, her new theory is not refuted. And she also gets some other unintended consequences which, along with the intended ones, she considers desirable; her new move is affirmed.

When a move fails to do what is intended and produces consequences considered on the whole to be undesirable, the inquirer surfaces the theory implicit in the move, criticizes it, restructures it, and tests the new theory by inventing a move consistent with it. The learning sequence, initiated by the negation of a move, terminates when new theory leads to a new move which is affirmed.

From the point of view of the logic of *confirmation*, the results of experiment remain ambiguous. Other theories of action or models might also account for the failure of the earlier move and the success of the later one. But in the practice context, priority is placed on the interest in change and therefore on the logic of *affirmation*. It is the logic of affirmation which sets the boundaries of experimental rigor.

The priority of the logics of affirmation and exploration over the logic of confirmation also becomes clear when we consider the other outcomes of experiment identified in our schema. In the second case, the inquirer's expectation is disappointed but the consequences taken as a whole are considered desirable. The associated theory is refuted but the move is affirmed. Petra might have designed the gallery as a pass-through, for example; she might then have decided that it worked badly as a pass-through but did fulfill a formal function, which justified it. In this case, Petra need not reflect on the theory which underlay her move. According to the logic of affirmation, the move has succeeded. Petra may wonder why her gallery failed to work as expected. But she need not reflect on it unless she wishes to consider the present case as a preparation for future cases where problems of circulation are also likely to arise.

In the third case, the move produces its intended outcome and its consequences are taken on the whole to be desirable. There is no need for reflection-in-action, unless the inquirer— again considering the present case as a preparation for future cases—were to ask himself to account for his present success.

In the fourth case, the move produces the expected results but it also causes unintended changes which are found, on the whole, to be unsatisfactory. Petra places the gym where she had wanted it, for example, in order to give direct access to the field. But she finds that her placement of it has constricted the space and spoiled the whole geometry of the buildings on the site. Here there will be reflection on the theory associated with the move, but it will focus on the theory's scope of relevance rather than its truth. Realizing that she has failed to consider the formal consequences of her move, Petra may consider new theories which take such factors into account. In the learning sequence which she then sets in motion, her new theories will refer not only to access but to the openness of the space and to the global geometry of the buildings on the site.

Thus the perceived changes produced by earlier moves determine the need for and the direction appropriate to reflection-in-action. The logic of on-the-spot experiment is threefold, and rigor in hypothesis testing is in the service of affirmation or exploration.

Virtual Worlds

The situations of Quist and the Supervisor are, in important ways, not the real thing. Quist is not moving dirt on the site. The Supervisor is not talking to the patient. Each is operating in a virtual world, a constructed representation of the real world of practice.

This fact is significant for the question of rigor in experimenting. In his virtual world, the practitioner can manage some of the constraints to hypothesis-testing experiment which are inherent in the world of his practice. Hence his ability to construct and manipulate virtual worlds is a crucial component of his ability not only to perform artistically but to experiment rigorously.

For Quist and Petra, the graphic world of the sketchpad is the medium of reflection-in-action. Here they can draw and talk their moves in spatial-action language, leaving traces which represent the forms of buildings on the site. Because the drawing reveals qualities and relations unimagined beforehand, moves can function as experiments. Petra can discover that her building shapes do not fit the slope and that her classrooms are too small in scale to do much with. Quist can find nooks in the intervals he has created and can see that his geometry works slightly with the contours of the site. Considering the gallery he has made, he can observe that "there is this which is repetitive and this again which is not repetitive."

Constraints which would prevent or inhibit experiment in the built world are greatly reduced in the virtual world of the drawing.

The act of drawing can be rapid and spontaneous, but the residual traces are stable. The designer can examine them at leisure.

The pace of action can be varied at will. The designer can slow down, to think about what he is doing. On the other hand, events that would take a long time in the built world—the carving of a slope, the shaving of the trees—can be made to "happen" immediately in the drawing.

No move is irreversible. The designer can try, look, and by shifting to another sheet of paper, try again. As a consequence, he can perform learning sequences in which he corrects his errors and takes account of previously unanticipated results of his moves. Petra can explore the size and shape of her classroom units and the placement of the administration building. Quist can propose that she "draw and draw" to determine the proper dimensions of her grid, figure out how to treat the "middle area" and "shave off the trees." Moves that would be costly in the built world can be tried at little or no risk in the world of the drawing.

It is possible to eliminate changes in the environment which would disrupt or confound experiment. In the drawing, there are no work stoppages, breakdowns of equipment, or soil conditions which would make it impossible to sink a foundation.

Some variables which are interlocking in the built world can be separated from one another in the world of the drawing. A global geometry of buildings on the site can be explored without any reference to particular construction methods. A building shape can be considered while deferring the question of the material from which the shape is to be made.

In order to capture the benefits of the drawn world as a context for experiment, the designer must acquire certain competences and understandings. He needs to learn the traditions of graphic media, languages and notations. Quist, for example, has a repertoire of media which enables him to choose the graphic system best suited to the exploration of particular phenomena. Sketches enable him to explore global geometries;

cross-sectional drawings, to examine three-dimensional effects; drawing to scale, to experiment with the dimensions of design; models, to examine relationships of building masses, comparative volumes, sun, and shade. He uses media selectively to address the issues to which he gives priority at each stage of the design process.

Quist has also learned to use graphic languages transparently. When he represents a contour of the site by a set of concentric lines, he sees *through* it to the actual shapes of the slope, just as practiced readers can see through the letters on a page to words and meanings. Hence he is able to move in the drawing as though he were moving through buildings on the site, exploring the felt-paths as a user of the building would experience them.

But the virtual world of the drawing can function reliably as a context for experiment only insofar as the results of experiment can be transferred to the built world. The validity of the transfer depends on the reliability with which the drawn world represents the built one. As an architect's practice enables him to move back and forth between drawing and building, he learns how his drawings will "build" and develops a capacity for accurate rehearsal. He learns to recognize the representational limits of graphic media. He learns, for example, how drawings fail to capture qualities of materials, surfaces, and technologies. He learns to remember that drawings cannot represent soil conditions, wind, costs of materials and labor, breakdowns of equipment, and man-made changes in the environment. Drawing functions as a context for experiment precisely because it enables the designer to eliminate features of the real-world situation which might confound or disrupt his experiments, but when he comes to interpret the results of his experiments, he must remember the factors that have been eliminated.

The Supervisor constructs, through his interactions with the Resident, a virtual world of talk which represents the experienced world of therapist and patient. Storytelling represents and substitutes for firsthand experience.

By his selective questions and acts of attention, the Supervisor shapes the experienced situation to which he will address interpretive inquiry. Like Quist, he is able to hold some features of the situation constant. Once a story has been told, it can be held as a datum, considered at leisure for its meanings and its relationships with other stories. Transient events, widely separate in time, can be held steady and juxtaposed with one another to permit exploration of such phenomena as dependency or guilt. Some stories can be ignored, or reduced to mere outlines, while others are expanded and elaborated. By attending to a few features which he considers central, the Supervisor can isolate the main thread of a story from the surrounding factors which he chooses to consider as noise. And by putting a term to his questioning or attention, he can set the boundaries of the universe of data which will serve as material for his experiments in interpretation. Trying now one interpretation, now another, he can make his experimental moves reversible and design his own learning sequences.

But in the therapeutic context, the practitioner's world is virtual in a twofold sense. The Resident's stories can be used to represent the therapeutic interaction, and the therapeutic interaction can be shaped to become a representation of the patient's life outside of therapy. In fact, the Supervisor tries to get the Resident to do precisely this when he urges him to tell his patient that "here, in the relationship with you, she can see what is going on and you can work it out together." The power of the transference lies in its use as a world representative of the patient's other relationships. In such a world, it becomes possible to slow down phenomena which would ordinarily be lost to reflection. Actions which might be otherwise irreversible can be examined for their meanings, revised, and tried again. Once the transference has become an object of shared inquiry, the therapist can experiment with moves that would ordinarily carry a risk of angering or alienating the patient.

The therapist's ability to use the transference as a virtual world depends on his ability to read its signs. He must become adept at listening to the patient's utterances as moves comparable to those she uses in the life outside. As the Supervisor comments,

> And yet she will find ways of distancing you, just as she does her boyfriend.

Further, the therapist must become adept at converting his relationship with the patient into a world of inquiry in which thoughts and feelings can be seen as sources of discovery rather than as triggers to action. The therapist's ability to make this happen depends both on his ability to reflect on his experience of being with the patient, detecting the signs of his own countertransference, and on his ability to elicit the patient's trust. This depends, in turn, on his ability to empathize with the patient, to establish and honor the norms of their mutual obligation, and to help the patient gain insight from revealed thoughts and feelings so that the effort of the special relationship comes to seem worthwhile. The creation and maintenance of the virtual world of therapy is both a method of inquiry and a strategy of intervention.

But the representative reliability of the virtual world has its limits. The Resident can guess, but cannot know, that the patient's decision to remain in therapy is a response to his becoming "the bastard she needs." He cannot be sure that her way of keeping herself frustrated in therapy is similar to her continual self-frustration outside of therapy. Only through further experience with the patient, as she risks bringing more of herself into the therapeutic relationship, can he test such inferences as these.

The therapist's use of the transference and the architect's sketchpad are examples of the variety of virtual worlds on which all the professions are dependent. A sculptor learns to infer from the feel of a maquette in his hand the qualities of a monumental figure that will be built from it. Engineers become adept at the uses of scale models, wind tunnels, and computer simulations. In an orchestra rehearsal, conductors experiment with tempo, phrasing, and instrumental balance. A roleplay is an improvised game in which the participants learn to discover properties of an interpersonal situation and to reflect-in-action on their intuitive responses to it. In improvisation, musical or dramatic, participants can conduct on-the-spot experiments in which, as improvisation tends towards performance, the boundaries between virtual and real worlds may become blurred.

Virtual worlds are contexts for experiment within which practitioners can suspend or control some of the everyday impediments to rigorous reflection-in-action. They are representative worlds of practice in the double sense of "practice." And practice in the construction, maintenance, and use of virtual worlds develops the capacity for reflection-in-action which we call artistry.

Stance Toward Inquiry

A practitioner's stance toward inquiry is his attitude toward the reality with which he deals.

According to the model of Technical Rationality, there is an objectively knowable world, independent of the practitioner's values and views. In order to gain technical knowledge of it, the practitioner must maintain a clear boundary between himself and his object of inquiry. In order to exert technical control over it, he must observe it and keep his distance from it—as Bacon said, commanding Nature by obeying her. His stance toward inquiry is that of spectator/manipulator.

In a practitioner's reflective conversation with a situation that he treats as unique and uncertain, he functions as an agent/experient.[10] Through his transaction with the situation, he shapes it and makes himself a part of it. Hence, the sense he makes of the situation must include his own contribution to it. Yet he recognizes that the situation, having a life of its own distinct from his intentions, may foil his projects and reveal new meanings.

From this paradoxical source derive the several features of a stance toward inquiry which are as necessary to reflection-in-action as the norms of on-the-spot experiment and the uses of virtual worlds.

The inquirer must impose an order of his own, jumping rather than falling into his transaction with the situation. Thus the Supervisor tries to get the Resident to recognize his contribution to the patient's stalemate and to see in the transference a medium for inquiry and intervention. Thus Quist tries to get Petra to see that coherence does not exist in the site but must be imposed upon it by the designer. But the inquirer must also take responsibility for the order he imposes. As Quist draws to scale and the Supervisor probes the Resident's stories, they engage in a disciplined pursuit of the implications of their chosen frames.

At the same time that the inquirer tries to shape the situation to his frame, he must hold himself open to the situation's back-talk. He must be willing to enter into new confusions and uncertainties. Hence, he must adopt a kind of double vision.[11] He must act in accordance with the view he has adopted, but he must recognize that he can always break it open later, indeed, *must* break it open later in order to make new sense of his transaction with the situation. This becomes more difficult to do as the process continues. His choices become more committing; his moves, more nearly irreversible. As the risk of uncertainty increases, so does the temptation to treat the view as the reality. Nevertheless, if the inquirer maintains his double vision, even while deepening his commitment to a chosen frame, he increases his chances of arriving at a deeper and broader coherence of artifact and idea.

His ability to do this depends on certain relatively constant elements that he may bring to a situation otherwise in flux: an overarching theory, an appreciative system, and a stance of reflection-in-action which can become, in some practitioners, an ethic for inquiry.

Technical Rationality and Reflection-in-Action Compared

As we have described similarities of patterns and principles in Quist's designing and the Supervisor's therapeutic inquiry, we have also begun to describe an epistemology of reflection-in-action which accounts for artistry in situations of uniqueness and uncertainty. On this view of professional knowing, technical problem solving occupies a limited place within the inquirer's reflective conversation with his situation; the model of Technical Rationality appears as radically incomplete.

The Positivist epistemology of practice rests on three dichotomies. Given the separation of means from ends, instrumental problem solving can be seen as a technical procedure to be measured by its effectiveness in achieving a pre-established objective. Given the separation of research from practice, rigorous practice can be seen as an application to instrumental problems of research-based theories and techniques whose objectivity and generality derive from the method of controlled experiment. Given the separation of knowing from doing, action is only an implementation and test of technical decision.

In the reflective conversations of Quist and the Supervisor, these dichotomies do not hold. For Quist and the Supervisor, practice is a kind of research. In their problem setting, means and ends are framed interdependently. And their inquiry is a transaction with the situation in which knowing and doing are inseparable.

These inquirers encounter a problematic situation whose reality they must construct. As they frame the problem of the situation, they determine the features to which they will attend, the order they will attempt to impose on the situation, the directions in which they will try to change it. In this process, they identify both the ends to be sought and the means to be employed. In the ensuing inquiry, action on the situation is integral with deciding, and problem solving is a part of the larger experiment in problem setting. For example, Quist applies his rules of thumb, about the uses of slopes appropriate to their various grades, as a component of the larger experiment in which he tries to impose a geometry of parallels onto the site. His frame experiment sets the problem to be solved, and his problem-solving is one element in his test of the frame.

Quist and the Supervisor reflect on their students' intuitive understandings of the phenomena before them and construct new problems and models derived, not from application of research-based theories, but from their repertoires of familiar examples and themes. Through *seeing as* and *doing as,* they make and test new models of the situation. But their on-the-spot experiments, conducted in the virtual worlds of sketchpad and storytelling, also function as transforming moves and exploratory probes. Hypothesis testing has the limited function of enabling them to achieve satisfactory moves or to surface phenomena which cause them to reframe the situation.

The values of control, distance, and objectivity, central to the model of Technical Rationality, take on new meanings in the reflective conversation. Here the inquirer tries, within the limits of his virtual world, to control variables for the sake of hypothesis-testing experiment. But his hypothesis is about the situation's potential for transformation, and in the testing process he steps into the situation. He produces knowledge that is objective, in the sense that he can disconfirm it. He can discover that he has not achieved satisfactory change or that he ought to undertake change of a different order. But his knowledge is also personal, bounded by his commitments to appreciative system and overarching theory. It is compelling only to members of a community of inquiry who share these commitments.[12]

In the following chapters, we will explore other examples of knowing-in-practice which exhibit, in greater or lesser degree, the process of reflective conversation with the situation which we have so far observed only in the practices of Quist and the Supervisor. We will examine how reflection-in-action varies with the context and domain-specific knowledge of other practitioners, and we will inquire into the contextual factors which set limits to reflection-in-action.

Reflective Practice in the Science-Based Professions

What Are the Science-Based Professions?

Medicine, agronomy, and engineering are prototypical examples of professions which have a basis in scientific knowledge. Many others, such as dentistry, optometry, meteorology, nursing, management, forestry, are, in Glazer's words,

> either based directly on science or contain a high component of strictly technological knowledge based on science in the education which they provide.[1]

Under the model of Technical Rationality, practitioners of these professions are seen as technical problem solvers. Physicians use techniques of diagnosis and treatment based on the physiology of disease. With research-based theories and techniques, agronomists solve problems of agricultural productivity, soil erosion, plant disease, and insect control. Production engineers use theories and techniques of statistical analysis and optimization to solve problems of product quality and production efficiency. Construction engineers apply the results of research on soil conditions and building structures to select types of building foundations.

According to the model of Technical Rationality, such problem solving is a manipulation of available techniques to achieve chosen ends in the face of manageable constraints. In Simon's more sophisticated language, there is an objective function which measures performance, a set of possible strategies of action, and a range of techniques of implementation; strategies and techniques may be compared in terms of their probable costs and their effectiveness in achieving the objective function. An occupation moves from craft to profession as it approximates this model of technical problem solving, and it becomes science based as its techniques are grounded in the theories of basic and applied research. According to the exchange relationship described early in this century by Veblen, practitioners give their problems to researchers, who give to practitioners new theories and techniques for problem solving.

Each practitioner of a science-based profession is seen as engaging in a very limited kind of on-the-spot inquiry. He asks, Have I selected the right problem from my stock of known problems? Have I selected the right problem-solving technique from my stock of known techniques? He makes a threefold *mapping* of the signs of the present situation onto known problems and techniques. Recent studies of medical diagnosis, for example, have shown that this mapping can become extraordinarily complex. Using the framework of artificial intelligence, some researchers have described the literally millions of facts, rules of inference, and heuristics which skillful clinicians use to describe and diagnose a present illness.[2] But for all of their complexity, these studies still treat the process of clinical diagnosis as a mapping of cues in the present situation to the clinician's theories of disease and methods of treatment.

If we turn from the model of Technical Rationality to the actual practice of science-based professionals, however, it is clear that technical problem solving is a radically incomplete description of what engineers, agronomists, and physicians actually do. They solve technical problems, but they also do other things.

When practitioners choose to address new or unique problems which do not fit known categories, their inquiry is not a threefold mapping of the kind I have just described, but a design process artistic in nature and fundamentally similar in structure to the reflective conversations analyzed in the previous chapter. And when science-based practitioners try to take account of the larger context of their inquiry, only some elements of which are within their control, they must construct a manageable problem from a problematic situation. In the first kind of case, the practitioner reflects-in-action on puzzling phenomena which are new to him, even though they fall within normal boundaries of a technical practice. In the second, he reflects-in-action on a larger situation that impinges on his activity even though it falls outside what are normally considered the boundaries of the profession.

The Art of Engineering Design

Engineering is a particularly interesting field in which to consider the relationship between technical problem solving and reflection-in-action, for in this field we have witnessed, in the period following World War II, both an attempt to redefine engineering as an applied science and a subsequent discovery of the limits of that redefinition.

After World War II, in the glow of engineering triumphs which would have been impossible without the contributions of physics, and later on under the shadow of Sputnik, the advocates of engineering science had succeeded in transforming the engineering curriculum into an education in applied physics. By the late 1960s, however, leading practitioners and educators were beginning to have second thoughts. Harvey Brooks, the dean of the Harvard engineering program, was among the first to point out the weakness of an image of engineering based exclusively on engineering science. In his 1967 article, "Dilemmas of Engineering Education,"[3] he described the predicament of the practicing engineer who is expected to bridge the gap between a rapidly changing body of knowledge and the rapidly changing expectations of society. The resulting demand for adaptability, Brooks thought, required an art of engineering. But the scientizing of the engineering schools had been intended to move engineering from art to science.

Aided by the enormous public support for science in the period 1953–67, the engineering schools had placed their bets on an engineering science oriented to "the possibility of the new" rather than to the "design capability" of making something useful; and with this shift of emphasis, the specialist in a discipline became the most powerful member of the engineering faculty. Brooks saw in this individual a set of values and attitudes not always compatible with the values and needs of the professional "who plans to devote himself to service, as the great majority must do." Like Glazer, he saw that the problem becomes more acute if the "intellectual stature of the disciplinary scientist within a professional school is sensibly above that of the faculty representing the profession itself." Practicing engineers are no longer powerful role models when the professors of highest status are engineering scientists. Under these circumstances, engineering schools confronted a new problem, "the relationship between science and art in the training of the professionals." But by 1967 engineering design had virtually disappeared from the curriculum, and the question of the relationship between science and art was no longer alive.

Brooks, who wished to bring this question back to life, perceived that the art of engineering design presents an educational dilemma. If this art is neither known nor invariant, then how can it be taught?

I propose that engineering design is understandable as a reflective conversation with the materials of a situation, a kind of process similar to the ones we have already observed in architecture and psychotherapy. Although it cannot be reduced to an application of general rules or theories, on the model of applied research, some of its main features are constant and amenable to description.

Let us consider, to begin with, an example of relatively unsophisticated engineering design. I have chosen an example from a university practicum in mechanical engineering where the technology is relatively simple and the outlines of the design process can be more readily discerned.

Some years ago, I met with faculty and students who were participating in an experiment in engineering education. In this program students worked, under faculty supervision, on real-world industrial problems. In our session together, we reviewed a project which had been submitted by a manufacturer of guns. The presenting problem was roughly this:

> We have a hundred-and-fifty-year-old process which produces a lovely blue patina on the hammers and triggers of our guns. We heat the metal in the presence of cow bone imported from Argentina, and then quench it in water. The process has always worked, though we have no idea why. Recently, we have learned that we will lose our supply of cow bone. We want you to develop a new process that duplicates the old colors exactly and reliably.

The project had been given to a small group of students who had very little to go on. The manufacturer's engineers had not been able to suggest a plan of attack. They had proposed investigating the surface chemistry of the metal, but this seemed merely a way of saying that the answer might lie in a field they knew nothing about.

The students quickly discovered that "there were a lot of variables." Given the fact that in the old process the metal had been heated to 1600 degrees Fahrenheit, the students decided to concentrate first on temperature and cooking time, and they tried to understand the oxide layer of the metal thermodynamically. This seemed to require a very long process of experiment, however, and as the pressure for performance increased, the students began to "fiddle with the variables" and "fly by the seat of our pants." They discovered that they could duplicate the colors pretty well by cooking the metal in an air furnace for seven minutes, then quenching the metal in water. But this left them with a new question: How was it that both the old and the new methods worked?

As one of the students said, "We knew it couldn't be the unique properties of cow bone!" In the factory, workers had heated the metal with cow bone in a closed container; then, when they quenched it in water, they exposed it to dissolved oxygen. Perhaps cow bone had functioned as a "sacrificial element," taking up oxygen from the surface of the metal, and perhaps the resulting oxygen deficiency had played an important role in the coloring process. By the end of the first semester's work, in any case, the students still had no firm explanation of the two processes, and their new process had proved erratic. Not all the triggers looked alike.

Later in the second semester, one of the manufacturer's engineers visited them and asked, "What have you been *doing?*" This stirred them to purchase a meter to measure dissolved oxygen, and they were able to convince themselves that dissolved oxygen was a key variable. As one of the students said, "Up to that point, we hadn't acted on our idea. When all the variables seem to be equally important, you do first what's easiest."

Now they still had some uncontrolled variables, but they thought they understood the problem well enough to begin to build a prototype to test their concept. They set about designing a furnace which would have a high rate of production and a low rate of rejection. They decided that the furnace should be continuous and automated. But immediately they encountered a new set of difficulties. A particularly annoying effect was the heat-sagging of the sides of the furnace, which interfered with experimentation. As a result, they decided to go back to a batch-type "muffler" furnace. When I asked whether they had been trying to design a production prototype or a vehicle for further experiment, the student who had taken on the project at this point said, "I was trying to give them what they wanted!" And the faculty supervisor explained that he had thought to himself, "Why continue to work on erratic results in an experimental setup when in the continuous furnace the whole situation may be different?"

In the muffler furnace, however, the student had been able to eliminate some of the earlier troubles. Heat-sagging had disappeared, and so had the blistering of the metal which had marred the results of some earlier experiments. But the student found that he could produce the desired color and hardness on only one side of the metal.

His next problem, as he saw it, was to get the desired results on both sides. He had said, "If you could get the pieces to fall in vertically, it would be okay," and he had begun the design of a vertical furnace.

Looking back on the whole process, it was clear that the students had begun with the problem of explaining why the old production method worked. They had tried at first to build a theory of the surface chemistry, but their experiments had yielded ambiguous results. Pressed by the client to solve the production problem quickly, they had come upon a new process which did not depend on exotic materials, but they were no more able to explain the new process than they had been able to explain the old.

Addressing this new problem of explanation, they developed the "dissolved oxygen" hypothesis. They now had a process which did not depend on cow bone and they had a plausible explanation of its effects, but the product quality was unreliable. In what context, now, should they carry out experiments to improve reliability—in the experimental setup they had been using, or in a production furnace where conditions might be "totally different"? They opted for the production furnace, which presented a new set of problems.

The entire inquiry can be represented as a reflective conversation with the materials of the situation, but in this instance the reflective conversation wove its way through stages of diagnosis, experiment, pilot process, and production design, as in figure 6.1.

FIGURE 6.1

Stages of Engineering Design, Conceived as a Reflective Conversation

Phenomena to be explained or remedied	Inquiry
The traditional process. ──────────→	Thermodynamic studies of the oxide layer. Experiments to duplicate results of the old process.
Why do both new and old processes work?	Experiments with dissolved oxygen.
Blistering, uncontrolled variables.	New experiments, coupled with design of production furnace.
Heat-sagging. Acceptable color and hardness on one side only.	Modified furnace design. Vertical furnace.

At each stage of this process, the students were confronted with puzzles and problems that did not fit their known categories, yet they had a sense of the kinds of theories (surface chemistry, thermodynamics) that might explain these phenomena. They used their theoretical hunches to guide experiment, but on several occasions their moves led to puzzling outcomes—a process that worked, a stubborn defect—on which they then reflected. Each such reflection gave rise to new experiments and to new phenomena, troublesome or desirable, which led to further reflection and experiment. Unlike Quist, these engineering students were able to make liberal use of research-based theory and technique, but their applications of research results were embedded in a reflective conversation with the situation similar in its general outlines to Quist's designing.

The Art of Scientific Investigation

Lest it be thought that engineering design takes a form such as this only in the relatively unsophisticated inquiry of engineering students, I shall turn now to a celebrated example in which technological invention and scientific discovery are interwoven—the development of the transistor. Here, too, experiment aimed at testing a particular hypothesis or achieving a particular technological effect repeatedly produces unexpected phenomena which trigger new hypotheses, goals, and questions. Experiment functions at the same time to test technological moves, discriminate among plausible scientific hypotheses, and explore puzzling phenomena. At some points in this process, a technological endeavor yields phenomena that provoke scientific discovery. In others, new technological possibilities are derived from a scientific explanation. In both cases, the "science" in question is not after the fact presentation of knowledge of the sort usually found in the scientific journals but before the fact, apparently disorderly research of the kind sometimes described as "the art of scientific investigation."[4]

In Richard Nelson's account of the development of the transistor at Bell Laboratories in the mid-1940s, he points out that long before World War II, scientists had been familiar with materials now called semiconductors which were known to have interesting though inexplicable properties.[5] "Cat whisker" (semiconductor) rectifiers were widely used in the early days of the radio industry, but the vacuum tube, whose functions and directions of possible improvement were better understood, overshadowed semiconductor rectifiers. Still, many scientists thought about making a semiconductor amplifier. Their thinking seems to have been motivated by a simple analogy with vacuum tubes.

Vacuum tubes rectified and, with the introduction of a grid, amplified. Semiconductors rectified. Therefore somehow, they should be able to amplify.[6]

Some researchers proposed inserting a grid into a semiconductor diode but, owing to the extreme thinness of the rectifying area, they were unable to do so.

Meanwhile a theory was taking shape which scientists would later see as an explanation of part of the behavior of semiconductors. This was A. H. Wilson's quantum mechanical model of a solid semiconductor, published in 1931. Wilson described a semiconductor as a crystal containing two different types of current carriers, electrons (negatively charged) and holes (positively charged). Wilson found that the number of holes and electrons free to carry current varies with the temperature and also with the purity of the crystal. A doped germanium crystal (an n, or negative, semiconductor) could be made so that it contained many more electrons than holes; in crystals of this type, electrons are the "majority" and holes the "minority" carriers. In crystals of the p, or positive, type, holes are the majority carriers. A junction of p- and n-type crystals conducts current much more easily in one direction than in another, because on the n side most of the charge carriers are negative while on the p side, most of them are positive. In this way, Wilson had explained how a p-n junction functions as a rectifier.

His model gave an adequate basis for understanding much of the behavior of p- and n-type semiconductors, including the crucial fact of the existence of minority carriers, but scientists missed some of the key points until the work of Shockley, Brattain, and Bardeen at Bell Laboratories. In the early stages of this work, just after World War II, Shockley's ideas about making amplifiers shifted from analogy with the vacuum tube to the use of an electric field, imposed from the outside without actually touching the material, to influence the number of movable electrons in the semiconductor. But devices based on this principle produced unexpected results. Sometimes even the sign of the effect was off, and even when the sign was right, the magnitude of the observed effect was a thousandth of its predicted value.

To explain this negative result, Bardeen proposed that electrons within the electric field were trapped at the surface in "surface states," and hence were unaffected by the presence of the field. In order to test this theory, and in an attempt to find a way to neutralize surface state "traps," the investigators performed a new set of experiments. In Nelson's words,

> These experiments did yield observed amplification from a field effect. But more important, in one of the experiments two contacts were placed quite close together on a germanium crystal. [Figure 6.2] It does not matter just why this particular experiment was performed with the hope of observing the most important result it yielded. For in the course of the experiment it was observed that connecting up the A battery increased the current flow in the B battery circuit. The device amplified. This was the first indication of the transistor effect.

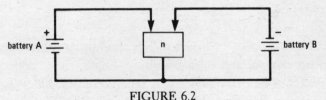

FIGURE 6.2
The Point Contact Transistor[7]

Experiments designed to make a field-effect amplifier had resulted in the construction of an amplifier working on quite different principles, which came later to be called a "point contact transistor." Later still, Shockley explained that current flow increased in the B circuit, as a result of connecting the

A circuit, because of electron "holes" flowing from top left to top right contact. The key concept was "the flow of minority carriers in a crystal, holes in *n*-type germanium."[8] As Nelson points out, there still is no really adequate quantitative theory of the point contact transistor. Nevertheless, experiments aimed at achieving amplification had produced unexpected observations indicating that an amplifier might be built on a design very different from the one originally intended, and the workings of this new amplifier could be explained in terms of injected minority carriers.

Shockley then set out to develop a theory of the role of minority carriers in semiconductor current flow. From this theory, he was able to design, in a conscious and deliberate way, the device later called the "junction transistor," shown in figure 6.3.

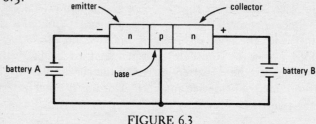

FIGURE 6.3
The Junction Transistor[9]

A junction transistor consists of a germanium or silicon crystal made up of *n, p,* and *n* (or "emitter," "base," and "collector" terminals). The two *n* regions are separated by a thin *p* region. Shockley showed that when voltage increased in the *A* circuit, there would be an increase in the flow of electrons between emitter and collector, the electrons flowing through the central *p* region. And he showed that, for appropriate battery biases, the transistor would amplify, because the induced change in voltage across the *A* circuit would produce a larger change across the *B* circuit. The invention depended directly on the role of minority carriers, which had grown out of the semiaccidental discovery of the point contact transistor.

The structure of inquiry into semiconductors at Bell Labs can be expressed in a schema, as in figure 6.4. Here we can discern two kinds of movement mediated by reflection. In the first, reflection on theory leads to experiment. In the second, reflection on the unexpected results of experiment leads to theory, or to invention. What is striking is that, in the interweaving of theory building and invention, experiment functions both to confirm or disconfirm hypotheses, to affirm or negate moves, and to explore phenomena. The *discovery* of new hypotheses occurs repeatedly in a process aimed primarily at design, and hypothesis-testing experiment leads repeatedly to invention. One should not say that what was learned from the surface-state experiments made the junction transistor a more promising alternative but that, before these experiments, the "path to an amplifier by way of junctions and minority carriers just was not clearly perceived."[10]

In the development of the transistor, experiments were sometimes designed to test hypotheses and existing theories

FIGURE 6.4

Stages of Development of the Transistor

Theories	Experiment, phenomena, invention
Pre-World War II model of semiconductor. ──────────→	Initial attempts to make semiconductor based on analogy with vacuum tube.
Shockley's theory of the electric ◄─── field. ──────────→	Field-effect experiments. Unexpected failure of predictions.
Bardeen's theory of surface states. ◄───	New experiments. Discovery of point contact transistor effect.
Theory of minority carriers. ◄─── ──────────→	Design of junction transistor.

were sometimes used to solve known problems. But both hypothesis testing and problem solving were parts of a reflective conversation with the situation in the course of which hypotheses were newly formed and problems newly framed.

Reflection on *Seeing-As*

In the examples just described, there was a crucially important step, one often attributed to "creativity" or "intuition." In the case of the gunmetal coloring problem, mechanical engineers devised a new heating/quenching process and a new hypothesis about the role of dissolved oxygen in coloring the metal. In the case of the transistor, several new theories were proposed and several new devices designed. Faced with unexpected and puzzling phenomena, the inquirers made initial *descriptions* which guided their further investigations.

Where do such descriptions come from? They are, at least on some occasions, outcomes of reflections on a perceived similarity, a process which in the previous chapter I called *seeing-as*. The perception of similarity before one can say "similar with respect to what," and the subsequent reflection on it, are essential both to the art of engineering design and to the art of scientific investigation.

Thomas Kuhn identifies this process in the development of theories of physics, for example, and he also finds it in the way in which a student of physics learns to solve the problems at the back of the book. Just as the student "learns to see his problem as like a problem he has already encountered," so scientists "model one problem solution on another, often with minimum recourse to symbolic generalizations."[11] Kuhn's example is worth quoting in full.

Galileo found that a ball rolling down an incline acquires just enough velocity to return it to the same vertical height on a second incline of any slope, and he learned to see that experimental situation as like the pendulum with a point-mass for a bob. Huyghens then solved the problem of the center of oscillation of a physical pendulum by imagining that the extended body of the latter was composed of Galilean point-pendula, the bonds between which could be instantaneously released at any point in the swing. After the bonds were released, the individual point pendula would swing freely, but their collective center of gravity, like that of Galileo's pendulum, would rise only to the height from which the center of gravity of the extended pendulum had begun to fall. Finally, Daniel Bernoulli, still with no aid from Newton's laws, discovered how to make the flow of water from an oriface in a storage tank resemble Huyghens's pendulum. Determine the descent of the center of gravity of the water in tank and jet during an infinitesimal interval of time. Next imagine that each partical of water afterwards moves separately upward to the maximum height obtainable with the velocity it possessed at the end of the interval of descent. The ascent of the center of gravity of the separate particles must then equal the descent of the center of gravity of the water in tank and jet. From that view of the problem, the long-sought speed of efflux followed at once.[12]

In "The Role of Analogies in Science," Robert Oppenheimer has told a similar story about the evolution of wave theory. Physicists had modelled theories of sound waves on existing theories of waves in liquids, and other physicists subsequently modelled electromagnetic wave theory on acoustics.[13]

Kuhn calls such processes "thinking from exemplars." Once a new problem is seen to be analogous to a problem previously solved, then "both an appropriate formalism and a new way of attaching its symbolic consequences to nature follow"[14]— "follow," that is, from reflection on the similarity earlier perceived. When the two things seen as similar are initially very different from one another, falling into what are usually considered different domains of experience, then *seeing-as* takes a form that I call "generative metaphor."[15] In this form, *seeing-as* may play a critical role in invention and design, as the following example suggests.

Some years ago, a group of product-development researchers was considering how to improve the performance of a new paintbrush made with synthetic bristles.[16] Compared to the old natural-bristle brush, the new one delivered paint to a surface in a discontinuous, "gloppy" way. The researchers had tried a number of different improvements. They had noticed, for example, that natural bristles had split ends, whereas the synthetic bristles did not, and they tried (without significant improvement resulting) to split the ends of the synthetic bristles. They experimented with bristles of different diameters. Nothing seemed to help.

Then someone observed, *"You know, a paintbrush is a kind of pump!"* He pointed out that when a paintbrush is pressed against a surface, paint is forced through the *spaces between bristles* onto the surface. The paint is made to flow through the "channels" formed by the bristles when the channels are deformed by the bending of the brush. He noted that painters will sometimes *vibrate* a brush when applying it to a surface, so as to facilitate the flow of paint.

The researchers tried out the natural and synthetic bristle brushes, thinking of them as pumps. They noticed that the natural bristle formed a *gradual curve* when it was pressed against a surface, whereas the synthetic brush formed a shape more nearly an angle. They speculated that this difference might account for the "gloppy" performance of the bristle brush. How then might they make the bending shape of the synthetic brush into a gentle curve?

This line of thought led them to a variety of inventions. Perhaps fibers could be varied so as to create greater density in that zone. Perhaps fibers could be bonded together in that zone. Some of these inventions were reduced to practice and did, indeed, produce a smoother flow of paint.

Paintbrush as pump is an example of what I mean by a generative metaphor. One can characterize the metaphor-making process by saying that the researchers, who had begun by describing painting in a familiar way, entertained the description of a different, already-named process (pumping) as an alternative description of painting; and that in their redescription of painting, both their perception of the phenomenon and the previous description of pumping were transformed. What makes the process one of metaphor making, rather than simply of describing, is that the new putative description already belongs to what is initially perceived as a different, albeit familiar, thing; hence, everything one knows about pumping has the potential of being brought into play in this redescription of painting. The researchers were engaged in seeing A as B where A and B are initially perceived, named, and understood as very different things—so different that it would ordinarily pass as a mistake to describe one as the other. It is the restructuring of the perception of the phenomena A and B which enables us to call "metaphor" what we might otherwise have called "mistake."

Not all metaphors are generative. In the researchers' talk about the paintbrush problem, for example, they also spoke of painting as "masking a surface." But this metaphor did not generate perceptions of new features of the paintbrush, nor did it give rise to a new view of the problem. Paintbrush as pump was a *generative* metaphor for the researchers in the sense that it generated new perceptions, explanations, and inventions.

It is important to note that the researchers were able to see painting as similar to pumping before they were able to say similar with respect to what. At first they had only an unarticulated perception of similarity which they could express by doing the painting and inviting others to see it as they did, or by using terms like "squeezing" or "forcing" to convey the pumplike quality of the action. Only later, in an effort to account for their earlier perception of the similarity, did they develop an explicit account of the similarity, an account which later still became part of a general theory of "pumpoids," according to which they could regard paintbrushes and pumps, along with washcloths and mops, as instances of a single technological category.

It would be seriously misleading, then, to say that in making their generative metaphor, the researchers first "noticed certain similarities between paintbrushes and pumps." For the making of generative metaphor involves a developmental process. It has a life cycle. In the earlier stages of the life cycle, one notices or feels that A and B are similar, without being able to say similar with respect to what. Later on, reflecting on what one perceives, one may come to be able to describe relations of elements present in a restructured perception of both A and B which account for the preanalytic detection of similarity between A and B. Later still, one may construct a general model for which a redescribed A and a redescribed B can be identified as instances. The new model is a product of reflection on the perceived similarity. To read it back onto the beginning of the process would be to engage in a kind of historical revisionism.

Thus in technological development as in scientific research, inquirers can sometimes figure out how to solve unique problems or make sense of puzzling phenomena by modelling the unfamiliar on the familiar. Depending on the initial conceptual proximity or distance of the two things perceived as similar, the familiar may serve as exemplar or as generative metaphor for the unfamiliar. In both cases, the inquirer arrives at a new description of the phenomena before him by reflecting-in-action on an earlier perception of similarity. The reflection on *seeing-as*, clearly present in Kuhn's example from the history of science and in my story of the paintbrush as pump, may also have been present in the engineers' invention of the dissolved oxygen hypothesis or in Bardeen's invention of the theory of surface-state electron traps. In these cases, we do not have the data on which to base such an interpretation. But the idea of reflection on *seeing-as* suggests a direction of inquiry into processes which tend otherwise to be mystified and dismissed with the terms "intuition" or "creativity," and it suggests how these processes might be placed within the framework of reflective conversation with the situation which I have proposed as a partial account of the arts of engineering design and scientific investigation.

The Context of Science-Based Practice

I have tried so far to show how reflection-in-action may play an important part in inquiry which falls well within the narrow definition of science-based practice. I shall turn now to the interaction between a practitioner's narrowly technical activity and the larger social context over which he has little control.

When a civil engineer worries over what road to build rather than how to build it, he comes up against the politics of land taking and the organized resistance of neighborhoods. Indeed, he comes up against the whole economic, social, and political life of the region upon which the road may be imposed. And when, having designed a road, he begins to convert his design to reality, he encounters such additional problems as the constraints on city budgets, the reactions of organized labor, and the political machinations of contractors. The engineer may deal with these messy factors by placing them beyond the boundaries of his professional life; he may try to clear a space for narrowly defined professional work, treating the rest of the situation as a necessary evil. Or he may accept the intrusions of the larger situation as a part of his legitimate professional concern, opening himself to complexity, instability, and uncertainty.

It is in the setting of technical problems and in the implementation of their solutions that science-based practitioners meet most directly the dilemma of "rigor or relevance." For neither problem setting nor implementation falls within the model of Technical Rationality, and in dealing with them an engineer encounters problematic situations of the sort that make up the everyday practice of such "minor" professionals as planners, social workers, or administrators. Yet he may bring to these messes the repertoire of a science-based practitioner.

I have had the good luck to meet and work with an engineer who fits this description. He is by no means typical of the engineering profession. Both the problems on which he has chosen to concentrate and the style of practice he has developed set him apart from most of his engineering colleagues. But just for this reason, his practice is of extraordinary interest, for it reveals how technical problem solving and reflection-in-action may be combined in a professional career which extends well beyond the boundaries often imposed on science-based practice.

This engineer, whose name is Dean Wilson, did his apprenticeship in a defense systems research laboratory. He worked on radar and on some of the early applications of computers. In the 1950s he became a member of the Department of Industrial Engineering at the University of Michigan. He was among those who believed that the methods of systems engineering could be transferred from the defense industry to the civilian sector, but he was unusual in that he took an entrepreneurial approach to this idea and stayed with it long after other engineers had dropped it. In the early 1960s, with a few of his students, he formed an organization which applied systems analysis to community institutions such as libraries and hospitals, and in the mid-1960s he became a Rockefeller Professor at the Universidad del Valle, in Cali, Colombia.

In his early work, Wilson developed two powerful guiding ideas which were to influence all of his later practice. The first of these was the idea of process-flow modelling; the second, the Cogwheel Experiment.

As a systems engineer, Wilson had been exposed to input-output models of materials handling and communications. In these models, inputs were seen as flowing through a series of operations which were described in terms of their effects, their costs, and their losses. Using formal descriptions of these variables, one could calculate, for a given objective function, the optimal process design. For Wilson, however, the idea of process flow had been raised to a high level of generality (he remembered vividly a lecture in which Kenneth Boulding had argued that everything in the world could be understood as a process), and he had developed a complex of theories and techniques associated with process models.

During his time at the defense systems laboratory, Wilson had learned of the Cogwheel Experiment. This was a method, developed at RAND's Systems Research Laboratory, to train teams of soldiers to defend the United States against enemy air attack. Crews of thirty to forty men ran simulated air defense experiments, each running about 200 hours, in which they had to detect and destroy enemy aircraft. Symbols came in from these simulated flights at an average of 300 a minute. Many training methods had been tried, always with unsatisfactory results. In the Cogwheel Experiments, however-er, the experimental crews kept up a highly effective defense even when air traffic reached a level three times as great as actual traffic anywhere in the United States. In this experiment, teams were freed from all standard procedures and were left free to invent new methods. They were given frequent, rapid, public feedback on team performance. And during the experiment, central displays gave each member of the crew a picture of the organization's way of responding to the task. Under these conditions, the teams invented simplified methods (for example, substituting hand signals, which could be seen at once by everyone, for complex telephonic equipment); and they learned to use less information, discarding by the end of the experiment 50 percent of the information they had needed in the beginning. Wilson treated this experiment in the broadest possible way, and was fond of quoting a student's observation that every problem should be subjected to a Cogwheel Experiment.

An example from Wilson's early work in Colombia illustrates his ability to frame the problems of new situations in terms of these two guiding ideas.

He had been asked to help solve a problem that had arisen at the teaching hospital in Cali. Doctors there had become aware of a high rate of error in the administration of drugs to patients. They blamed the nurses and believed that the solution was to put all of them through a master's program, but they knew that this would be time consuming and costly. Wilson began by mapping the "flow process" involved in the conversion of a doctor's order to an administered drug. He found an error rate of 33 percent, compared to an average error rate of 5 percent in the United States; and by applying the method of binary search (that is, by measuring error rate at the midpoint of the process, and then at the midpoints of the remaining segments) he found that errors were evenly distributed throughout the whole process.

He presented these results to a meeting of doctors, nurses, and orderlies, and asked them for their ideas about ways to reduce errors. In the corridor, in full view, he placed a chart which showed the previous week's error rate at each stage of the process. As the staff found ways to reduce errors, the changes were recorded on the chart. Gradually, over a period of three months, error rates dropped to the U.S. norm. Wilson had framed the problem as a flow process and had solved it by creating the conditions for a Cogwheel Experiment. Under these conditions, the doctors and their staff—who might have figured, in a more conventional approach, as part of the social context of the problem—functioned both as problem solvers and as implementers of their own solutions. There was no need to worry about the implementation of an expert solution.

Wilson took a similar approach to the more important and complex problem which he decided to place at the center of the rest of his work in Cali, the problem of malnourishment.

Malnourishment in children under the age of six was (and is) endemic in Colombia. In the region of the Cauca Valley, around Cali, it is not uncommon to see the swollen bellies, thin arms, and light hair associated with kwashiorcor and marasmus. As Wilson began to learn about malnourishment, he discovered that many researchers were already at work on it. There was consensus about the urgency of the problem, yet there was little agreement about its definition. Researchers representing a variety of professions and beliefs were approaching the problem from a multiplicity of conflicting perspectives.

Some nutritionists, as in Herbert Simon's "diet problem," sought to relieve malnourishment by choosing the best diet that could be selected from available foods at current prices. But Wilson showed that Colombia's total nutrient production, divided by total population, would yield a daily intake below minimum protein/calorie requirements. Given a national "nutrient gap," the malnourishment problem called for more than the best selection from available foods.

Agronomists who had established agricultural research stations in Colombia saw the problem as one of agricultural productivity. They tried methods of bringing more land under cultivation and studied the introduction of high-lysine corn and strains of high-protein rice and soya. But some village experiments, undertaken by public health physicians, had shown that when malnourished children were fed increased amounts of protein and calories they tended to remain malnourished. These children lost nutrients because of diarrheas caused by intestinal parasites. Public health specialists therefore thought in terms of improvement in water quality, replacement of open sewers with modern plumbing, and family education in the elements of hygiene.

Some economists thought differently. They traced poor sanitation and low-protein diets to a single cause, poverty. Poor families must become more productive in order to raise their income levels to the point where malnourishment-reducing strategies would become economically feasible. These economists thought in terms of training, creation of village industries, and relocation of workers to places of high employment. Some of them argued that the roots of malnourishment were in the low rate of national economic growth and could only be removed by more effective policies for economic development.

Other observers noted that in the Cauca Valley, the very fertile lowlands consisted of large plantations whose owners grew sugarcane and cattle for export, while on the eroding mountainsides the peasants eked out a bare living from their small farms. Colombia needed a redistribution of land and wealth. In a country where approximately 5 percent of the population consumed some 80 percent of the agricultural production (and almost all of the domestic meat), and where the best land was used for export, malnourishment was a problem of political economy. The more radical members of this group despaired of conventional political solutions. They looked to revolution, pointing to Castro's Cuba as a shining exception to the general rule of malnourishment in Latin America.

Researchers who took a historical perspective saw that a protein gap at the national level was a recent phenomenon. Twenty years before, Colombia's total agricultural production would have been sufficient, had it been distributed, to nourish the whole population. But in twenty years population had grown much faster than agricultural production. The national protein gap had resulted from the success of public health interventions, especially from the World Health Organization's near-eradication of malaria in the 1950s. The malnourishment problem was a problem of population control.

In this *Rashomon* of problem settings, each profession framed the problem according to its expertise, its ideology, and its interests.

As a systems engineer, Wilson's impulse was to reconcile the conflicting perspectives by including the many different factors they named within a larger system, a flow process whose output was the nutritional status of children. He envisaged a system of nutrient flows which began in the fields and ended in the body of the child. He wanted to devise a method which would enable him to estimate the losses of nutrients incurred at each stage of the process. By ascertaining the "nutrient gap" at each stage (as he had measured the error rate at each stage of the drug-administration process), he would be able to learn the points at which interventions would be most likely to reduce malnourishment.

A simplified version of this "nutrient flow model" is shown in figure 6.5.

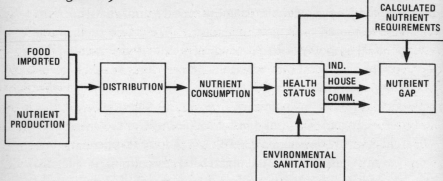

Wilson intended to use models of this kind to calculate nutrient gaps for whole regions, villages, and individual households. He would begin at the community level, determining, as he put it, "what are the practical methods of closing the nutrient gap and, of these, which combination is the least costly within a time constraint of a few years?"[17] He organized a project team, drawing on his Colombian and North American students and colleagues, and got support to develop and test his nutrient flow model in six communities in the Cauca Valley. But the methodological problems proved formidable. There were serious problems in the choice of measures of malnourishment, in the calculation of nutrient gaps, and even in the analysis of such fundamental ideas as "nutrient distribution" and "household." In some villages, for example, children ate most of their meals not in their own houses but in informal daycare settings where they stayed while their parents worked in the field. Determination of nutrient gaps at the household level depended on reliable measures of consumption which were extraordinarily difficult to obtain, if only because families tended to raise their levels of consumption to their image of the observer's standards.

The full range of methodological problems began to make it seem doubtful that it would be possible, in a single model, to encompass all of the variables involved in nutrient flow. At the same time, Wilson became intensely aware of difficulties in implementing the model. Who would carry out the community-level interventions? If outside professionals did so, they would reinforce the pattern of passive dependence on outsiders which was so much a part of the community predicament. There were many examples of externally motivated and engineered interventions which had failed in the later stages of implementation. Moreover, there seemed to be no reliable technique of intervention which could be generalized across all communities. Increasingly, Wilson began to conceive of the nutrient flow model not as a general technique of diagnosis for use by outside experts but as a framework of analysis with which community residents could set and solve their own problems of malnourishment.

An opportunity to act on this idea arose when Wilson and his colleagues were invited to participate in an educational project in the small village of Buenos Aires, which lay in the mountains some two hours away by jeep from Cali. A physician who had grown up in this village was a colleague of Wilson's at the Valle medical school. He had been working with the children of local peasants who were living at a *Hogar*, a boarding school and farm located just outside the village. This *Hogar* was one of some two hundred that had been established throughout Colombia to provide secondary education for children from rural villages, who would otherwise have no chance of going beyond the primary grades. The children—about a hundred of them, between the ages of thirteen and nineteen—worked a small farm, contributing to their own subsistence, and received instruction in the usual secondary-school subjects. To Wilson, the *Hogar* at Buenos Aires offered the opportunity he had been seeking. Over the next several years, the village of Buenos Aires became the setting in which he taught systems engineering to the children of peasants.

Wilson and a former Peace Corps volunteer, Kip Ekroad, began to spend a great deal of time at the *Hogar*, getting to know the children and the staff. It had been decided that they would meet with the students every Wednesday afternoon, when the regular school was not in session.

As they puzzled over finding a good way to introduce the problem of malnourishment, the nutrient flow model, and the idea of experiment, it occured to Wilson that a colony of laboratory rats, which had been used to demonstrate the effects of different diets, might intrigue the children. The rat cages were arranged in the form of a matrix, so that it was possible, reading from the upper left to the lower right-hand corner, to see dramatic differences in the size and behavior of the rats as a function of their diet. The display never failed to interest visitors, and it was decided to do something similar at Buenos Aires.

On the first Wednesday, the staff brought out nine rats and told the students, "We'd like you to keep these rats, and of course it will be necessary to feed them. What do you suggest?"

The students disagreed about the best diet for the rats. There were three main proposals: *yuca* and *platano* (two popular local foods containing no protein), the same foods the students were eating in the *Hogar*, and a standard laboratory diet for rats. Wilson and Ekroad suggested, "Let's divide the rats into three groups of three rats each, and feed each a different diet. Then we can see if they look any different."

The students ran the experiment. They were responsible for feeding and caring for the rats and for weighing them once a week, all of which they did with enthusiasm. After one week, the first results were astonishing to the students. The groups on the *Hogar* diet and on the laboratory diet had gained weight considerably, while the groups on the *yuca* and *platano* diet had actually lost weight. After four weeks of this, students became concerned that "these rats were going to die," and a general discussion took place. It was decided to switch the rats' diets and then observe and plot the results. The curves actually crossed.

From this early experiment, the group moved to more complex experiments with diets for rats (one of these led to an inquiry into the apparently magical properties of vitamins) and then to explorations of malnourishment in human beings.

Shortly after the first experiment, the students were shown pictures of a group of children, all aged seven or eight. They were asked, "What do you see?"

The students noticed that some were small and some were big, but they noticed other things as well. "The little ones look sad," they said. "They do not have any muscles." Staff did not use the word "malnourishment," nor did they ask what the children in the picture might be eating. They hoped to elicit such responses spontaneously, as a test of the transfer of learning (from rats to people) that might already have taken place. But no such responses were forthcoming.

Some of the students, those who lived near enough to the *Hogar* to make the trip, made visits home once a month. After the first few weeks, these students were asked to bring back information about the members of their households, including name, sex, age, and relationship, and they were asked to weigh their brothers and sisters. Upon their return, the data were plotted on a scatter graph. Staff analyzed these data independently, and found a number of examples of mild and serious malnourishment, but the students themselves had few com-

ments about the data. They did not yet have concepts sufficient for such analysis.

Once the data of weight for age were plotted, the students
were told they could now tell the relative nutritional status of
their brothers and sisters, but they could not yet tell the abso-
lute levels of malnourishment. They were then asked what the
next step should be. Their answer was that they should find
out what their families were eating. When they were asked
how to do this, they first said, "Go ask our mothers," and then,
"Go weigh the food," quickly identifying the two principal
methods used in the diagnostic procedure.

One of the students, Aida, wrote these comments about her
experiences in these early sessions:

> I became completely convinced that platano and yuca are not as
> good foods as I considered them. They do not contain all the ele-
> ments necessary for growing and developing normally. . . . I, Aida,
> see nothing funny, thanks to this experiment, since it makes us
> realize what good nourishment is and of what it consists.

> In the class, we received some instructions on measuring and
> weighing children under 5 years old and, as with the rats, the age
> and size of the children tells us, more or less, if they are malnour-
> ished or not . . . Before going to our houses to weigh our younger
> brothers and sisters, we practiced on children in the homes near
> the school with some girls who taught us to weigh children.

> Then we went to our homes to weigh the younger children. We
> weighed many children and brought back a great quantity of data
> that shows the bad malnourishment state.

> This system of teaching appears to be good to me. I like this kind
> because it is practical. Because what one *does* is difficult to forget.
> It is easier to forget when something is only said.

> I have learned that one must analyze his own problems and then
> look for the solution to devise his own way of overcoming, and
> not to expect others to do it for us.

> I am still waiting since this course began to learn how we are going to fight the malnourishment that affects so much our country.[18]

When the students were asked what "problems" they had found at home, they were puzzled. They could identify no problems—finding it odd, perhaps, to describe as a "problem" what they observed routinely in their surroundings. They did, however, become interested in the diets of siblings, and this led later on to questions about the cultivation and consumption of higher-protein foods—notably soya. With this, over several months, the students turned to the problems of agricultural productivity. Thinking of experiments they might carry out at their own farm at the *Hogar,* they debated, as they had become used to doing, over methods for increasing productivity, and they tried to resolve their disagreements by conducting an experiment.

Their first such experiment consisted in testing natural versus synthetic fertilizer, and no fertilizer at all, on three patches of corn planted on a hill. One of the students at the Hogar explained to a visitor that this was "the same as the rat experiment," and when the visitor did not immediately see the point, she said, "Can't you see? It's the same as the rat feeding, only here we're feeding plants instead of rats!"

But what the students found was that the tallest corn grew in none of the three patches, but at the bottom of the hill where the soil had washed down. When they saw this, their attention shifted from fertilizer to erosion of the soil, a problem that plagued all of the farmers who tried to cultivate the red claylike soil of the hills around the Cauca Valley. Wilson and Ekroad then began some instruction in soil erosion and its control, following which the students undertook a series of experiments. When it came to the problem of measuring the rate of erosion, one of the students invented a simple but elegant device. A hollow cylinder was planted in the ground at the bottom of the hill, and the height of the soil that accumulated in the cylinder showed the rate of erosion.

Meanwhile, the fathers of the children at the *Hogar* became increasingly curious about the education the children were receiving. These gaunt, dignified men had travelled by burro from village to village, collecting money to make up their matching share of the costs of the *Hogar,* and they did not take the school for granted. They observed the children's work and discussed it among themselves. Several of them decided to plant soya at their own farms. Others introduced experiments in irrigation and erosion control.

The lessons that Aida and other children had drawn from the program began to make themselves felt in other ways as well. When the mayor of Buenos Aires received money from the municipality and announced that it would be used to pave some roads, a group of the children decided to confront him. They asked why the money should be used to build roads when none of the villagers owned a car, and why it should not be used to improve the quality of the water which they had measured and found badly polluted. The mayor, temporarily nonplussed, eventually decided to go along with the children's suggestion. But when the episode came to the attention of the local coffee planters who helped to support the *Hogar,* they had a less benign reaction. The *Hogar,* as they saw it, had been designed to make the children into good workers, not to make them challenge the established order. They dropped their support, but because the *Hogar* had other sources of support it was able, nonetheless, to survive.

In all of their teaching in the Buenos Aires project, Wilson and Ekroad developed a mode of practice which they thought a great deal about but could only partially articulate. (They always trusted their practice more than their articulations of it.)

The early rat-feeding experiment became an exemplar for them. They sought out concrete, dramatic contexts which would capture the students' attention and would also serve as simulation models for human nutrition. They tried to create situations in which students could discover relationships—for example, relationships between diet and age-weight ratio—for themselves. Similarly, the students were led to experience the experimental method before any explicit mention of its principles was made, and were given a great deal of control over events in the classroom and therefore over their own learning. Wilson and Ekroad designed experiments to test the students' hypotheses but also held themselves ready to respond to happy accidents, such as the discovery of highest corn growth at the bottom of the hill.

What the students seem to be learning was, as Aida said, to take initiative in solving problems for themselves, to be skeptical of outside authority, to settle disagreements by experiment. But they may have been learning more than this. Some students were able to understand the fertilizer experiments as versions of the rat-feeding ones, and some turned their attention to soil erosion when they saw that plants grew best at the bottom of the hill. These students, at any rate, seemed to be learning to model the unfamiliar on the familiar and to reframe their questions around the changes which resulted unexpectedly from their actions.

Something similar had been happening in Wilson's work on malnourishment. He had begun with the image of a nutrient flow model that would organize all of the variables recognized by the conflicting research perspectives on malnourishment, and he had intended that outside experts would use that model to diagnose and cure the malnourishment problems of particular communities. Nevertheless, as he became more fully aware of the methodological difficulties in constructing the model and of the dilemmas of implementing it, he was led to restructure his image of intervention. It would not be outside experts but community members themselves who would use the nutrient flow model idea to diagnose their own malnourishment problems and design their own interventions. With this change, community learning became an objective equal in importance to the reduction of malnourishment. And as a consequence, community members—who might have figured as parts of the social context of technical practice—became problem-solving agents. As Wilson sought to create at the *Hogar* the conditions for a Cogwheel Experiment on malnourishment, he had to frame and reflect on a new problem, that of involving and guiding the community members he wished to adopt as co-inquirers. His practice as a systems engineer merged with his practice as a teacher.

In some respects, the Buenos Aires project produced ambiguous results. Although it led to a number of village-level experiments on the production and consumption of soya, there were no dramatic effects on the local malnourishment rate, at least in the first few years of the project's life. Indeed, it was not clear what future effects on malnourishment would be, for many of the children living at the *Hogar* (about 50 percent, according to one study) would probably move after graduation to one of the nearby cities. But the project did capture the imagination of those who came in contact with it. The Colombian organization that sponsored the *Hogares* became interested in the Buenos Aires experiment and took steps to reproduce it in other settings. Professional observers of the project were excited by its use of education in experimental method as a response to community-level malnourishment.

The Buenos Aires project reveals Wilson's unusual way of being an engineer and thereby epitomizes the main themes of this chapter. The kind of reflection-in-action which engineers sometimes bring to engineering design, and scientists to scientific investigation, Wilson has brought to a practice in which technical analysis and social intervention are joined together. As scientists and engineers learn to model unfamiliar problems on familiar ones and build new theory by reflecting on perceived but as yet unarticulated similarities, so Wilson has evolved a repertoire of powerful exemplars on which he draws to make sense of unique and complex socio-technical situations. He has not expunged technical problem solving from his practice but has embedded it in relevant and, in its own way, rigorous reflection-in-action.

7

Town Planning: Limits to Reflection-in-Action

The Evolving Context of Planning Practice

Town planning has a charter membership in Glazer's society of minor professions. The institutional context of planning practice is notoriously unstable and there are many contending views of the profession, each of which carries a different image of the planning role and a different picture of the body of useful knowledge. At the present time, for example, planners function variously as designers, plan makers, critics, advocates of special interests, regulators, managers, evaluators, and intermediaries. In planning as in other professions, each role tends to be associated with characteristic values, strategies, techniques, and bodies of relevant information. But in the planning profession, images of role have evolved significantly in relatively brief periods of time. The profession, which came into being around the turn of the century, moved in succeeding decades through different ideas in good currency about planning theory and practice, partly in response to changes in context shaped by planners themselves. The history of the evolution of planning roles can be understood as a global conversation between the planning profession and its situation.

With the development of the city planning movement in the early years of this century, planners first gained visibility, power, and professional status. The growth of comprehensive and master planning and the widespread establishment of local planning commissions in the United States paralleled the formation of the coalition supportive of town planning in Britain.[1] Following World War II, probably as a result of military and economic planning in wartime America, the idea of central planning extended its scope from comprehensive and master planning for towns to such fields as urban renewal, urban and regional transportation, health services, public education, mental health, and criminal justice.

In these domains, among many others, the centralist planner operated from the base of institutions created and legitimized through legislation brought into being by a coalition of political forces. The planner framed his role at the center of a system for which he planned, in relation to agencies which would implement his plans and clienteles who would benefit from them. His system of knowledge-in-practice dealt with the framing of objectives and goals, the imagining of a desirable future, the description of baseline conditions, the identification of alternative strategies of action, the description of constraints to be circumvented or removed, the mapping of the system to be influenced, and the prediction of the consequences of action. Later, planners also came to be concerned with the feasibility of implementing plans and the political problems of "selling" them.

Through the mid-1960s, centralist planning proceeded in this mode. Its operations were based on two main assumptions:

1. There is a working consensus about the content of the public interest, sufficient for the setting of planning goals and objectives, and

2. There is a system of knowledge adequate for the conduct of central planning.

It does not matter that these assumptions may never have been true. They were widely believed to be true, and they set the terms of reference for the planning profession. But by the mid-1960s, both assumptions were in trouble.

The public at large, and planners themselves, were becoming increasingly aware of the counterintuitive consequences, the harmful side effects and the unwanted by-products of implemented plans. Plans designed to solve problems either failed to solve them or created problems worse than the problems they had been designed to solve. Some of the phenomena planners were most anxious to influence—poverty, crime, urban congestion and decay—seemed tenaciously resistant to intervention. The most broadly believed predictions (those relating to school enrollment, for example) turned out to be mistaken. Attempts to build formal, quantitative models of social phenomena foundered in complexity. Attempts to conduct social experiments were confounded by unanticipated and uncontrollable changes in the experimental context. Planners were found sometimes deliberately, sometimes unintentionally, to be serving interests incongruent with their espoused values. Social critics and angry political pressure groups demonstrated that plans had meanings and consequences well beyond those envisaged by urban planners. And as the perceived scope and complexity of planning increased, planners found that their techniques and models were inadequate to the tasks of analysis, diagnosis, and prediction. Planning "problems" came to seem more like dilemmas made up of conflicts of values, interests, and ideologies unresolvable by recourse to the facts.

By the mid-1960s, the apparent consensus about the content of the public interest—perhaps even about the feasibility of establishing such a consensus—had faded away. As the harmful consequences of centralist planning and governmental action were discovered, special interest groups formed around issues of injustice, hazard, and neglect. By the late 1970s, it was clear that there was no national consensus about the public interest. There was rather a field of special interests: minority groups, women's groups, environmentalists, consumers' groups, advocates of health and safety at work, the handicapped, the protagonists of special education and basic education, neighborhood conservationists, advocates for neighborhood schools, energy conservationists, advocates of zero population growth, advocates for and antagonists of abortion, moral and religious fundamentalists, advocates for guns or gun control, advocates for crime prevention, and advocates for de-institutionalization of prisons and mental hospitals. These constituencies had learned to organize themselves, enter into public debate, and take political action in order to bring their concerns to legislative and judicial reality.

In some cases, special interest groups took positions which were in direct and explicit conflict with one another. In other cases, conflicts of interest became clear only as the success of one movement led to consequences contrary to the interests of another. In still other cases, conflict became evident as the different movements found themselves competing in hard times for scarce resources.

Throughout the 1960s, a new breed of social planners began

to criticize established institutions because they rode rough-shod over the less powerful. Herbert Gans, Jane Jacobs, Francis Piven, and Mark Fried, among other students of urban renew-al, showed how planners acting ostensibly in the public interest actually served the interests of real estate developers and large corporations by displacing the poor and ethnic minorities.[2] The social critics and advocate planners operated in a social field made up of the constituents they sought to protect, the established institutions they fought, the media they tried to influence, the courts through which they often sought redress of grievances, and the legislatures through which they tried to shape laws that would regulate the behavior of established in-terests. Their knowledge-in-practice had to do with issues such as these: expressing the interests of the dispossessed, or empow-ering the dispossessed to express their own interests; demystify-ing the professional personas of the centralist planners, show-ing up their intended or unintended alliance with established interests; explaining how the actions of government and busi-ness affect the less powerful; formulating policies and programs to protect the less powerful and identifying the practices of established interest groups which needed most to be watched and controlled; figuring out how to gain visibility and political voice for the dispossessed; building connections to legislators, regulators, and executive agencies.

As these critics, advocates, and organizers were able to bring their ideas into good currency, they succeeded in influencing the legislative process either to regulate the actions of estab-lished institutions or to establish programs of service or income support for special interest groups. As a partial consequence of their success, the present social context of planning has be-come a field of institutions organized around contending inter-ests. Regulatory systems have been established by law to moni-tor and control the actions of agencies such as businesses, schools, hospitals, universities, and real estate developers. The courts play a large and increasing role as adjudicators of doubtful cases, interpreters of the law, dispensers of sanctions for violation of the law, and sometimes as direct monitors or managers of systems in default.

Within these institutional fields, planners no longer follow the centralist planning model. They practice in relation to a growing variety of special interest groups and regulatory systems, and they have developed a variety of new or modified roles. They may function as spokesmen, strategists, or technical staff for parties to the regulatory process. They may perform watchdog functions, reviewing, for example, the environmental impact statements of developers or the affirmative action plans of government agencies. They may position themselves in the neutral space between regulators and regulated, functioning as mediators who convene interested parties, helping them to understand one another's position, to identify common interests, or to fashion an acceptable compromise.

In these intermediary roles, more like the traditional roles of the lawyer than the sometime centralist planner, knowledge must be developed and brought to bear on issues such as these: understanding the field of actors and interests with its potentials for satisfaction, frustration, mutual constraint or mutual enhancement; formulating issue-specific targets for negotiation, mediation, or inquiry; creating conditions for effective control or evasion of control, for successful negotiation, or for productive inquiry; designing intermediary interventions and assessing their effectiveness; maintaining the conditions of credibility and legitimacy on which the intermediary roles depend.

In the case that follows, I shall consider an example of this most recent form of planning practice, showing how one intermediary planner has evolved knowing-in-practice which enables him to address issues such as those listed above. In this case study, however, I shall explore several more general features of professional knowledge.[3]

A professional role places skeletal demands on a practitioner's behavior, but within these constraints, each individual develops his own way of framing his role. Whether he chooses his role frame from the profession's repertoire, or fashions it for himself, his professional knowledge takes on the character of a system. The problems he sets, the strategies he employs, the facts he treats as relevant, and his interpersonal theories of action are bound up with his way of framing his role. In the case that follows, I shall describe such a system of knowing-in-practice.

Further, a system of this sort tends to be self-reinforcing. Depending on the kind of role frame he has constructed and on the kind of interpersonal theory of action he has evolved, a practitioner's reflection-in-action may be more or less limited in scope and depth. In the case that follows, I shall try to show how limits to reflection-in-action are set and maintained.

Some of What One Planner Knows

The individual whose practice we will be examining in this chapter is a town planner concerned primarily with the physical development of the town he serves. Yet he makes no comprehensive plans and prepares no designs for neighborhoods or regions. He has defined his job as one of reviewing proposals submitted by private developers to local regulatory bodies, and has positioned himself as an intermediary between these two parties. He seeks, by advising and negotiating with developers, to influence the direction and quality of physical development in the town. Substituting these functions for the more traditional preparation of plans, he plans by proxy.

Given his way of framing his role in the town and his image of the dilemmas associated with that role, the planner has learned to treat his practice as a balancing act in which he tries continually to advise and negotiate with developers while at the same time preserving his credibility with all the parties on whom his role depends.

In the following protocol, a transcript of a videotape of one of the meetings recorded in the planner's office, a developer presents drawings and plans for remodelling an apartment building which he and his uncle own in the town. Under the town's development bylaws, the planner must review such plans before submitting them to the Zoning Board of Appeals which has authority to grant or withhold variances.

As the tape begins, the planner rolls up his sleeves, consults his notes, and leans across the table to look at the developer and his architect.

PLANNER: I'll give you a review here. I think we ought to base some of the discussion we had a couple of weeks ago. You've got plans, and what I suggested is that we go over the zoning bylaw to see exactly how they conform. The building plans, the structure itself, is no problem, but I think that within the zoning bylaws we've got to have some areas that we have to look at very closely in the site plan. Okay? Now, uh, and as far as the building is concerned, I think we can work out the details with the building inspector about the code requirements.

ARCHITECT: Right

PLANNER: . . . which you work with all the time anyway . . .

The planner has defined the meeting's purpose, which is to review the developer's plans to see "exactly how they conform" to the zoning bylaw. He divides the plan into two parts, one that he finds acceptable ("the structure itself") and one that he finds problematic ("the site plan"). From here on, he will review elements of the site plan which he has listed for comment.

First, however, he checks to see whether the developer is familiar with the bylaws.

> PLANNER: ... but, Tom, have you had a chance to look at the development bylaws?
> (Developer looks at architect.)
> ARCHITECT: Well, I've gone through it roughly.
> PLANNER: Why don't we look at the lot?
> DEVELOPER: We've blown the plans up quite a bit for you ...
> ARCHITECT: They were real small, you couldn't see 'em.

Now the planner zones in on the first item on his list, the question of lot size.

> P: All right, now. Under the new apartment controls in our town, before the new bylaw enactor, you had to have 20,000 square feet of lot area; you had only 14,341. As you know, it's apparently impossible to get any more.
> D: Uh-hum.
> P: Now, what you wanna do is add a couple apartment units to this building. That is gonna require a variance ... because ... you are ... adding to a multi-family building in an apartment zone where the lots aren't large enough. So you're gonna need a variance on lot size. ... At the same time, you'll need a special permit because you are dealing with an apartment structure, but that can be handled. As I look at it, without seeing a more detailed site plan (but that can be put together eventually), the only variance you need is on lot area. Everything else is all right.

The developer, still preoccupied with the visibility of his plans (as though that might remove the difficulty), questions whether he is really in violation of the bylaw.

D: I don't know. I think I have something a little bit larger for us to look at. I don't know that we violate too much of the thing, especially if we get involved in taking down that little thing up front there.

The planner explains how the developer may be able to justify a variance on lot size, ignoring the latter's hint that there may be no need for it.

P: Obviously you have no problems with the floor area.
D: We don't.
P: You have no problem with land area per dwelling unit, and when you go to the Zoning Board of Appeals, obviously that's gonna be one thing you want to play out. Even though you don't have the 20,000 square feet of land, you're not even approaching the zoning limit, because you're dealing with existing buildings.

Without pausing to sound out the developer's reaction to these suggestions, the planner goes on to point out additional requirements in the bylaw.

P: The new zoning bylaw does have two open-space requirements, and they're slightly different from other bylaws you may have worked with. You must have a landscaped area, which is ten percent of the gross floor area of the buildings on the lot, not ten percent of the lot area, unless you have a usable open-space area of 25 percent of the building. Now look closely at the definitions of the bylaw: What constitutes landscape? What constitutes usable?
D: Uh-hum.
P: Essentially, the section of your landscaped area can be met perhaps here, or along part of the site.

The developer checks out what is included under the term "usable open space."

D: When they say usable, are they referring to space that's been paved for parking?
A: No.
D: No, so that's over and above that.
P: So its unpaved.
A: Unpaved.
D: Unpaved.
P: Unpaved.

With this chorus of "unpaved"s confirming the existence of the problem, the architect moves to suggest how the problem could be solved:

A: You take that door down, that's how you could solve that very easily.

But the developer does not show much interest in this idea. His attention has shifted to a new consideration which leads him to depart from the planner's carefully prepared list of possible violations of the bylaw:

D: You know, when I went back after our last meeting I discussed with my uncle, who is the other owner of the building. He said something and he made a lot of sense. Well, look, he said, if we've got to take down the store, he said, and if we violate (and it appears to me that the biggest thing is the 20,000 flipper rule that we don't violate too badly from what I can see—but you're the planner, you know better than I). If we're violating only that anyway, he says, why don't we ask for a couple more apartments? Why are we settling for eleven? Because then we'd be able to do other things, even with maybe keeping the same structure. And I have no answer for that.

If there is only one variance needed on lot size, what about the possibility of increasing the number of apartments on the lot? To which the planner responds:

P: Now, I'm not going to say yes or no.
D: All right.
P: Because I think there's only so much you can put on this land.
D: Right.
A: Legally.
P: That's the criterion. Now, I don't know if it's nine, ten, eleven, twenty, or fifty. But I do know that as long as you're dealing with existing buildings, you know, 14,000 square feet of land is not, I think, going to be a serious problem. But I'm not the Zoning Board of Appeals. That's their decision. If you then begin to overbuild on the land, you have to have variances for open space.
D: We don't want that.
P: Right. Now all you have to worry about is one variance.

Having disposed of the developer's question, the planner proceeds to the next item on his list:

P: The other thing I think you want to look at very carefully is the article on parking. The parking requirements are slightly different than they used to be. In an apartment house, you have to have one parking space for each efficiency, one and a half for each two-bedroom, two for each three- or four-bedroom. I'm not sure exactly how much parking you have provided here now.
D: Right, I think we have seventeen there.

But the parking requirement is complicated by two further provisions of the bylaw:

P: Also in the parking section, I want you to look at Section 812, there are setback requirements for parking areas. We want to keep them off the lot line. Now that's gonna limit your area a little bit.

A: You mean side and rear.

P: Once again, I'm just urging you to lay it out. Now, this is just a simple layout here. There are other ways, I'm sure, to do it.

A: Oh, every one that you eliminate, the better off you are, there's no question about it. Now, if it comes down to the 20,000 square feet variance, and even the parking variance, that's still not too bad.

P: Okay, but it's gonna take some layouts to determine what you can and can't do. These parking spaces were thrown in without looking at the new ratios. Because we looked at them very carefully, and I think we found that you have four extra spaces.

D: Yes.

The planner now turns to his concluding piece of advice:

P: When you go down the road and actually apply for the variance and go to the public hearing, make sure you're prepared to answer these questions. Now, uh, I don't want to prejudge, but the one question they're going to ask is, what hardship do you have with this particular piece of property? Why do you need the variance to do what you want to do?

D: Well, based on what I told you, is that a sufficient hardship?

P: As I say, I don't prejudge.

D: No.

P: There are certainly economic considerations. Generally, you know, you've got a situation where you've owned a piece of property for a long time. In order to do something in these times when costs are different, you need to increase the income potential of the building. . . .

D: Exactly.

P: But they're gonna want to know specifics, and I think that's the kind of thinking you ought to work on. O.K.?

And here the architect raises a new possibility:

A: With regard to the fact that he has to go for a variance anyway, what's the possibility of going for a new building?

P: I think then you're gonna run into difficulties, because you're
asking for a new variance. Now, if you're asking for a new
building to replace the eight units that you have there, then
I seriously doubt that a variance will be granted. The town
has made it very clear that in order to build new apartments
you've got to have 20,000 square feet of land. And I know
of no case where they've granted a variance for a new building on a lot under 20,000 square feet.

In the remaining few minutes of the meeting, the developer
agrees that he had "pretty much ruled out going that route."

What happens in the protocol. Most of the planner's behavior in this meeting can be understood as an attempt to follow
rigorously an agenda which he establishes at the outset: to review the developer's plans in order to see exactly how they conform to the zoning bylaw. Hence the planner takes up, in turn,
the factors of lot size, open space, and parking. The developer
and his architect respond by questioning the meanings of such
terms as "open space," or by suggesting how the various problems might be solved. On two separate occasions, however, the
developer or his architect makes a proposal and the planner
responds to it in a way that suggests a kind of bargaining. Early
in the meeting, the developer quotes his uncle's suggestion that
as long as they need a variance because of the "20,000 feet
flipper rule," why shouldn't they go for a couple more apartments? The planner responds with "Now, I'm not going to say
yes or no . . . ," but he goes on to spell out the factors that
will govern the board's response, all the while setting limits to
his own authority to give such an answer ("I'm not the Zoning
Board of Appeals"). At the very end of the protocol the architect raises the question of going for a new building, and here
the planner answers firmly, "I know of no case where they've

granted a variance for a new building on a lot under 20,000 square feet."

Elsewhere the planner prepares the developer for a future meeting with the Zoning Board of Appeals, rather as though he were preparing a student for an exam. He signals questions to be asked, answers that will be acceptable, and homework to be done. (" . . . they're going to ask what hardship do you have . . . ? Why do you need the variance to do what you want to do? . . . think about that.") At the same time, he tries to avoid giving the impression that he can make such decisions himself. ("As I say, I don't prejudge.")

Thus the planner undertakes three main tasks. As he *reviews the plans* and notes possible violations of the zoning bylaw, he *advises* the developer about the need for variances. He *prepares him for the examination* he can expect when he puts his case before the Zoning Board of Appeals. And he *bargains with the developer,* responding guardedly to proposals the developer uses, apparently to discover how much he will be allowed to get away with.

The planner's conduct of his meeting with the developer can be understood in terms of his attempt to solve problems he has framed around these three main tasks.

In his review of the plans, he is meticulous. He takes pains to document his evaluations ("Don't forget these items . . . When you work on the site plan, I'll give you a copy of this if you want"). At the same time, he continually exhibits a concern with the limits of his own authority, announcing frequently that he can only anticipate the board's actions and can make no decisions by himself. He behaves, in other words, as though he must conduct a rigorous preliminary review of plans which is in constant danger of being misconstrued as final.

Occasionally he calls attention to a possible violation of the bylaw, communicating information he appears to think the developer may regard as negative. At each such point, he behaves as though he wishes to avoid discouraging the developer:

> As I look at it, without seeing a more detailed site plan (but that can be put together eventually), the only variance you need is on lot area.

Here he stresses that only *one* variance will be necessary, pointing out that he has not yet seen the final site plan, but plays down the difficulty of preparing such a plan. When he points out a potential problem, he makes the remedy seem easy:

> Now, this is just a simple layout here. There are other ways, I'm sure, to do it.

And he tries to make the negative information palatable by surrounding it with "good news":

> The building plans, the structure itself, is no problem, but I think that, within the zoning bylaws, we've got to . . . look at very closely in the site plan. Okay? Now, uh, and as far as the building is concerned, I think we can work out the details with the building inspector about the code requirements   something you work with all the time anyway."

The planner deals with negative information by minimizing it, making the remedy seem easy, and surrounding it with good news.

As he preps the developer, he suggests the form of an acceptable answer but makes clear that someone else will finally grade the exam:

> Now, uh, I don't want to prejudge, but the one question they're going to ask is, what hardship do you have with this particular piece of property?

He is careful to say that the developer will have to work out the details by himself:

P: In order to do something in these times when costs are different, you need to increase the income potential of the building, and in order to do that, you need to rehabilitate the building.

D: Exactly.

P: But they're gonna want to know specifics, and I think that's the kind of thinking you ought to work on. Okay?

The planner's problem seems to be this: without usurping the board's evaluative role or doing the developer's work for him, he must make sure that the developer will be able to give the right answers.

When he responds to proposals for a few more apartments or a new building, he behaves again as though he had to meet conflicting requirements. He tries to prevent the developer from putting forward proposals the board will reject:

. . . there's only so much you can put on this land. . . . That's the criterion.

But he also tries to avoid discouraging proposals the board may accept:

. . . as long as you're dealing with existing buildings, you know, 14,000 square feet of land is not, I think, going to be a serious problem.

Having thus conveyed the impression that he can predict or even influence the Board's behavior, he ends by setting a limit to his own authority.

. . . I'm not going to say yes or no. . . .
. . . I'm not the Zoning Board of Appeals . . . That's their decision.

Thus as he reviews the developer's plans, prepares him for this forthcoming session with the Board of Appeals, and bargains with him, the planner performs a balancing act. He tries to criticize the developer's plans without discouraging him. He tries to be stringent in his review of plans and at the same time permissive. He tries to lead the developer along the right lines without reducing the developer's responsibility for his own proposal. And he behaves authoritatively while presenting himself as devoid of authority.

Framing the role and the situation. Just as we can understand the planner's behavior in terms of the problems he has set for himself, so we can see these problems, and the resulting balancing act, as a consequence of the way he has chosen to frame his role.

When the planner began to work for the town, he knew that several roles were open to him. Like his predecessor, he could have made himself into a writer of plans, covering the walls of his office with maps and charts. Or he could have become a community organizer and advocate. He chose, instead, the intermediary role.

He seeks to bring to reality his image of what is good for the town, but he cannot initiate anything. Like a labor mediator, marriage counselor, co-ordinator, or broker, he must solicit and respond to the initiatives of others. He can only plan by proxy, through his influence on the plans of others. In this intermediate function, he is interdependent with those who initiate and with those who have regulatory authority. Without the planner's advice and help, the developers cannot understand and negotiate the hurdles they must jump in order to gain permission to build in the town. Without their proposals, the planner cannot realize his image of what is good for the town. Without the Zoning Board of Appeals, the planner has no function. Without the planner's screening and tailoring of development projects, the board could not do its regulatory job.

These interdependencies are essential conditions for the "review game" which the planner plays with the developers. The developers come to the planner for advice and review of plans, and he uses this to bargain with them. In return for their concessions to his image of what is good for the town, he will help them get what they want from the board. As he remarks in an interview,

> When a person gets in a variance case or a special zoning case, I immediately see an opportunity for negotiation and an opportunity for us to lend some assistance, and maybe give away a little within bounds, but also extract something for the town.

The planner tries to win the review game by wringing concessions from the developer, while at the same time helping him to pass the board's review. The developer tries to win by getting concessions from the planner without paying too great a price for them. The planner can lose the game in two ways: by allowing bad projects to get through, or by discouraging good ones. The developer can also lose in two ways: by failing to get his project through, or by paying too high a price for getting it through.

In order to be able to play the review game, the planner must maintain his credibility both with the developers and with the Zoning Board of Appeals. With both groups, he has worked hard to shape the attitudes and expectations which are essential to his intermediary functions. At the beginning, he had to create the institutional arrangements which legitimize his role. As he explained,

> Under the old zoning bylaws, there was no requirement that we file a report. We took it upon ourselves to file. Under the new zon-

ing bylaws, which we wrote, there are more stringent standards. We will continue our same policy, but by addressing specific items in various cases. These are now in the bylaws.

He had also to create, in developers and board members, a network of expectations. Board members had to learn to respect his expertise; developers, to respect his influence with and knowledge about the board. These expectations had to become routine and, once routinized, they had to be continually reinforced.

Thus the planner has a dual objective. In order to improve the town he must win the review game, but he must also maintain the credibility on which his role depends. In these two requirements, which turn out to conflict with one another, lie the origins of his balancing act.

As the planner reviews the developer's plans, he must search out mismatches between the plan and the pertinent rules. For each mismatch, he must estimate the likelihood that the board will grant or withold an exception to the rule. He must invest ways of circumventing their negative responses, and he must predict their reactions to such efforts at circumvention. His knowledge-in-practice must be adequate to all of these activities. But in addition, he must avoid being perceived as a usurper of the board's regulatory function. For if he is so perceived, both members of the board and developers will cease to regard him as an intermediary. On the other hand, if he is perceived as lacking in knowledge or influence, he will be unable to bargain successfully. Similarly, he must be tough enough to screen out unacceptable projects, or he will lose his credibility with the board. Yet he must not exclude acceptable projects, or he will shut off the flow of proposals.

As he preps the developer, the planner must anticipate the board's questions, distinguish the less from the more important of these, and determine the direction of acceptable answers. He must also gauge the developer's understanding of the problems, distinguish what he can and cannot do for himself, and motivate him to do the necessary homework. At the same time, he must avoid becoming identified with the developer's proposals or he will cease to be regarded as an intermediary.

The planner's bargaining with the developer follows a familiar schema. There are two parties, each of whom has a stake in the outcomes of interaction. Each must communicate his own wants, learn what the other wants, formulate proposals, and learn the other's responses to them. Each gives something in order to get something, trying to get as much as he can while giving as little as possible, and the process continues until each party gets what he is willing to settle for, or until one party decides to stop. In order to bargain effectively, the planner must know a great deal about costs and benefits of interest to the developer, and he must know a great deal about the board's likely responses to proposed concessions and about the effects of such concessions on the quality of building in the town. But the planner must conduct his bargaining without appearing to usurp the board's role.

The problems the planner sets for himself are the problems of balancing these several constraints. In order to review effectively while preserving his credibility as an intermediary, he strives for thoroughness and clarity but also insists on presenting his review as preliminary. In order to insure that acceptable projects will be approved while at the same time protecting his intermediate status, he tries to make sure that the developer understands how to answer the board's questions while at the same time distancing himself from the developer's proposal. In order to bargain effectively without discouraging the flow of proposals, he tries to convey negative information and also to make it palatable, and he tries to convey his ability to make or withold concessions while at the same time remaining within the bounds of his legitimate authority.

In the bargaining process, especially, the planner's balancing act leads to strange effects. Clearly, planner and developer bargain with one another. Privately, the planner states explicitly that they do so. Yet in their public meeting, they give the impression of attempting to conceal what they are doing.

When the developer makes a bid for concessions, he does so indirectly, by referring to a conversation with his uncle. And when the planner responds, he says,

> [I don't think it's] going to be a serious problem. But I'm not the Zoning Board of Appeals.

The developer bids indirectly, by appearing to transmit his uncle's request for a clarification of the rules, and the planner responds indirectly, by guardedly predicting the board's reaction.

Why this indirectness, as though the success of the game depended on appearing not to play it? In the planner's case, the explanation lies in the conflicting requirements that flow from his dual objective. He must negotiate with developers, and in order to do so, he must claim, at least implicitly, to be able to make or influence the board's decisions on requests for variances. But this claim makes him vulnerable to the danger that developers will put him in place of the board. The board might resent this usurpation of their authority, and developers might take it as a cue for increased pressure or even, perhaps, for bribery. Hence the planner's frequent "I'm not the Zoning Board of Appeals!", uttered just when he has made an implicit claim to authority.

In the developer's case, he acts as though he were colluding with the planner by appearing to share the assumption that the latter has no authority. If the planner is to appear to have no authority, the developer must appear to make no bids for concessions.

But this collusion, which makes the review game into an "open secret," adds a new layer of ambiguity to a process that is already ambiguous. In the review game, each possible violation of the bylaw is also a possible bargaining point. When the planner brings up such an item, he may or may not be communicating an invitation to negotiation. If, in addition to this, the planner and the developer cannot admit to the game they are playing, then ambiguous invitations and ambiguous responses can never be publicly clarified.

The self-reinforcing system of knowing-in-practice. The planner's balancing act flows from the particular way in which he has framed his intermediary role. It is true that his twofold objective is inherently conflictual, requiring that he negotiate with developers without infringing on the board's authority, but this is not by itself sufficient to create the conditions for the balancing act. These follow from the theory of action he uses to set and solve the problems of his interactions with developers and members of the board.

The planner's interpersonal theory of action conforms to a model that Chris Argyris and I have called Model I.[4] An individual who conforms to Model I behaves according to characteristic values and strategies of action. His values include the following:

- Achieve the task, as I define it.
- In win/lose interactions with others, try to win and avoid losing.
- Avoid negative feelings, such as anger or resentment.
- Be rational, in the sense of "Keep cool, be persuasive, use rational argument."

Among the strategies by which he tries to satisfy these values, there are the following:

- Control the task unilaterally.
- Protect yourself unilaterally, without testing to see whether you need to do so.
- Protect the other unilaterally, without testing to see whether he wishes to be protected.

When the several parties to an interaction behave according to Model I, there are predictable consequences. The behavioral world—the world of experienced interpersonal interaction—tends to be win/lose. The participants in it act defensively and are perceived as doing so. Attributions to others tend to be tested privately, not publicly, for public testing carries a perceived risk of vulnerability. Hence, attributions tend to become self-sealing; the individual cannot get the data that would disconfirm them. And individuals tend to employ strategies of mystery and mastery, seeking to master the situation while keeping their own thoughts and feelings mysterious.

The planner in our protocol frames the problems of his meeting with the developer in a Model I way and brings a Model I theory of action to their solution. He perceives the review game, which he plays with the developer, as a win/lose game. He sets and tries to solve problems by a strategy of mystery and mastery.

He has decided ahead of time, for example, what the developer needs to know. In order to make sure that the developer gets the right message, he sets up the meeting in his own office and asks the architect to be present, because he believes the architect will help the developer to pay closer attention to what is going on. He introduces his agenda at the beginning of the meeting and follows it rigorously throughout. He stamps in the messages he regards as important, and uses his expertise (as in the matter of parking spaces) to reinforce his strategy of control.

In order to keep the developer from reacting defensively to negative information, he uses a variety of techniques to soften or mask the impact of his criticisms of the plans. He preps the developer for his presentation to the Zoning Board of Appeals, while indicating to the developer that he must treat the proposal as his own. And he negotiates with the developer, exhibiting the authority he denies, and induces the developer to collude with him in appearing not to be negotiating.

The intermediary role, by itself, requires none of these strategies of action. But the planner's framing of the intermediary role does require them. The balancing act follows from the fact that the planner keeps the conflicting demands of the intermediary role to himself and attempts to manage them by unilaterally controlling the impressions he creates in the minds of others. Thus his framing of the role, his setting of the problems of the meeting, and his Model I theory of action, make up a self-reinforcing system. One could say either that he has framed role and problems to suit his theory of action, or that he has evolved a theory of action suited to the role and problems he has framed.

Limits to Reflection-in-Action

The planner is an individual who likes to reflect on his practice. Indeed, his willingness to participate in our research grew out of this interest. But he limits his reflection to his *strategies* of unilaterial control. He mentioned in an interview, for example, that he spends time experimenting with such rhetorical devices as delivery, intonation, and eye contact. He reflects on the strategies by which he tries to create the desired impressions in others, but he does not reflect on the role frame, problem setting, or theory of action which lead him to try to create one impression rather than another.

Indeed, his balancing act and his strategy of mystery and mastery are bound together in a system of knowing-in-practice which tends, in several ways, to make itself immune to reflection. Since the planner is doing one thing while appearing to do another, he cannot easily make his assumptions public or subject them to public testing. His sense of vulnerability discourages reflection. And he is so busy managing the balancing act, manipulating the impressions he makes on others and defending against vulnerability to exposure, that he has little opportunity to reflect on the problem settings that drive his performance. Moreover, for the same reason, he is unlikely to detect errors of interpretation which might provoke broader and deeper reflection.

Our protocol contains, as it turns out, an example of just such an error.

In an interview following his meeting with the planner, the developer revealed that he had decided against going forward with his project *because he would have to apply for a single variance.* He had other opportunities for investment, he explained, and he did not want to spend his energies on what he thought would be a long and cumbersome process of appeal. He had made this decision during his meeting with the planner, but he had chosen not to reveal it.

When he learned of the developer's decision, the planner was shocked. He had based his strategy on minimizing variances, but he had assumed that a single, easily obtainable variance on lot size would not stand in the project's way.

Nevertheless, to the developer, the need for a single variance had loomed large. And he had responded with a strategy of mystery and mastery similar to the planner's. He had run a private test of project feasibility, and when it produced negative results, he had decided unilaterally to abandon the project.

The planner's and developer's theories of action had combined to produce a behavioral world in which each withheld negative information, tested assumptions privately, and sought to maintain unilateral control over the other. In this sort of climate, the developer was unlikely to reveal his negative decision. To do so would have violated the "open secret" of the review game into which the planner had drawn him, and it would also have called for a degree of trust unlikely within a Model I behavioral world. For similar reasons, the planner was unlikely to make a public test of his assumptions about the developer's decisions.

As a result, the planner was unaware that his efforts had been futile from the moment the developer learned of the need for a single variance. The planner had no access to information that might have put this pivotal assumption in doubt.

It is of interest, nevertheless, to ask what *might* have happened if, contrary to fact, the planner had become aware of his mistake. In what directions might his inquiry then have taken him?

This is a peculiar sort of question because, in order to have become aware of this information, the planner would have had to behave according to a very different theory of action, one conducive to the public testing of private assumptions. Argyris and I have proposed a model of such a theory of action, which we call Model II. The question stated above then becomes the following: What might have happened if the planner had operated on a Model II theory of action?

An individual who conforms to Model II tries to satisfy the following values:

- Give and get valid information.
- Seek out and provide others with directly observable data and correct reports, so that valid attributions can be made.
- Create the conditions for free and informed choice.
- Try to create, for oneself and for others, awareness of the values at stake in decision, awareness of the limits of one's capacities, and awareness of the zones of experience free of defense mechanisms beyond one's control.
- Increase the likelihood of internal commitment to decisions made.
- Try to create conditions, for oneself and for others, in which the individual is committed to an action because it is intrinsically satisfying—not, as in the case of Model I, because it is accompanied by external rewards or punishments.

These three values are interconnected in several ways. Valid information is essential to informed choice. Freedom of choice depends on one's ability to select objectives that challenge one's capacities within a tolerable range, which again depends on valid information. An individual is more likely to feel internally committed to a freely made decision.

Among the strategies for achieving these values, there are the following:

- Make designing and managing the environment a bilateral task, so that the several parties to the situation can work toward freedom of choice and internal commitment.
- Make protection of self or other a joint operation, so that one does not withold negative information from the other without testing the attribution that underlies the decision to withhold.

- Speak in directly observable categories, providing the data from which one's inferences are drawn and thereby opening them to disconfirmation.
- Surface private dilemmas, so as to encourage the public testing of the assumptions on which such dilemmas depend.

When the several parties to an interaction behave according to Model II, they tend to be seen by others as minimally defensive and open to learning. They tend to be seen as firmly committed to their positions but equally committed to having them confronted and tested. Discussions tend then to be open to the reciprocal exploration of risky ideas. Assumptions are more likely to be subjected to public test and are less likely to become self-sealing. Learning cycles—not only with respect to the means for achieving one's goals but with respect to the desirability of the goals—tend to be set in motion.

If the planner had been operating on a Model II theory of action, he would not have devoted his energies to maintaining unilateral control of his own agenda, but would also have tried to elicit the developer's agenda. He would have tested for the developer's responses to the information that a variance would be required, and he would therefore increase the likelihood of discovering that for the developer the need for a single variance was enough to make the project unattractive.

Had he become aware of this negative information, the planner might have gone on to reflect on his approach to the conflicting demands of his intermediate role. He might ask, for example, why he finds himself in the position of having to bargain with the developer without appearing to do so—a condition that exacerbates the problem of getting access to crucial information about the developer's intentions. This condition grows out of the planner's balancing act which depends, in turn, on his attempt to manage the conflicting demands of his role by a strategy of mystery and mastery—that is, by keeping his conflicting objectives private while controlling the impressions he creates in the minds of developers and members of the board.

If he were operating on a Model II theory of action, the planner might ask himself, "What if I were to make my dilemma public?" This would have implications for his conduct both with board members and with developers. It would carry risks, but it would offer the possibility of important benefits.

In a more open discussion of his role in the town, the planner might describe to the board his strategy of using "review of plans" to seek out opportunities for negotiation with developers. He might point out that he cannot negotiate effectively unless he can exercise some authority of his own, without fearing that the board will later reverse his decisions. At the same time, he might indicate his recognition of the fact that final decisions do remain with the board. He might invite the board to monitor his negotiations, working with him to keep the lines of authority clear and at the same time flexible. By surfacing these issues, it is true, he might irritate some members of the board; but he might also confirm publicly what many of them had already privately suspected.

With developers, the planner might admit that, while his actions are subject to the board's final approval, he does have some discretionary freedom to decide on requests for variances. In doing this, he might open himself to more vigorous attempts on the part of developers to subject him to pressure or persuasion. It is hard to see how this would be a very great risk, however. Since the developers already bargain with him, they must believe that he has some freedom to carry out his end of the bargain.

Under these conditions, the planner would have reframed his balancing act. The central conflict of his intermediary role would remain but it would be a public conflict. There would be no need to bargain while appearing not to do so. The planner would be less likely to make undetected errors. At the same time, he would experience new demands for Model II behavior. He would no longer measure his effectiveness in terms of the successful performance of his balancing act but in terms of his ability to bargain openly, to share control of the interaction, to advocate his own goals firmly while inquiring effectively into the goals of others. He would also reduce some of the impediments to his further reflection-in-action.

Conclusion

The case of the town planner illustrates, in one small episode drawn from the practice of one planner, how and with what sorts of consequences planning roles are framed. I have tried to show how planning roles have evolved in a global conversation with the planning situation which has led, at various times over the past decades, to the salience of centralist planning, advocacy, regulatory, and intermediary roles. But I have also tried to show, in the case of a practitioner of intermediary planning, how knowing-in-practice consists of a self-reinforcing system in which role frame, strategies of action, relevant facts, and interpersonal theories of action are bound up together.

The intermediary role, in which a practitioner places himself between those who propose and those who dispose, carries inherent potentials for conflict. Nevertheless, the meaning of this conflict for practice varies greatly with the way in which each practitioner frames his role. Role frame is interdependent with interpersonal theory of action, and the resulting system of knowing-in-practice has consequences both for the practitioner's ability to detect crucial errors and for the scope and direction of his reflection-in-action. In our example, the planner's balancing act is tied to his Model I theory-in-use. In the alternative that I have outlined, a Model II theory-in-use would be linked to a framing of the intermediary role in which private dilemmas would be made public and private assumptions would be subjected to public test. In the first case, attributions tend to become self-sealing, and reflection-in-action tends to be limited to consideration of the effectiveness of strategies of unilaterial control. In the second case, errors of attribution are more likely to surface and reflection-in-action is more likely to extend in scope to the entire system of knowing-in-practice, including the framing of the role itself.

So long as a practitioner chooses to play an intermediary role, he cannot avoid the conflicts inherent in the role. But within these constraints, he has considerable freedom to choose the role frame he will adopt and the theory of action according to which he will behave. Depending on these interdependent choices, he will increase or constrict his capacity for reflection-in-action.

8

The Art of Managing:
Reflection-in-Action
Within an Organizational
Learning System

The Split in the Field of Management

The field of management has long been marked by a conflict between two competing views of professional knowledge. On the first view, the manager is a technician whose practice consists in applying to the everyday problems of his organization the principles and methods derived from management science. On the second, the manager is a craftsman, a practitioner of an art of managing that cannot be reduced to explicit rules and theories. The first view dates from the early decades of the twentieth century when the idea of professional management first came into good currency. The second has an even longer history, management having been understood as an art, a matter of skill and wisdom, long before it began to be understood as a body of techniques. But the first view has gained steadily in power.

The idea of management science, and the complementary idea of the manager as a technician, has been carried by a social movement which has spread out from its center in the United States to encompass the whole of the industrialized world. The origins of this movement are difficult to identify, but a critically important milestone in its development was the work of Frederick Taylor who, in the 1920s, conceived of management as a form of human engineering based on a science of work.[1] While Taylor may not have invented these ideas, he was certainly the first to embody them in a practice of industrial management and consultation, and he popularized them in a way that has had enormous influence in industry, in business, and in the administration of public agencies.

Taylor treated work as a man/machine process which could be decomposed into measurable units of activity. Every industrial process, from the shovelling of coal to the processing of steel, could be subjected to experimental analysis. The design of tools, the bodily movements of the worker, and the sequencing of production steps, could be combined in an optimum configuration, a "one best way." Taylor saw the industrial manager as a designer of work, a controller and monitor of performance, and a distributor of rewards and punishments carefully selected and applied so as to yield optimally efficient production. Above all, he saw the manager as an on-line experimenter, a scientist in action, whose practice would consist in the trial and measurement of designs and methods aimed at the discovery and implementation of the one best way.

Taylor's views were by no means unique. Thorsten Veblen, to take one extraordinary example, also perceived that industry had taken on the characteristics of an organizational machine within which managers of the business enterprise must be increasingly concerned with standards, measures of performance, and the articulation of interlocking activities. But it was Taylor who embodied these ideas in practiace, and it was Taylor's version of the practice of industrial engineering, efficiency expertise, and time and motion study which has evolved into the management science of the present day.

World War II gave an enormous impetus to the management science movement, first, because of the general rise in prestige of science and technology, and second, because of the birth of operations research and systems theory. These disciplines, which grew out of the use of applied mathematics to solve problems of submarine search and bomb tracking, were later exported to industry, commerce, and government. In the wake of World War II, management science grew to maturity. Teachers and researchers in the new schools of management, in partnership with managers in public and private sectors, have engendered a plethora of new techniques. There is no field of management which has been immune to the incursions of management science. What was once true only of industrial production has now become true of sales, personnel selection and training, budgeting and financial control, marketing, business policy, and strategic planning. Technical panaceas have appeared on the scene with clocklike regularity, old ones making way for new. Value analysis, management by objectives, planning programming and budgeting, and zero-based budgeting are only a few of the better-known examples. Even the human relations movement, which had originated as a reaction against Taylorism, has tended increasingly to present itself as a body of techniques.

Yet in spite of the increasingly powerful status of management science and technique, managers have remained persistently aware of important areas of practice which fall outside the bounds of technical rationality. This awareness has taken two forms.

Managers have become increasingly sensitive to the phenomena of uncertainty, change, and uniqueness. In the last twenty years, "decision under uncertainty" has become a term of art. It has become commonplace for managers to speak of the "turbulent" environments in which problems do not lend themselves to the techniques of benefit-cost analysis or to probabilistic reasoning. At least at the level of espoused theory, managers have become used to the instability of patterns of competition, economic context, consumer interests, sources of raw materials, attitudes of the labor force, and regulatory climate. And managers have become acutely aware that they are often confronted with unique situations to which they must respond under conditions of stress and limited time which leave no room for extended calculation or analysis. Here they tend to speak not of technique but of "intuition."

Quite apart from these exceptions to the day-to-day routine of management practice, managers have remained aware of a dimension of ordinary professional work, crucially important to effective performance, which cannot be reduced to technique. Indeed, they are sometimes aware that even management technique rests on a foundation of nonrational, intuitive artistry.

Among theorists of management, the nonrational dimension of managing has had several notable exponents. In chapter 2, I have cited Chester Barnard's description of "nonlogical processes," Geoffrey Vickers's analysis of the art of judgment, and Michael Polanyi's reflections on tacit knowing. More recently, a Canadian professor of management, Henry Mintzberg, has caused a considerable stir with studies of the actual behavior of top managers that reveal a virtual absence of the methods that managers are "supposed to" use.[2] And in some of the most prestigious schools of management, where the curriculum depends on cases drawn from the actual experience of business firms, there is a widely held belief that managers learn to be effective not primarily through the study of theory and technique but through long and varied practice in the analysis of business problems, which builds up a generic, essentially unanalyzable capacity for problem solving.

It is no exaggeration, then, to say that the field of management is split into two camps, each of which holds a different view of the nature of professional knowledge. At the same time that management science and technique have grown increasingly in power and prestige, there has been a persistent and growing awareness of the importance of an art of managing which reveals itself both in crucially important situations of uncertainty, instability, and uniqueness, and in those dimensions of everyday practice which depend upon the spontaneous exercise of intuitive artistry. One sign of this split is that in some schools of management, representatives of the two tendencies—the professors of management science and the practitioners of case-method—no longer speak to one another. The representatives of each school of thought go about their business as though the other school of thought did not exist.

But a split of this kind, which is barely tolerable in a professional school, creates for thoughtful students and practitioners a particularly painful variant of the dilemma of "rigor or relevance." For if rigorous management means the application of management science and technique, then a "rigorous manager" must be selectively inattentive to the art which he brings to much of his day-to-day practice, and he must avoid situations—often the most important in organizational life—where he would find himself confronted with uncertainty, instability, or uniqueness.

But if the art of managing can be described, at least in part, and can be shown to be rigorous in a way peculiar to itself, then the dilemma of rigor or relevance need not be so painful. Indeed, it may be possible to bring the art of managing into dialogue with management science.

The Art of Managing

In management as in other fields, "art" has a two-fold meaning. It may mean intuitive judgment and skill, the feeling for phenomena and for action that I have called knowing-in-practice. But it may also designate a manager's reflection, in a context of action, on phenomena which he perceives as incongruent with his intuitive understandings.

Managers do reflect-in-action. Sometimes, when reflection is triggered by uncertainty, the manager says, in effect, "This is puzzling; how can I understand it?" Sometimes, when a sense of opportunity provokes reflection, the manager asks, "What can I make of this?" And sometimes, when a manager is surprised by the success of his own intuitive knowing, he asks himself, "What have I really been doing?"

Whatever the triggering condition, a manager's reflection-in-action is fundamentally similar to reflection-in-action in other professional fields. It consists in on-the-spot surfacing, criticizing, restructuring, and testing of intuitive understandings of experienced phenomena; often it takes the form of a reflective conversation with the situation. But a manager's reflection-in-action also has special features of its own. A manager's professional life is wholly concerned with an organization which is both the stage for his activity and the object of his inquiry. Hence, the phenomena on which he reflects-in-action are the phenomena of organizational life. Organizations, furthermore, are repositories of cumulatively built-up knowledge: principles and maxims of practice, images of mission and identity, facts about the task environment, techniques of operation, stories of past experience which serve as exemplars for future action. When a manager reflects-in-action, he draws on this stock of organizational knowledge, adapting it to some present instance. And he also functions as an agent of organizational learning, extending or restructuring, in his present inquiry, the stock of knowledge which will be available for future inquiry.

Finally, managers live in an organizational system which may promote or inhibit reflection-in-action. Organizational structures are more or less adaptable to new findings, more or less resistant to new tasks. The behavioral world of the organization, the characteristic pattern of interpersonal relations, is more or less open to reciprocal reflection-in-action—to the surfacing of negative information, the working out of conflicting views, and the public airing of organizational dilemmas. Insofar as organizational structure and behavioral world condition organizational inquiry, they make up what I will call the "learning system" of the organization. The scope and direction of a manager's reflection-in-action are strongly influenced, and may be severely limited, by the learning system of the organization in which he practices.

These distinctively organizational aspects of a manager's reflection-in-action must enter into any good description of the art of managing. In the examples that follow, I shall sample a range of organizational phenomena with which reflective managers concern themselves: the problem of interpreting the external environment's response to organizational action, the diagnosis of signs of trouble within an organization, the process by which an organization learns from its experience, and the effects of an organizational learning system on the way in which organizational problems are set and solved. I shall limit myself to the experience of business firms, not because business managers are more reflective than others but because they are the source of my freshest examples. In the business context, the kinds of organizational phenomena noted above may be illustrated by the behavior of a market, the problems of a production plant, the acquisition of knowledge about product development, and the learning system of a product development organization.

In all of these examples, I shall describe processes that managers often undertake but on which they seldom reflect. Managers do reflect-in-action, but they seldom reflect on their reflection-in-action. Hence this crucially important dimension of their art tends to remain private and inaccessible to others. Moreover, because awareness of one's intuitive thinking usually grows out of practice in articulating it to others, managers often have little access to their own reflection-in-action. The resulting mysteriousness of the art of managing has several harmful consequences. It tends to perpetuate the split in the field of management, creating a misleading impression that practitioners must choose between practice based on management science and an essentially mysterious artistry. And it prevents the manager from helping others in his organization to learn to do what he can do. Since he cannot describe his reflection-in-action, he cannot teach others to do it. If they acquire the capacity for it, they do so by contagion. Yet one of a manager's most important functions is the education of his subordinates.

For all of these reasons, it seems to me critically important to begin to describe how managers do reflect-in-action and how their reflection-in-action is limited.

Interpreting market phenomena. A business firm is continually in interaction with its markets, and markets are often in a state of flux—some of which is induced by the action of the business firm itself. In the contemporary business setting, inquiry into market phenomena has become a specialized function in its own right. Market researchers and strategists have developed principles of marketing, models of market behavior, and techniques of market exploration and analysis. Nevertheless, much of what managers encounter in the marketplace resists the application of ready-made theories and procedures.

Market research cannot say very much about consumer response to a radically new product. People cannot readily answer questions about their interest in something of which they have neither direct nor indirect experience. At best, if they are helped to carry out the imaginative feat of supposing themselves in possession of a nonexistent product, they may speculate on their future responses to it. But speculation of this sort is usually a very poor predictor of their behavior toward an actual product, more or less like the one described, which will appear one day, in a particular package and at a particular price, on supermarket shelves. If prototypes of the new product are produced (and it takes money to develop and produce them), then consumer panels may provide information from which managers can make inferences about actual market behavior. But the gap between panel response and market response is significant. Only with the introduction of large-scale market tests do manufacturers begin to get reliable information about market behavior, and regional market tests can also produce misleading results.

At each stage of the development of a radically new product, managers must make investment decisions in the absence of adequate information or rules for rational decision. Each such judgment is a unique case, and the market tests, which may reduce uncertainty, come only at the price of further investment.

The full-scale marketing of a product is also a test of sorts, and managers often find themselves confronted with surprising data that demand interpretation.

Shortly after World War II, to take one rather celebrated example, the 3M Corporation put on the market a clear cellulose acetate tape, coated on one side with pressure-sensitive adhesive, which they called Scotch Tape. They had intended it for use as a book-mending material, a way of preserving things that would otherwise have to be thrown away; hence the name Scotch. But in consumers' hands, the product came to be used in many different ways, most of which had nothing to do with mending books. It was used to wrap packages, to fasten pictures to the wall, to make labels, to decorate surfaces, even to curl hair. 3M's managers did not regard these surprising uses as a failure of their initial marketing plan, nor did they merely accept them as a happy accident. They *noticed* them and tried to make sense of them as a set of messages about potential markets. The company began to market types of Scotch Tape specially designed for use in such applications as packaging, decorating, and hair curling.

3M's marketing managers treated their product as a projective test for consumers. They reflected on unanticipated signals from the marketplace, interpreted them, and then tested their interpretations by adapting the product to the uses that consumers had already discovered. But their tests were also moves aimed at strengthening market position and probes which might yield additional surprises. Their marketing process was a reflective conversation with consumers.

Interpreting organizational troubles. When a manager first gets signals that something is going wrong in his organization, he usually has no clear, consensual account of the trouble. Various members of the organization, who occupy different positions and have different interests, tell different and often conflicting stories. If the manager is to take action, he must make some sense of the organizational *Rashomon;* but by inquiring into the situation, he also influences it. Hence he faces a twofold problem: how to find out what (if anything) is wrong, and how to do so in a way that enhances rather than reduces his ability to fix what is wrong.

Consider a case drawn from the recent experience of a manufacturer of scientific instruments.

The company, based in a developing country, was founded some fifteen years ago by a nuclear physicist who, with a small group of former students and colleagues, built a very narrow product line into a $100 million dollar business. The company's main offices are in its home country, but it has sales and service facilities in thirteen foreign countries. It has captured about 15 percent of the market in its field.

The founder, now chairman of the board, attributes his success to two main principles: stay in close touch with the market, and deliver fast responses to changes in the field.

From these two principles, many organizational consequences have been made to follow. In order to get product improvements to the market quickly, the company often puts instruments in the field before all development problems have been resolved. They depend on highly skilled technical servicemen to complete the development task. In order to achieve fast response to market demand, customers' orders are frequently changed. About 30 percent of all manufacturing orders are subject to engineering changes. As a result, manufacturing has become a highly sophisticated job shop where speed and flexibility take precedence over efficiency, which depends on long production runs.

The company has deliberately refrained from establishing a fixed organizational structure. There are no organization charts. Roles are frequently overlapping and informal group problem solving is the norm. As the founder says, "This is no place for people who can't live with uncertainty."

Role flexibility is carried to an extreme. The present vice-president for finance is a former nuclear physicist who has learned finance as he might have learned a new branch of physics. And every member of the top-management team has filled virtually every major corporate function. The president of the company, G, who began with the company fifteen years ago, has worked in budgeting, finance, sales, and manufacturing. He is still regarded as "the best engineer in the company." Along with the founder and the vice-president for finance, he regards work as "fun," likes to put "impossible" demands on himself, and expects others to do likewise.

G is used to reaching down into the company to deal with whatever crisis presents itself. He has done this three or four times. Within the last year, for example, he spent three months at a computer console in order to resolve a critical software problem that threatened to stall a major new development.

The crisis presently facing G concerns a new production plant established a year ago to make metal parts for instruments manufactured in the two main production facilities. It is located in a development zone of the country, where it is eligible for generous government subsidies, although it lacks access to labor force and services which would have been available in one of the larger cities. The new manager of the plant, M, has been hired away from a large electronics firm. He has been in his position for a year, and during that time there have been increasingly troublesome production delays. Recently one of the managers of the two main instrument plants brought the problem to G, who discussed it with the manager of the other instrument plant, the vice-president for manufacturing, and the manager of the new plant, M.

The manager of the first plant describes the situation as follows:

> I want the parts on time and M wants efficiency! And I want 100 different kinds of parts. Opening the new plant caused a lot of crunches in our system. We worked night and day all last year to solve this problem. For a while, things were okay. Then, when the head of the metals section left because he couldn't get along with M, we had a big decline. M tried to manage the metals section by remote control. He should get in there and manage metals for himself. Or perhaps we should take the operation and bring it back to Central, in a metals shop of our own. M lacks the capacity to manage the problem. I see no light at the end of the tunnel.

Manager of the second plant:

> M's is a new plant built around new people. There are communications problems, because people there don't adapt to flexible demands. M is pressed between demands for efficiency and for fast response, and he's not solving the problem. They need new staff functions. They have problems with orders because they don't know what's going on. They must see their raison d'etre as giving service to us, but they won't accept that definition. They are not equal. They feel second class.

M, manager of the new plant:

> There's informal problem solving at Central, but between here and Central, it can't work. You have to have more rules, even with less flexibility, because as you grow, without new rules, you have a mess. G prefers that we use 50 percent of our capacity and hold people on standby to respond to orders when they come in, but that teaches people to be inefficient. And so I sell to outsiders,

but I have to give preference to the company. It's an axiom that you should produce efficiently, but I have to be inefficient in order to get the parts in on time. Management attention is split.

Vice-president for manufacturing:

> Right now, the new plant is G's crisis. First we must clean up the channels of communication, providing better, more sophisticated management tools. And we must resolve the conflict of priorities. Most of the problems grow out of the frequent engineering changes which are vital to the company. Two-thirds of the problem is to get the right man in the right place. One of our main problems is a shortage of upper-middle management.

The first plant manager, who brought the problem to G, says,

> I know G is working on the problem, because he hasn't erased all the figures we put on the blackboard!

And he is right, G is working on the problem.

G has listened to the several stories about the production delays at M's plant, but he has chosen not to decide among them or even to try to put them all together to make a single coherent picture of the trouble. He has read the *Rashomon* as a sign of two main difficulties: a lack of effective communication among the several parties, and a split between the new plant and central operations. He has seen his problem as one of creating a process to deal with these two difficulties.

He has decided to treat the diagnosing of the problem as a central part of the resolution of the problem, and has assigned the task of diagnosis to those who are most centrally concerned. He has asked the vice-president for manufacturing, together with his staff of three, to spend two days a week at the new plant over the next three months. They will work with their counterparts there to trace the sources of delays, to review and repair reporting systems, to fix whatever problems in operations they discover.

G has followed company traditions in turning the full force of management attention onto the crisis point. But this time he has not gone down to deal with the problem himself. He has seen his role as one of designing and putting in place a process to identify and fix the problem, leaving to others the task of working out their conflicting views of it. He has set up an organizational experiment, the essence of which is to bring into close interaction those who have been distant from one another.

M has reacted favorably to this move. He says, "For the first time, I think they are learning what it is really like here. New capacity won't solve our problem; it will barely let us keep up with growth. But as the atmosphere improves and we get a better handle on the problems, we'll gradually remove the delays. I'm optimistic."

And G says, "Perhaps as M comes to feel that people here understand his situation better, he will begin to feel more a part of the company, and then he may commit more fully to his frame of reference."

G has responded to the organizational crisis by designing a process which will involve the key participants in collective reflection-in-action.

Learning about product development. A large American consumer products firm has an extraordinary reputation as a developer of new products. Inside the firm, individual managers are very well aware of their corporate reputation, and attribute it to their success in learning about the process of conceiving, inventing, and commercializing new products.

What is remarkable about this firm is the consciousness that managers bring to this process, the sense they have of being members of a corporate culture which includes a great deal of knowledge about it, and the extent to which each manager sees himself both as a user of the store of corporate knowledge and a contributor to it. It is possible to dig down into the firm at least four layers deep without losing access to the corporate reservoir of knowledge about product development.

These are some examples of what product development managers believe they have learned.

1. "The target is a variable."

One of the heads of technology remarks, "Product development is a game you can win, so long as you keep it open—so long as you remember you can redefine the target." Typically, a product development project is worked out among representatives of marketing, technology, and general management. Once a target has been defined, general management commits the necessary resources. But as development proceeds, technical people learn more about the feasibility of the initial target and more about the properties of the materials with which they are working. They discover unexpected difficulties in achieving the target originally chosen, and they also discover technical possibilities they had not suspected at the outset. They can redefine targets to reflect these discoveries, so long as they also understand the marketing implications of their redefinition of the target.

Thus, in one project concerned with disposable paper products, the development director observes, "We found that the critical variable was not absorptive capacity but rate of absorption!" It was much more difficult to increase absorptive capacity than rate of absorption, but it was the latter that mattered most to the consumer. In the words of one researcher, "We knew we were on the right track when our panels no longer hated us!"

In order to treat the target as a variable, the development team must be able to see a technical property of materials in terms of its meaning to consumers, and they must be able to see a marketing target in terms of the technical demands that follow from it. Such a team cannot afford a "seesaw" between marketing and technology, in which marketing says to technology, "Make what we can sell!" or technology says to marketing, "Sell what we can make!" Technical and marketing specialists must be able to share the uncertainty which they convert to risk by redefining the development target. And, like the marketing managers at 3M, they must be willing to give up the assumption that they *know* the target, once and for all, at the beginning of the development process. As they discover new properties in the phenomena and new meanings in the responses of consumer panels, they learn to restructure not only the means but the ends of development.

2. "The unit of development is not a new product but a game with the competition."

Members of the development team think of themselves as engaged in a game with the competition. For each major product line, there is a national market within which many companies struggle for position. Winning this game consists in establishing, maintaining, and extending market position at the expense of the competitors. Moves in the game consist in product improvements, advertising campaigns, and new product introductions. And for every move, competitors make counter moves. The game lasts for the duration of the life cycle of the product line.

Playing the game well means forming and implementing a development *strategy*. A given development (a paper product with a higher rate of absorption, for example) is likely to trigger competitive developments, and good strategy includes anticipation of the likely countermoves. The development team tries to have in the wings a set of long-term developments which they can activate in response to competitors' moves, when the time is right. Thus, the unit of development is not an individual product but a full cycle of the competitive game.

Within the game, however, there is always the question, "What is the situation now?" Depending on one's interpretation of the situation, construction of an appropriate strategy may vary significantly. In the case of the paper product described above, for example, there was a period in which the team believed that they had established the basic acceptability of their product and needed mainly to get the price down. But a competitor introduced a new product which came in at a higher price and achieved greater consumer acceptance than theirs. How should they interpret their situation in the game? A corporate vice-president made the suggestion, "Why don't you come up with a Cadillac?" This was surprising to the development team, because it ran counter to their strategy. They did not reject it out of hand, however. They waited to see what the market would do. Then, as they said, "When we discovered that our product was holding its own among the low-priced brands, we were freed to work on the Cadillac. Had we brought out a low-priced improvement, we would have cannibalized our own brand."

The new signals from the marketplace enabled the development team to construct a new picture of their situation, one which required them to revise their understanding of their position relative to other brands. And from the new description of the situation, they evolved a new strategy which they would test with the introduction of the "Cadillac" (a familiar metaphor which, like "cannibalizing," is a part of the repertoire they bring to their inquiry).

3. "The important thing is to keep the dialectic moving."

It is unusual to find the term "dialectic" in common usage within a corporate culture. But in this corporation, managers talk freely about dialectic, by which they mean the surfacing and working out of conflicting views among participants in the development process.

The vice-president of technology goes so far as to define his role in terms of the dialectic. He says, "I feel good when I see that engineering and development, advertising and manufacturing, are really surfacing and talking about their differences. It's my job to keep the dialectic alive."

And a general manager says, "You must keep the conflicts alive and on the surface. Once you have identified the conflicts, you see to it that *they* resolve them and that they let you know the results. If they agree ahead of time, too quickly, that can shield you from legitimate conflict. It breaks your heart when you see people have stopped talking about it."

The expectation is that "legitimate conflicts" will surface. The complexity of development situations is such that engineering and research, advertising and manufacturing, general management and finance, will have different and conflicting views of situation and strategy, all of which are important to the organization. A manager's task is to make sure that such conflicts are neither surpressed nor circumvented. Organizational learning about a present situation, and about product development more generally, depends on the "working out" of such conflicts. But no one can say ahead of time *how* they will be worked out, which will depend on the reciprocal reflection-in-action of the parties to the conflict.

Limits of the Organizational Learning System

The very same company that is so conscious of organizational learning about product development also provides a very good example of the ways in which an organizational learning system may constrain reflection-in-action.

As a consultant to this organization, I was asked to address the problem of the "burn-out" of product development directors. These individuals, who work at the intersection of general management, advertising, and research, are hard to find, expensive to develop, and difficult to keep. They experience an unusually high incidence of alcoholism, health problems, divorce, and mental breakdown, and the vice-president for technology wanted to know why.

We agreed that my study would take the form of an analysis of a case of product development—Product X, as I will call it, a product for use in household appliances. The story of Product X was already famous in the company when I began my study. Nearly everyone described it in the same way: "A case in which we nearly failed because of problems we ought to have anticipated and dealt with better than we did. But we came through and bailed ourselves out."

Initially, there were three questions about the case:

- Why were we so late in detecting and admitting the problems?
- Why were we so unwilling to ask for help and to accept help once it was offered?
- How did we bail ourselves out?

The product had originated in a "brainstorming" session where development specialists had asked themselves, "What benefits can we deliver through products designed for use in household appliances?" When they had arrived at a basic product definition, they began to explore the technologies they would need, and they hit on a particular technology, owned by a private inventor, which they could turn to their purposes.

Their development process proceeded, as usual in this company, through a series of tests. They tested the product's effectiveness in delivering its intended benefit, and they tested it for possible harmful side effects. The testing process began in the laboratory where, for example, standard corrosion tests were performed by immersing steel plates in a bath made up of the product's components. And the process continued through "blind" tests with consumer panels (a standard element in all of their development processes), and finally to regional test markets. It is important to note that a successful passage through such a sequence of standard tests functioned, in this company, as an essential part of the dialogue between technical development specialists and general managers. The general managers, who controlled the commitment of resources, depended on the results of standard tests to make their decisions.

The product performed very well in panel tests, and was placed in its first regional test market. Two months into the test market, however, an appliance company which had been asked to test the product sent back word, "This product can get stuck in the machine, and if it does, you can get overheating. There is a risk of fire." Members of the development team at first said, "We don't think so." But the appliance company wrote a formal, threatening letter to general management: "If you market this product, we'll put stickers on our machines telling people not to use it."

With this exposure of the problem, everyone started to talk about it. General management, who had known nothing of the problem, were furious. Three different task groups were set up and they arrived at two different solutions. Both of these were subsequently accepted and incorporated in a new version of the product. But this created a new problem. What should be done with the existing test market? The old product had been successful in consumer panel blind tests, and general management said, "We'll keep the old test market going. It's the original product we invested in. It passed our tests." The technical group nearly mutinied. But general management took the position, "We can assume a liability if we want to; your job is to tell us the odds."

The sense of general management's position was, "The product is a black box. We make decisions about things that pass our tests. But we don't take the cover off the box because we get confused." And the sense of the technical group's position was, "We make decisions about particulars, not general probabilities. We understand what it is that makes a product pass tests. And we don't always trust the tests!"

A year later, the first test market was dropped and a new one, based on the revised product, was instituted. But technical people felt that the issue had "put them into short pants."

At this point, the development was some two years old, with $30 million invested.

A second major embarrassment occurred in the midst of the second test market. The product had been doing well, when a sprinkling of complaints came in from the field to the effect that the product caused rust in appliances. These complaints came in after the "sticking" problem, and after the laboratory immersion tests which had revealed no rusting. The technical team chose to ignore the complaints. The rusting detected by a few users of the product must have been produced by other causes.

Members of the corporate research laboratory who heard about the problem took a different view. One member of the research group lathered some of the product's ingredients on a tin can and left it overnight; in the morning the can had rusted. The researchers took the rusted can to the vice-president for technology, who said, "There's no red light. Don't worry about it. We can handle it." But as letters from the field multiplied, the laboratory team became convinced that the rusting effect was real. They developed a model that would explain the rusting process, used X-ray spectroscopy to test the model, and brought in high-powered consultants from a university. The product development team reacted by asking, "Are you really sure of this? Why are you doing this to us? Why don't you do something constructive?"

The laboratory group was disillusioned. The head of the laboratory sent out a memo which forbade researchers to do more work on Product X. At this point, however, the vice-president for technology fired the head of the development team and appointed a researcher from the laboratory to become the new head. This man quickly satisfied himself, with the help of his former colleagues in the laboratory, that the rusting effect was real. This produced a new crisis.

The vice-president for technology then held a meeting with members of the two teams. At this meeting he said, "Are you guys men enough to keep this problem from general management and go ahead on faith, without knowing that you can really do it, to make an alternative work?" This set in motion a new process which led, eventually, to solution of the rusting problem. The laboratory group, who had been told not to work on the problem, continued to do so. They came up with a new ingredient which they believed not only solved the rusting problem but actually protected machines. The product development team criticized them for "shooting from the hip" and "overstepping their bounds." But the new head of the laboratory team proposed a technical-political compromise: the new ingredient was to be combined with 10 percent of the old. New tests showed that the rusting effect had been overcome and the product worked as well as ever. As one member of the laboratory group said, "It was all played out under the tent, for fear of tipping off general management and breaking their commitment to the product. But at each replay of the problem there was the same issue: Did the new element really work? What about negative side effects? It was a guerrilla war, and we used science as a weapon."

The interactions between product development team and research laboratory can be represented as a cycle of action and reaction, roughly as follows.

The product development team sought to protect themselves, to control the task and territory, and to win credit for their work and credibility with general management. To these ends, they

- resisted the problems pointed out by the laboratory,
- discredited the laboratory findings,
- kept them in their place by confining them to narrow and unimportant problems,
- kept their own work quiet.

The laboratory team became angry and frustrated, distrusted the product development team, and felt a low sense of their own worth. They retaliated by

- taking an aggressive stance as they proved their points,
- seeking to win through science,
- continuing to work on the problem even when the boss told them not to,
- trying to capture the task,
- circumventing product development to get to management.

These strategies made the product development team angry, frustrated, fearful, and distrustful, and reinforced them in their efforts to win and protect themselves.

The consequences of the cycle were wasted effort, duplicated work, and delay in the recognition of problems. The product development team could not, under these circumstances, ask for help nor use it when it was offered. As the cycle amplified, researchers and developers were less and less able to work together. But management injected stopgap solutions. They shifted people around and they intervened directly at moments of crisis.

The pattern was one of "heroism under a tent." To quote some of the observations of the participants, "Three people told me not to work on Product X, but I wouldn't stop," "Don't tell management what you're doing," "Fix the problem first, then tell them about it."

What accounts for such a pattern? In order to answer this question, we must turn to the larger context in which the research/development cycle arose. For researchers and developers were involved in a more comprehensive process which I shall call "the product development game." The game has mainly to do with four variables: corporate commitment, credibility, confidence, and competence.

In order to set a new product in motion, general management must commit the necessary resources. But management commitment is deliberately made hard to win. This is partly a matter of thoroughness. As one of the managers said, "We're a very thorough company; we do our research well, and we don't accept just anything." But management commitment is also hard to win because managers tend to distrust research and development. As one manager said, "They are likely to flimflam and fool us if we're not careful." On the other hand, managers are aware of their dependence on research and development. They know that corporate growth depends on it.

Thus managers must commit to a process which they distrust. They respond by making the commitment of resources hard to win; and once resources are committed, they hold the product development director wholly accountable for performance, loading him with the full burden of uncertainty. And the maintenance of corporate commitment becomes touchier as investment in the product increases and the company becomes more exposed.

Under these circumstances, product development people try to win the game by gaining and retaining management commitment, while maintaining their own credibility within the company.

A participant's credibility behaves like a stock on the stock market, going up or down with the perception of his success or failure. There is a corporate market for credibility. Each person strives to maintain his credibility at all costs, because a loss of credibility can make it impossible for him to perform. As the former head of the product development team reported, "When the problems hit the fan, my credibility was shot and I was dead in the company."

Confidence and competence are closely tied together. An individual has a "confidence tank" whose level rises or falls, depending on his perception of his status in the company.

Credibility, commitment, confidence, and competence are interdependent, in this sense.

"The more credibility I have, the more confident I can be."

"The more confident I am, the more confident I appear."

"The more confident I appear, the more I am seen as credible and competent."

Conversely,

"If I lose credibility, I may lose confidence,"

"If I lose confidence, I appear to be incompetent and I lose more credibility."

As a result, the company is full of very confident-seeming people. It is seen as necessary to appear to be confident, no matter what the problems are, in order to maintain credibility. Indeed, old-hands in technology management advise younger ones along the following lines:

"Tell management enough of what you're doing to capture commitment, but not enough to make them uneasy. Commit yourself to do the things that are necessary, even if you're not sure you can do them. And do the work you see to be necessary, even if your boss says no."

Thus heroism and secrecy (mastery and mystery) are essential elements of the strategy for winning the product development game.

The game yields a double bind, even for winners. It puts the players into a situation in which they lose, eventually, whatever the consequences. A participant says to himself,

"I must commit to what I'm not sure I can do, in order to secure corporate commitment. To this end, I lay my credibility on the line, without which I cannot function. So I must be heroic and secretive. If I fail, I lose big. But unless I play, I cannot win."

But old-time managers say,

"If you're up, you can stay up, and it's a winnable game, because there's plenty of resource and time and room for the redefinition of targets, if you have the competence and the confidence. But you must keep it up."

So product-development is a high-wire act in which you eventually fall. Moreover, you don't whine or complain, because you would be seen to lack confidence. The effect is to put product development directors, those who occupy the pivotal position between general managers and the laboratory, under a great deal of strain. They strive to protect their own credibility, keeping problems "under a tent," with the result that in midstream, problems tend to be ignored. In order to retain corporate commitment, the product is changed as little as possible. Once a problem has been exposed, however, they "climb all over it." And they strive to retain ownership of the task, which makes them treat offers of help as though they were threats to security.

In the light of this product development game, most of the questions with which the case study began can be given plausible answers. It is clear why problems encountered in midstream tend to be ignored until they are unavoidable, and it is also clear why, upon unavoidable exposure, they are "oversolved." It is clear how the corporation bails itself out of its crises, through stopgap "patching" solutions which resolve the crisis at hand without affecting the underlying processes that produce crises. It is also clear how product development directors are placed under extraordinary stress, which might well cause them to "burn out."

Considered more broadly as an organizational learning system, the product development game determines the directions and the limits of reflection-in-action. When crises present themselves, managers subject them to inquiry—often with successful results—but they do not reflect publicly on the processes which lead to such crises, for this would surface the games of deception by which product development deals with general management. While these games are "open secrets" within the organization, they are not publicly discussable.

Managers reflect on the strategies by which product development can be made into a "winnable game". But neither general managers nor product development directors reflect on the Model I theories-in-use which create the conditions for the game. All participants try to achieve their objectives as they see them: general managers, to keep the burden of uncertainty on the shoulders of product development; product development directors, to retain corporate commitment while maintaining their own credibility. Each participant tries to protect himself unilaterally from being tagged with failure and from the resulting loss of credibility. Each seeks to gain unilateral control over the situation, to win and avoid losing in a situation he perceives as irretrievably win/lose. And each one withholds negative information from the other, as long as he believes it is a winning strategy to do so. Participants may be aware of these strategies, particularly as they are evinced by other players in the game, but they do not subject them to public reflection-in-action. To do so would be to make oneself vulnerable in an intensely win/lose world and, in the context of the product development game, might look like a failure of confidence.

This is not to say, however, that members of the organization are not able to recognize the game when it is described for them. When the results of the study of Product X were presented to those who had been involved in the story, there was a generally favorable reaction. Although most participants had never put the whole picture together for themselves, they recognized its validity. Some were highly amused. They seemed to feel that the study elaborated the open secret with which they were all familiar. But with very few exceptions, they did not believe that the system was susceptible to change. The risks seemed too great, the stakes too high, and the chances of success too low.

The Art of Managing and Its Limits

Returning now to the questions with which we began this chapter, let us consider the lessons that may be drawn from the several examples of managerial practice which have occupied our attention.

It is clear that managers do sometimes reflect-in-action. Beginning with questions like, What do consumers really see in our product? What's really going on underneath the signs of trouble in our organization? or What can we learn from our encounters with the competition? managers sometimes try to make sense of the unique phenomena before them. They surface and question their intuitive understandings; and in order to test their new interpretations, they undertake on-the-spot experiments. Not infrequently, their experiments yield surprising results that cause them to reformulate their questions. They engage in reflective conversations with their situation.

The reflection-in-action of managers is distinctive, in that they operate in an organizational context and deal with organizational phenomena. They draw on repertoires of cumulatively developed organizational knowledge, which they transform in the context of some unique situation. And as they function as agents of organizational learning, they contribute to the store of organizational knowledge. G's inquiry into production delays becomes a corporate exemplar for diagnosis of the troubles of the internal environment. In the consumer products firm, managers build up a corporate repertoire of cases, maxims, and methods which becomes accessible to new generations of managers.

But managers function as agents of organizational learning within an organizational learning system, within a system of games and norms which both guide and limit the directions of organizational inquiry. The case of Product X reveals a learning system that creates a pattern of corporate crises and at the same time prohibits public reflection-in-action on their causes.

As a consequence, the organizational learning system becomes immune to reflection-in-action. It is not publicly discussable; and because managers do not discuss it, they are often unable to describe it—although they may recognize the descriptions constructed by an outsider to the organization. Public discussion of the product development game would reveal the strategies by which general managers distance themselves from the uncertainties inherent in product development and the complementary strategies by which technical personnel protect themselves against the loss of corporate commitment. To reveal these strategies publicly, in an actual present instance where some action might be taken, would violate the norms of the product development game and would carry a perceived risk of vulnerability and loss of control.

Thus organizational learning systems, of the sort revealed by the case of Product X, become diseases that prevent their own cure. Managers could not extend the scope of reflection-in-action to their own learning systems without transforming the theories of action which they bring to their lives within the organization. And these, under the normal conditions of corporate life, are also immune to reflection-in-action.

We might begin to heal the split in the field of management if we were to recognize that the art of management includes something like science in action. When practicing managers display artistry, they reveal their capacity to construct models of unique and changing situations, to design and execute on-the-spot experiments. They also reveal a capacity to reflect on the meanings of situations and the goals of action. A more comprehensive, useful, and reflective management science could be built by extending and elaborating on what skillful managers actually do. Practitioners might then become not only the users but the developers of management science.

But extending and elaborating on artistry means reflecting on artistry and its limits, that is, on the ways in which managers do reflect-in-action and on the theories-in-use and organizational learning systems that constrain them.

Patterns and Limits of Reflection-in-Action Across the Professions

Having considered a sample of professional fields and having studied episodes of reflection-in-action in each of them, we are now in a position to return to two of the questions with which we began this study:

1. What are the patterns of similarity and difference in reflection-in-action across professional fields?
2. What have we learned about the limits to reflection-in-action?

Constancy and Variation

I have tried in Part II to show how practitioners in very different sorts of professions reveal an underlying similarity in the art of their practice, and especially in the artful inquiry by which they sometimes deal with situations of uncertainty, instability, and uniqueness. This is the pattern of reflection-in-action which I have called "reflective conversation with the situation." In chapter 5, I showed how architectural designing and psychotherapy can both be seen as variations on this underlying process, and in the subsequent chapters on the science-based professions, planning, and management, I have described what I take to be versions of the same process.

In all of these examples, inquiry begins with an effort to solve a problem as initially set. In some cases, the initial problem is framed as a problem of making something (a semiconductor amplifier, a higher-absorbency paper product); in some cases, it is framed as a problem of understanding something (why a traditional industrial process works, the sources of malnourishment). However the problem is initially set, in the later stages of inquiry both making and understanding interests come into play.

The inquirer remains open to the discovery of phenomena, incongruent with the initial problem setting, on the basis of which he reframes the problem. Thus, the discovery of a new metal-coloring process, which also works, leads to a new question, "How to account for the effectiveness of both the traditional and the new processes?" As the Bell Laboratory scientists tested Bardeen's theory of surface-state "electron traps," they observed an unexpected amplifying effect which they saw as requiring a new explanation. Having constructed his initial nutrient flow model, and having discovered the problems of implementing it, Wilson was led to ask how community members themselves could be helped to treat reduction of malnourishment as an experimental task. Product development researchers, seeking higher-absorbency paper products, discovered phenomena which led them to recast the development target from high "absorption capacity" to "high rate of absorption."

Thus, in all of these examples, inquiry, however it may initially have been conceived, turns into a frame experiment. What allows this to happen is that the inquirer is willing to step into the problematic situation, to impose a frame on it, to follow the implications of the discipline thus established, and yet to remain open to the situation's back-talk. Reflecting on the surprising consequences of his efforts to shape the situation in conformity with his initially chosen frame, the inquirer frames new questions and new ends in view.

In this shared pattern of inquiry there are two critically important processes, which I have also noted in my comparison of Quist's designing and the Supervisor's psychotherapeutic interpreting. Faced with some phenomenon that he finds unique, the inquirer nevertheless draws on some element of his familiar repertoire which he treats as exemplar or as generative metaphor for the new phenomenon. So Wilson thought of the malnourishment process in terms of nutrient flow, and the product researchers saw the synthetic-bristle paintbrush as a pump. Further, as the inquirer reflects on the similarities he has perceived, he formulates new hypotheses. But he tests these hypotheses by experimental actions which also function as moves for shaping the situation and as probes for exploring it. In the later examples, as in Quist's designing, the reflective conversation includes and depends upon this threefold transactional experimenting.

I have so far stressed similarities of pattern in the various arts of reflective professional practice, but there are also important differences. These go beyond the familiar distinctions between "hard" and "soft" professions, "helping professions" and "mechanical arts," "learned professions" and "professionalizing occupations." I have in mind differences in the *constants* that various practitioners bring to their reflection-in-action:

- the media, languages, and repertoires that practitioners use to describe reality and conduct experiments
- the appreciative systems they bring to problem setting, to the evaluation of inquiry, and to reflective conversation
- the overarching theories by which they make sense of phenomena
- the role frames within which they set their tasks and through which they bound their institutional settings.

In calling these things constants, I do not mean to suggest that they are absolutely unchanging. They do change, sometimes in response to reflection, but at a slower rate than theories of particular phenomena or frames for particular problematic situations. Hence they give the practitioner the relatively solid references from which, in reflection-in-action, he can allow his theories and frames to come apart. Indeed, depending on the robustness of these constants, practitioners are more or less able to recognize and engage that which is shifting and turbulent in their practice. And depending on differences in these constants, taken individually and as whole patterns, we can account for significant differences in reflection-in-action within and across the professions.

Although it would be beyond the scope of this book to pursue this line of inquiry very far, I would like in a few paragraphs to suggest how it might be pursued.

What does it matter that the medium of reflection-in-action is the architect's sketchpad, the relation between patient and therapist, the drawings and experimental models of an engineering laboratory, the dialogue of planner and developer, or the interactive relations among managers in a corporation? Media cannot really be separated in their influence from language and repertoire. Together they make up the "stuff" of inquiry, in terms of which practitioners move, experiment, and explore. Skills in the manipulation of media, languages, and repertoires are essential to a practitioner's reflective conversation with his situation, just as skill in the manipulation of spoken language in essential to ordinary conversation.

Quist's designing depends on his feel for the sketchpad and the scale model, and for the drawing/talking language in which he works. Similarly, the engineers' experimental designing depends on their feel for the behavior of metals under varying conditions of temperature, exposure to air, or immersion in water. For Wilson, the Supervisor, the town planner, the managers, media are kinds of social fields. Because they have developed a feel for the media and languages of their practices, the individuals we have studied can construct virtual worlds in which to carry out imaginative rehearsals of action. Because of the importance of this feel for media and language, an experienced practitioner cannot convey the art of his practice to a novice merely by describing his procedures, rules, and theories, nor can he enable a novice to think like a seasoned practitioner merely by describing or even demonstrating his ways of thinking. Because of the differences in feel for media, language, and repertoire, the art of one practice tends to be opaque to the practitioners of another, obscuring such underlying similarities as I have outlined above.

We know very little about the ways in which individuals develop the feel for media, language, and repertoire which shapes their reflection-in-action. This is an intriguing and promising topic for future research.

Constancy of appreciative system is an essential condition for reflection-in-action. It is what makes possible the initial framing of the problematic situation, and it is also what permits the inquirer to reappreciate the situation in the light of its back-talk. Thus Quist's valuing of coherent design, nooks and soft back areas, artifices, and the softening of hard-edged forms makes it possible for him both to give his initial framing of the problem of the design of the school and to reframe that problem in the light of his discovery of the meaning of the gallery. And Wilson's valuing of experimental modelling, trying things out, finding things out for oneself, seeing connections between apparently disparate phenomena, showing up the defects of an orthodox view, underlies both his initial framing of the malnourishment problem in terms of the nutrient flow model and his later reframing of it in terms of community-based Cogwheel Experiments. If, in the midst of such inquiries as these, there were a sudden shift of appreciative system, inquiry would no longer have the character of a reflective conversation. It would become a series of disconnected episodes.

It is also because of the constancy of his appreciative system that an inquirer engaged in on-the-spot experiment can tell when he is finished. He bounds his experimenting by his appreciation of the changes he has wrought.

Overlap in appreciative system has much to do with the shape of professional communities of inquiry, and differences of appreciative system have much to do with differences in reflection-in-action both across professions and within them. Partly because of such differences, architects from different schools will approach the same site and program in very different ways and produce dissimilar products, even though their design processes may conform in broad outline to my description of Quist's designing. Similarly, different planners, managers, or systems engineers may enter what would seem to an outsider to be the same situation and carry out very different inquiries, leading to different kinds of results, even though they are all engaged in reflective conversation with the situation. This variability, partly rooted in difference of appreciative system, leads to a special version of the problem of objectivity. Within a process of inquiry, evaluations of methods and products may be objective in the sense that they are independent of mere opinion. Across processes of inquiry, differences in evaluation may not be objectively resolvable. Resolution of such differences depends on the little-understood ability of inquirers to enter into one another's appreciative systems and to make reciprocal translations from one to the other.[1]

Quist has access to special theories of building structures, soil conditions, and the circulation of people through spaces. The engineers working on the gun-coloring problem have access to theories of the surface properties of metals. Both Quist and the engineers can *apply* their special theories to particular instances so as to derive a rule for the prediction or control of the phenomena at hand. Quist can use his structural theories, for example, to figure out the minimum dimensions of a beam that must carry a given load. But neither Quist nor the engineers appear to have access to what I have called overarching theories. An overarching theory does not give a rule that can be applied to predict or control a particular event, but it supplies language from which to construct particular descriptions and themes from which to develop particular interpretations. Psychoanalytic theory functions in this way for the Supervisor, and process-flow modelling does so for Wilson. In both cases, the practitioner does not consider that he has formed a satisfactory account of phenomena in any practice situation *until* he has framed it in terms of his overarching theory.

If a practitioner has such a theory, he uses it to guide his reflection-in-action. The nature of the reflective conversation varies, from profession to profession and from practitioner to practitioner, depending on the presence or absence, and on the content, of overarching theory.

In the several cases we have examined, we have observed how practitioners frame their roles. In one case, the town planner's, we have traced the consequences of role-frame for the system of knowing-in-practice. Because role-frame remains relatively constant from situation to situation, it bounds the scope of practice and provides a reference which allows a practitioner to build a cumulative repertoire of exemplars, facts, and descriptions.

Differences in role frame help to determine what knowledge is seen as useful in practice and what kinds of reflection are undertaken in action. Consider, to take a particularly important example, how practitioners treat their institutional contexts. All professional roles are embedded in an institutional context, but not all practitioners take it seriously. A mechanical engineer may see himself as a technical problem solver, treating his relations with his clients as an unavoidable but essentially nonprofessional activity. Or, like Wilson, he may frame his tasks in such a way that a larger social context moves to the foreground and technical problem solving becomes a piece of the larger social puzzle. If institutional context occupies a central place in a practitioner's role frame, then he pays attention to phenomena for which there is no satisfactory off-the-shelf theory. He must construct a theory of his own. And if he treats his theory of the context as an object of reflection (as the town planner does only to a slight extent), then he will perceive that others in the situation meet his frames and theories with frames and theories of their own. He will see them not only as objects to be planned for but as planners in their own right, and his interaction with them will take the form of a reflective conversation.

In these ways, among others, differences in the constants brought to inquiry affect the scope and direction of reflection-in-action. But the constants—media, language, repertoire, appreciative system, overarching theory, and role frame—are also subject to change. They tend to change over periods of time longer than a single episode of practice, although particular events may trigger their change. And they are sometimes changed through the practitioner's reflection on the events of his practice. The study of these sorts of reflection, crucial both to professional development and to the epistemology of practice, would require a more sustained longitudinal analysis than any I have attempted in the chapters of this book.

The Limits of Reflection-in-Action

What is it that constrains our ability to reflect-in-action? To what extent are such constraints inherent in the human situation or in the epistemology of practice, and to what extent can we learn to transcend them?

Our examples suggest that practitioners do frequently think about what they are doing while doing it. In professional practice, reflection-in-action is not a rare event. On the other hand, we have also seen how systems of knowing-in-practice may limit the scope and depth of reflection.

The first finding disconfirms the rather widespread belief that thinking must interfere with doing. The second draws attention to the self-limiting character of knowing-in-practice, both in individuals and organizations, and suggests the directions in which such limits might be extended.

According to conventional wisdom, thinking interferes with doing in two ways. First, artistry being indescribable, reflection *on* action is doomed to failure; and second, reflection-*in*-action paralyzes action. Both arguments are largely, though not entirely, mistaken. They owe their plausibility to the persistence of misleading views about the relation of thought to action.

As to the first argument, I have already noted that "artistry" has two meanings. It may designate intuitive knowing, like the intuitive judgments of a skilled craftsman or the intuitive theories-in-action of an expert block balancer. It may also designate reflection-in-action on intuitive knowing, as in Quist's designing or the Supervisor's interpreting. In both of these senses, artistry is describable. When practitioners reflect-in-action, they describe their own intuitive understandings. And it is possible to describe reflection-in-action itself, as I have done in the previous chapters.

It is true, nevertheless, that there is always a gap between such descriptions and the reality to which they refer. When a practitioner displays artistry, his intuitive knowing is always richer in information than any description of it. Further, the internal strategy of representation, embodied in the practitioner's *feel for* artistic performance, is frequently incongruent with the strategies used to construct external descriptions of it. Because of this incongruity, for example, people who do things well often give what appear to be good descriptions of their procedures which others cannot follow. Everyone who has tried to learn from a book how to ski or write a story knows how difficult it can be to act from such a description.

But the gap between artistry and its description need not obstruct reflection-in-action. In such examples as Quist's reflection on Petra's framing of the problem of the site or the block balancer's reflection on his geometric center theory of balancing, the description of intuitive knowing feeds reflection, enabling the inquirer to criticize, test, and restructure his understandings. Incompleteness of description is no impediment to reflection. On the contrary, anything like a complete description of intuitive knowing would produce an excess of information. Nor is it a fatal impediment that reflection-in-action converts one's intuitive feel for performance to knowledge-in-practice which involves a different strategy of representation. Reflection-in-action does not depend on a description of intuitive knowing that is complete or faithful to internal representation. Although some descriptions are more appropriate to reflection-in-action than others, descriptions that are not very good may be good enough to enable an inquirer to criticize and restructure his intuitive understandings so as to produce new actions that improve the situation or trigger a reframing of the problem.

Even if reflection-in-action is feasible, however, it may seem dangerous. The baseball pitcher who claims never to think about his pitching in the midst of a game, and the famous story of the centipede paralyzed by the attempt to explain how he moves, suggest that reflection interferes with action. It may seem to do so for four different reasons:

1. There is no time to reflect when we are on the firing line; if we stop to think, we may be dead.
2. When we think about what we are doing, we surface complexity, which interferes with the smooth flow of action. The complexity that we can manage unconsciously paralyzes us when we bring it to consciousness.
3. If we begin to reflect-in-action, we may trigger an infinite regress of reflection on action, then on our reflection on action, and so on ad infinitum.

4. The stance appropriate to reflection is incompatible with the stance appropriate to action. As Hannah Arendt has said,

> Every reflection that does not serve knowledge and is not guided by practical needs and aims is . . . "out of order" . . . it interrupts any doing, any ordinary activities, no matter what they happen to be. All thinking demands a *stop-and-think* . . . it is, indeed, as though thinking paralyzed me in much the same way as an excess of consciousness may paralyze the automatism of my bodily function.[2]

So understood, reflection-in-action is a contradiction in terms.

These arguments admit the possibility of reflecting *on* action (even the pitcher who never "thinks" during the game is happy to review films of the game in the privacy and safety of the locker-room), but they point to the dangers of reflection *in* action. They contain grains of truth, but they depend on a mistaken view of the relationship between thought and action. Fused together in the conventional wisdom, they have become a myth that reinforces the ever-present tendency to mystify the art of practice.

There are indeed times when it is dangerous to stop and think. On the firing line, in the midst of traffic, even on the playing field, there is a need for immediate, on-line response, and the failure to deliver it can have serious consequences. But not all practice situations are of this sort. The action-present (the period of time in which we remain in the "same situation") varies greatly from case to case, and in many cases there is time to think what we are doing. Consider, for example, a physician's management of a patient's disease, a lawyer's preparation of a brief, a teacher's handling of a difficult student. In processes such as these, which may extend over weeks, months, or years, fast-moving episodes are punctuated by intervals which provide opportunity for reflection.

Even when the action-present is brief, performers can sometimes train themselves to think about their actions. In the split-second exchanges of a game of tennis, a skilled player learns to give himself a moment to plan the next shot. His game is the better for this momentary hesitation, so long as he gauges the time available for reflection correctly and integrates his reflection into the smooth flow of action. And we have observed how practitioners like architects, musicians, and therapists construct virtual worlds in which the pace of action can be slowed down and iterations and variations of actions can be tried. Indeed, our conception of the art of practice ought to give a central place to the ways in which practitioners learn to create opportunities for reflection-in-action.

The argument from the inherent complexity of intuitive knowing raises again the question of what constitutes a good description of action. Speaking of the centipede's paralysis, Seymour Papert once observed that the difficulty is not in the inherent complexity of the material brought to consciousness but in our ways of representing complexity. Certain descriptions are more useful for action than are others. The centipede might have given a nonparalyzing answer to the question, "How do you do it?" by saying simply, "I move forward in a wavy motion." A good coach learns to capture the complexity of action in metaphor ("Lean into the slope!") that helps to convey the feel for the performance.

On the other hand, some very useful prescriptions for action do temporarily interfere with performance. Someone learning to play tennis or golf or a musical instrument may be asked to change his grip (or his embouchure) with the expectation that he will lose spontaneity for a time before recapturing it at a higher level of quality. Here we are not surprised to find that reflection does temporarily inhibit action. Whether or not we are prepared to pay this price depends on our ability to find a context in which we can practice at low risk, or on our judgment of the value of incurring a temporary loss of spontaneity. In any case, we are most likely to initiate reflection-in-action when we are stuck or seriously dissatisfied with our performance. Our question then is not so much *whether* to reflect as *what kind* of reflection is most likely to help us get unstuck.

The fear that reflection-in-action will trigger an infinite regress of reflection derives from an unexamined dichotomy of thought and action. If we separate thinking from doing, seeing thought only as a preparation for action and action only as an implementation of thought, then it is easy to believe that when we step into the separate domain of thought we will become lost in an infinite regress of thinking about thinking. But in actual reflection-in-action, as we have seen, doing and thinking are complementary. Doing extends thinking in the tests, moves, and probes of experimental action, and reflection feeds on doing and its results. Each feeds the other, and each sets boundaries for the other. It is the surprising result of action that triggers reflection, and it is the production of a satisfactory move that brings reflection temporarily to a close. It is true, certainly, that an inquirer's continuing conversation with his situation may lead, open-endedly, to renewal of reflection. When a practitioner keeps inquiry moving, however, he does not abstain from action in order to sink into endless thought. Continuity of inquiry entails a continual interweaving of thinking and doing.

Finally, Hannah Arendt's observation that reflection is "out of order" in action may seem valid or invalid depending on the kind of reflection one has in mind. It is not hard to imagine reflection "not guided by practical needs and aims" which might distract an actor or cause him to cease acting altogether. This may appear a good or bad thing, depending on one's view of the action in question. Some advisors to President Johnson during the Vietnam War years have recorded the feeling that in the councils of war their skeptical reflections always seemed impractical and out of order.[3] In such a case, the interruption of action by reflection might seem heroic. In other, less dramatic instances, reflection incongruent with a present course of action may be maintained through double vision. Double vision does not require us to stop and think, but the capacity to keep alive, in the midst of action, a multiplicity of views of the situation. It does not interfere with action but contributes to the inquirer's readiness for the mode of action I have called reflective conversation with the situation.

There is nothing in reflection, then, which leads necessarily to paralysis of action. The fear of paralysis may spring from worst-case analysis which ignores the opportunities for reflection within the action-present, from neglect of our ability to construct virtual worlds in which the pace of action can be slowed down, from ignorance of double vision, from inability to imagine descriptions useful for action, or from an inappropriate dichotomy of thinking and doing.

In actual practice, practitioners do, without paralysis, reflect-in-action. The fear of a paralysis induced by reflection, like the belief in the indescribability of artistry, comes not from the experience of practice but from a lingering model of practical rationality which is much in need of reflection.

Quite different from the mythical limits to reflection, celebrated in the conventional wisdom, are the self-reinforcing systems of knowing-in-practice that we have encountered in some of our case studies of professional practice.

The town planner in our example reflects on his strategies of problem solving but not on his problem settings or on the role frame and theory of action from which they derive. The consumer product managers reflect on their organizational crises but not on the organizational learning system that fosters crises. Their reflections operate *within* their systems of understanding. The town planner, who takes his balancing act as a given, reflects only on the techniques best suited to its performance. The product development managers, who treat their learning system as unchangeable, think only about the best ways of patching it. Similarly, in the dialogues of Quist and Petra and the Supervisor and the Resident, there is a great deal of artistry (which involves reflection-in-action) but very little second-order reflection either on artistry or on the interaction between teacher and student.

It seems to me that the processes which maintain the constancy of individual and organizational systems of knowing-in-practice are also the ones that keep the art of practice mysterious. When a practitioner does not reflect on his own inquiry, he keeps his intuitive understandings tacit *and* is inattentive to the limits of his scope of reflective attention. The remedy to the mystification of practice and to the constriction of reflection-in-action is the same: a redirection of attention to the system of knowing-in-practice and to reflection-in-action itself. Quist and the Supervisor should be thinking about the art that they demonstrate for their students, and about the interactions in which they demonstrate it. The town planner should be thinking about his limited reflection-in-action, and about the balancing act within which he frames his practice. The managers of the consumer products firm should be reflecting on their patching exercises and on the organizational learning system that requires patching.

But this is circular. What keeps the planner, for example, from reflecting on his balancing act is his self-reinforcing system of knowing-in-practice. The system makes itself immune to reflection, thereby protecting the planner from the uncertainty (and perhaps also from the paralysis) he would experience if he were to allow his system to come apart. A practitioner might break into a circle of self-limiting reflection by attending to his role frame, his interpersonal theory-in-use, or the organizational learning system in which he functions. Whatever his starting point, however, he is unlikely to get very far unless he wants to extend and deepen his reflection-in-action, and unless others help him see what he has worked to avoid seeing.

The pursuit of these questions, critical to a theory of education for reflection-in-action, would take us well beyond the scope of this book.

Part III

CONCLUSION

10

Implications for the Professions and Their Place in Society

Introduction

In parts I and II of this book, I have advocated an epistemology of practice based on the idea of reflection-in-action. I shall now explore several of its implications—for the professional's role in society, his autonomy and authority in relation to his clients, the kinds of research likely to be useful to him, the institutional contexts conducive to reflective practice, and the visions of social progress and well-being which may be used to justify professional activity. In considering these questions, I shall contrast reflective practice with the model of technical rationality and with a more recent tradition of radical criticism of the professions. The concept of professional as technical expert is closely bound to the utopian imagery of the Technological Program, and the radical demystification of the professions is also linked to a utopian vision, one of liberation from the domination of established interests and professional elite. Although the social implications of the idea of reflective practice do not lie midway between these utopian extremes, they may be illuminated by the threefold comparison.

Within the dominant tradition which has grown up over the past four hundred years, the professional's claim to extraordinary knowledge is rooted in techniques and theories derived from scientific research undertaken for the most part in institutions of higher learning. The status of professional experts, their claims to social mandate, autonomy, and license, are based on the powerful ideas of Technical Rationality and the technological program. There is no more vivid sign of the persistence of these ideas than the hunger for technique which is so characteristic of students of the professions in this decade.

Within the tradition of radical criticism, the attack on professionals as elite instruments of the establishment is combined with a critique of Technical Rationality. Both the Technological Program and the professional's claim to extraordinary knowledge are treated as mystiques. In a critical literature most dramatically, though perhaps not most rigorously, represented by Ivan Illich,[1] the mystique of technical expertise is seen as an instrument of social control of the have-nots—the poor, the dispossessed, ethnic and racial minorities, women—by a social elite. The mandate, autonomy, and license of the technical expert work toward a distribution of social benefits which is profoundly unjust, and they tend toward the creation of a technocratic society in which most human beings do not want to live. Professional expertise, when it is exposed to careful scrutiny, dissolves into empty claims. The professions are vehicles for the preemption of socially legitimate knowledge in the interest of social control.

These arguments are used to justify the thoroughgoing demystification of the professions and to buttress either of two remedial strategies: development of a new breed of professional advocates who will work in the interests of the powerless client-victims of the professions, educating them to their rights and organizing them to defend their rights; or creation of a new breed of citizen-practitioners—citizen-planners, citizen-builders, citizen-physicians—who will be equipped to take over the territories of the professional experts.[2]

Paradoxically, it is not uncommon to discover that the very same students of the professions who hunger for the "hard" technical skills which they believe will assure them of jobs in established institutions also espouse the radical vision of demystification.

But demystification of professional knowledge may have two quite different meanings. It may consist in treating professional knowledge as the emperor's new clothes; or it may mean that professionals do know something worth knowing, a limited something that is inherently describable and, at least in some measure, understandable by others. In this second sense, mystification consists in making knowledge-in-practice appear to be more complex, private, ineffable, and above all more once-and-for-all, more closed to inquiry, than it needs to be. In this sense, both professional and counter-professional may be mystifiers. And in this sense, demystification is not a showing up of the falsity of the practitioner's claims to knowledge but a bid to undertake the often arduous task of opening it up to inquiry.

Those who would demystify professional knowledge, in the sense of showing it up, would explode the professional's claim to extraordinary knowledge, including its basis in scientific research, and would deny his claims to mandate for social control, autonomy in practice, and license to keep the gates of the professions. But I shall argue that radical critique cannot substitute for (though it may provoke) the qualified professional's critical self-reflection. Unreflective practitioners are equally limited and destructive whether they label themselves as professionals or counterprofessionals.

The Professional-Client Relationship

In the social context of professional practice which is accepted as routine in our society, the professional is a provider of services. The names given to the recipients of service vary with the profession. Thus lawyers, accountants, architects, and consulting engineers have "clients"; physicians, dentists, and therapists have "patients"; teachers have "students" or "advisees"; the recipients of the social worker's services may be called "clients," "cases," or "counselees." Although these different names often connote important shades of difference in relationship, it is customary to use "client" as the generic term.

The professional-client relationship is essential to what is meant in our society by a profession. This fact is supported, rather than denied, by the existence of professions in which it is difficult to identify those who stand in the client's role. In cases where the professional's role has more to do with social control than with help, or where the relationship between help and control is a matter of ambiguity and debate, then it seems paradoxical to call the objects of professional attention "clients." This is true of policemen, and may also be true of teachers, managers, or social workers. In cases where the professional works within a bureaucracy, as more and more professionals— managers, engineers, architects, planners, even physicians and lawyers—are coming to do, then it is also paradoxical to speak of the professional's superiors, subordinates, or peers as clients. Here, however, the paradox has to do with the use of "client" to refer to individuals who occupy roles of formal authority, subordination, or exchange in a specialized task system. In cases where the professional—a town planner, superintendent of schools, or public official—occupies a position which requires him to interact with many different groups, then we are apt to speak of "constituents" or "stakeholders" rather than clients.

But in all of these cases where it is paradoxical, ambiguous, or simply inappropriate to speak of "clients," the matter is a source of trouble to the members of the profession. The absence of a clearly identifiable professional-client relation has the effect of undermining the service provider's view of himself as a professional. Policemen, who are apt to have strongly protective feelings about their professional status, frequently present themselves in terms of the helping, social service dimensions of their roles, in the light of which they can more readily identify the citizens who receive their services as their clients.[3] Engineers, architects, managers, and other bureaucratized professionals are given to public debate, in the forums of their professional societies, over the threat posed by bureaucratization to the maintenance of their status as professionals.[4] And for planners, school principals, and organizational consultants, it is often a matter of urgency to determine, "Who is the client?" The meaning of this question is, I think, "to whom should we define ourselves as standing in the essential professional relationship?" for professionals must be able to offer the benefits of their extraordinary knowledge to other individuals in relation to whom they can exercise authority and enjoy the autonomy to which they lay claim.[5] These observations suggest what must be some of the features essential to the traditional professional-client relationship, and they also suggest how that relationship may change with changes in our understanding of professional knowledge.

The traditional professional-client relationship, linked to the traditional epistemology of practice, can be described as a contract, a set of shared norms governing the behavior of each party to the interaction. These norms, some of which have a formal basis in the legal system and others a basis in informal understandings, enable professional and client to know what they can expect from one another.

In the traditional professional-client contract, the professional acts as though he agreed to deliver his services to the client to the limits of his special competence, to respect the confidences granted him, and not to misuse for his own benefit the special powers given him within the boundaries of the relationship. The client acts as though he agreed, in turn, to accept the professional's authority in his special field, to submit to the professional's ministrations, and to pay for services rendered. In a familiar psychological extension of the informal contract, the client agrees to show deference to the professional. He agrees not to challenge the professional's judgment or to demand explanations beyond the professional's willingness to give them. In short, he agrees to behave as though he respected the professional's autonomy as an expert.

Within the bare outlines of such a contract, there are large zones of discretionary freedom for both parties. The client may show more or less deference, more or less compliance with the professional's advice, may present a greater or lesser challenge to the professional's opinions. In turn, the professional may show more or less sympathy with the client's problems, evince more or less effort at understanding his situation, reveal more or less of the special knowledge available to him, all of which may depend on the professional's perception of the client's status, his ability to pay, or on prior relations of friendship or obligation.

Under the traditional contract, the professional's accountability for his performance is mainly to his professional peers. He is, of course, directly accountable to his client; but often the client has limited ability to determine whether or not legitimate expectations have been met. The professional's accountability within the legal system arises only on the occasion of claims of an egregious violation of contract, as in a medical malpractice suit. Within the broader range of accountability, short of a possible violation of the law, it is the professional's peers who are best equipped to determine whether he has performed satisfactorily within his contract. But the professional-client relationship is usually characterized by privacy and there are often no routinely available means for a professional's peers to get access to his performance. The failure of institutional mechanisms of accountability have contributed a great deal to the current disenchantment with the professions, for example, in the nursing home scandals, the well-publicized abuses of Medicare, and the behavior of some lawyers in the Watergate affair. It is true that in these highly public scandals, outrage at the violation of professional norms is triggered by their exposure, which suggests that some mechanism of accountability is working. There is, nevertheless, a widespread worry that the relatively rare instances of public exposure signal a far wider pattern of violation of the professional contract, which existing mechanisms of accountability are insufficient to reveal or correct.

The prototypical examples of the contract which I have called traditional are the physician's relation to his patients and the lawyer's to his clients. These are the cases in which the status, authority, and autonomy of the professional are most secure. In Glazer's minor professions—the ministry, teaching, social work, for example—the traditional professional-client contract may be deficient in one or more of the features described above. Even in these cases, however, the professional often takes the physician's or lawyer's relation to his client as a norm and tries to emulate it.

The radical criticism of the professions carries significant implications for the professional-client contract. Because the radical critic denies the legitimacy of the professional's authority and of the client's submission to it, he rejects a fundamental element of the traditional contract. He would place client and professional in an essentially adversarial relationship. Insistence on the rights of patient, prisoner, or welfare recipient is a way of establishing the client's adversarial equality to the professional, empowering him to resist the professional's efforts to control him. The movement to create "citizen professionals," on the other hand, is an effort to replace the professional-client contract by a new contract in which exchanges of service and remuneration would occur between laymen.

But these remedies carry defects of their own. When advocates organize clients to defend their rights against excessive professional control, the organized advocacy and the adversarial process may become as controlling and as unreflective as traditional professional practice at its worst. Poverty lawyers who construe the housing problem as one of "getting the landlords off the tenants' backs" may provide a legitimate defense against exploitation of the powerless, but they may also generate a militant orthodoxy which ignores the deeper causes of the housing problem and may even worsen tenants' lot over the long run, causing landlords to abandon properties and reduce the stock of available housing. Citizen healthworkers, planners, or builders may serve as a useful corrective to the excesses of doctrinaire or peremptory professionals; but they may also make a virtue of ignorance, paying insufficient attention to the legitimate parts of the professional's claims to extraordinary knowledge, misleading their clients. The defects of such measures seem to hinge on one or another of two issues. First, there is the difficulty of combining an adversarial stance toward the professional with a wish to benefit from his special knowledge. And second, there is the sense in which a professional advocate or citizen-professional still takes a professional stance, claiming special knowledge and autonomy which he may abuse in his relations with his clients.

What, then, does the idea of reflective practice imply for the nature of the professional-client contract?

It is important to note, first of all, that reflective practice does not free us from the need to worry about client rights and mechanisms of professional accountability. My concern is to show how the professional-client contract may be transformed, within a framework of accountability, when the professional is able to function as a reflective practitioner.

Just as reflective practice takes the form of a reflective conversation with the situation, so the reflective practitioner's relation with his client takes the form of a literally reflective conversation. Here the professional recognizes that his technical expertise is embedded in a context of meanings. He attributes to his clients, as well as to himself, a capacity to mean, know, and plan. He recognizes that his actions may have different meanings for his client than he intends them to have, and he gives himself the task of discovering what these are. He recognizes an obligation to make his own understandings accessible to his client, which means that he needs often to reflect anew on what he knows. If he is a physician, to take one example, he may urge his patient to stop smoking, but he may also be alert to discover whether, in *this* patient's life, smoking is a way of handling a level of stress that might have other serious consequences if it were given up. If he has a patient with leukemia who never mentions her disease by name, he may explore the meaning of her failure to utter the dread word; and if he discovers that she has been unable to accept the reality of her disease, he may work with her to say the word, and then to understand the varieties of leukemia and the place of her own version of it in the overall pattern of the disease. In this sort of example, and in the examples of reflective teaching, managing, and therapy which I have given earlier, there is the recognition that one's expertise is a way of looking at something which was once constructed and may be reconstructed; and there is both readiness and competence to explore its meaning in the experience of the client. The reflective practitioner tries to discover the limits of his expertise through reflective conversation with the client.

Although the reflective practitioner should be credentialled and technically competent, his claim to authority is substantially based on his ability to manifest his special knowledge in his interactions with his clients. He does not ask the client to have blind faith in a "black box," but to remain open to the evidence of the practitioner's competence as it emerges. For this relationship to work, however, serious impediments must be overcome. Both client and professional bring to their encounter a body of understandings which they can only very partially communicate to one another and much of which they cannot describe to themselves. Hence the process of communication which is supposed to lead to a fuller grasp of one another's meanings and, on the client's part, to an acceptance of the manifest evidence of the professional's authority can only begin with nonunderstanding and nonacceptance—but with a willing suspension of disbelief.[6]

Thus, in a reflective contract between practitioner and client, the client does not agree to accept the practitioner's authority but to suspend disbelief in it. He agrees to join the practitioner in inquiring into the situation for which the client seeks help; to try to understand what he is experiencing and to make that understanding accessible to the practitioner; to confront the practitioner when he does not understand or agree; to test the practitioner's competence by observing his effectiveness and to make public his questions over what should be counted as effectiveness; to pay for services rendered and to appreciate competence demonstrated. The practitioner agrees to deliver competent performance to the limits of his capacity; to help the client understand the meaning of the professional's advice and the rationale for his actions, while at the same time he tries to learn the meanings his actions have for his client; to make himself readily confrontable by his client; and to reflect on his own tacit understandings when he needs to do so in order to play his part in fulfilling the contract.

Within such a contract, the professional is more directly accountable to his client than in the traditional contract. There is also room here for other means of assuring accountability, that is, for peer review, for monitoring by organized clients, and for the "default procedures" of public protest or litigation. But in the reflective contract, where the professional seeks to open his special knowledge to public inquiry, these other mechanisms of accountability would have to function differently. Built as they are on an essentially adversarial structure, they would have to be implemented so as to encourage public inquiry within that structure—a point to which we will return later in this chapter.

Clearly there are serious constraints on the applicability of the reflective contract. Its establishment is difficult and time-consuming, and the matter at hand must seem of sufficient importance to make the effort worthwhile. There are occasions when the client wants nothing more than the notarization of a deed, or the prescription of a conventional remedy, and to be done with it. There are also situations of crisis, when the practitioner ought to do nothing more than the bare task required; conversation, reflective or otherwise, would be irrelevant.

In situations which are neither emergencies nor routine cases, the establishment of a reflective contract is possible and may seem worthwhile; but as compared with the traditional contract, it is difficult. The difficulty lies in the different demands on competence, and the different sources of satisfaction, that are presented both to the professional and to the client.

Let us consider, first, the situation of the professional. When he is a member of a "major" profession, whose role carries a strong presumption of authority and autonomy, then the problem of moving to a reflective contract involves giving up his initial claim to authority and sharing the control of the interaction with the client. When the professional's initial position is weak, when he tends to be regarded as a mere service provider rather than an authority, then the problem is reversed. I think, for example, of the principal of a school anguished by her inability to confront what she believes to be the unreasonable demands of parents; of engineers in large companies who feel coerced by the directives of general managers too ready to sacrifice product quality or safety to immediate commercial advantage; of human service personnel in public bureaucracies who feel that agency procedures prevent them from attending to the clients they are supposed to serve. It is not unusual in such cases to find that individuals aspire to a professional status that they are only tenuously, or partially, given. Their difficulty in establishing a reflective contract with their clients is to acquire enough voice in the situation to be able to do so.

Whether the professional occupies a position of initial

strength or weakness, the reflective contract calls for competences which may be strange to him. Whereas he is ordinarily expected to play the role of expert, he is now expected from time to time to reveal his uncertainties. Whereas he is ordinarily expected to keep his expertise private and mysterious, he is now expected to reflect publicly on his knowledge-in-practice, to make himself confrontable by his clients.

As the professional moves toward new competences, he gives up some familiar sources of satisfaction and opens himself to new ones. He gives up the rewards of unquestioned authority, the freedom to practice without challenge to his competence, the comfort of relative invulnerability, the gratifications of deference. The new satisfactions open to him are largely those of discovery—about the meanings of his advice to clients, about his knowledge-in-practice, and about himself. When a practitioner becomes a researcher into his own practice, he engages in a continuing process of self-education. When practice is a repetitive administration of techniques to the same kinds of problems, the practitioner may look to leisure as a source of relief, or to early retirement; but when he functions as a researcher-in-practice, the practice itself is a source of renewal. The recognition of error, with its resulting uncertainty, can become a source of discovery rather than an occasion for self-defense.

Indeed, it can be liberating for a practitioner to ask himself, "What, in my work, really gives me satisfaction?" and then, "How can I produce more experiences of that kind?" For some teachers in the MIT Teachers' Project who asked themselves that question for the first time, the most satisfying experiences were ones in which they "gave the child reason" and put themselves into the role of student, allowing themselves to experience and reveal the confusions they had always assumed they were expected to suppress or keep private.

These differences in sources of satisfaction and demands for competence might be expressed as follows:

Expert	Reflective Practitioner
I am presumed to know, and must claim to do so, regardless of my own uncertainty.	I am presumed to know, but I am not the only one in the situation to have relevant and important knowledge. My uncertainties may be a source of learning for me and for them.
Keep my distance from the client, and hold onto the expert's role. Give the client a sense of my expertise, but convey a feeling of warmth and sympathy as a "sweetener."	Seek out connections to the client's thoughts and feelings. Allow his respect for my knowledge to emerge from his discovery of it in the situation.
Look for deference and status in the client's response to my professional persona.	Look for the sense of freedom and of real connection to the client, as a consequence of no longer needing to maintain a professional facade.

Just as the reflective contract demands different kinds of competences and permits different sources of satisfaction for the practitioner, so it does for the client.

For one thing, the problem of choosing a practitioner presents itself to the client in a new way. He must choose not only on the basis of the practitioner's reputed expertise (always a more or less "black box") but on the basis of his amenability to the reflective contract. Is the practitioner willing to talk about the issue at hand, to consider it from more than one point of view, to reveal his own uncertainties? Is he interested in the client's perceptions of the issue? Is he open to confrontation, without defensiveness? Is he willing to carry out experiments on the spot and to be open about such experimenting, including the conditions under which he would regard his views as confirmed or refuted? What is his stance toward his own knowledge? Does he claim only to 'know," or is he interested in, rather than threatened by, alternative ways of seeing the phenomena that do not fit his models?

It is not easy for a client to adopt these attitudes if he really wants the security of having someone who "knows" with the comforting certainty of expertise. In order to choose in the way I have just described, a client must be able to distance himself from his own attraction to the professional mystique. And he must develop a new kind of skill in asking questions. How, for example, is a client to question a practitioner's claim to knowledge when the client cannot readily distinguish a reasonable claim from one that is overblown? His problem is similar to the problem of a manager committed to the management of people whose technical knowledge in certain areas exceeds his own. Some of the methods familiar to managers can be useful to the client, for example:

- "Judge the man rather than his knowledge." Challenge him, and see how he responds to challenge. Look for the combination of confidence and humility, advocacy of a position, and openness to inquiry which is characteristic of reflective competence.
- "Use your own ignorance." Do not be afraid to admit ignorance, ask for help in understanding, and expect to get it.
- "Ask for sources of risk." Push for the limits of the other's confidence. Ask what risks are attendant on a proposed course of action.
- "Seek out more than one view." Assume that it is normal and legitimate to compare practitioners' approaches to a problem. Use multiple meetings to build up a sense of the proper questions to ask and the criticisms of a particular approach that need to be answered.

To be able to use strategies like these effectively, the client must have some of the good manager's skills. He should be able to question and confront claims to expert knowledge without hostility, that is, without making himself the cause of the other's defensiveness. He should have a sense of the *limits* of expert knowledge, which shape his expectations of the professional's appropriate behavior at the boundaries of his expertise.

In short, the competent client should really function in many ways as a reflective practitioner. He need not pretend to take matters into his own hands (like the "lay physician" or "citizen planner"), but he should cultivate competence in reflective conversation with the professional, stimulating him to reflect on his own knowledge-in-practice.

The competences and satisfactions appropriate to clients in the reflective contract can be summarized and contrasted with the traditional contract roughly as follows:

Traditional Contract	Reflective Contract
I put myself into the professional's hands and, in doing this, I gain a sense of security based on faith.	I join with the professional in making sense of my case, and in doing this I gain a sense of increased involvement and action.
I have the comfort of being in good hands. I need only comply with his advice and all will be well.	I can exercise some control over the situation. I am not wholly dependent on him; he is also dependent on information and action that only I can undertake.
I am pleased to be served by the best person available.	I am pleased to be able to test my judgments about his competence. I enjoy the excitement of discovery about his knowledge, about the phenomena of his practice, and about myself.

On the left hand side of the page there is the comfort and the danger of being treated as a child. On the right, there is the gratification, and the anxiety, of becoming an active participant in a process of shared inquiry.

For any professional or client who wishes to move from traditional to reflective contract, there is the task of reshaping the norms and expectations which the other party brings to the interaction. If one party to an institution wishes to begin acting in a nontraditional way, he is apt to create new sorts of dilemmas for himself. Should a professional, for example, risk losing his patient's confidence in order to create the possibility of a reflective contract? Should he risk exploring the client's meanings when the client might regard such exploration as an intrusion? Should he reveal the complexity of the situation at the risk of frightening or confusing his client?

The way in which such risks present themselves is a function of the sort of behavioral world in which professional and client encounter one another. Their behavioral world may be conducive to the avoidance of risks, the suppression of dilemmas, the exercise of mystery and mastery, and in these ways may foil a practitioner's efforts to establish a reflective contract with his client. But the behavioral world is an artifact which professional and client jointly create. They can change it in the directions required by the reflective contract if they have the will and competence to do so. Indeed, one of them may initiate such a change and gradually gain the other's support in bringing it about.

Normal professional-client behavior is what I have earlier described as Model I. It tends to take the form of win/lose games of control. This is true whether the professional is weak or strong. For example, a client may feign compliance, and then proceed, when he is out of the professional's sphere of control, to do what he sees fit. The client may seek to play one professional off against another, using "second opinion" to evade control. Or the client may impugn the professional's expertise in order to reduce the professional's control. To all of these strategies, the "strong" professional may respond by threatening the client who fails to comply with his advice ("You'll learn better!" or "You do this at your own risk!"). Or the professional may "pull rank," refusing to have anything further to do with a client so long as he remains rebellious. The professional may extend his claim to know beyond the limits of his expertise, or he may use the mystery of his expert knowledge so as to enhance his control over the client.

Games such as these can have serious consequences. The client may refuse to comply with the professional's advice, in order to show the professional that he cannot be controlled. When the professional exaggerates his claim to know, he may fail to perceive a line of inquiry which would yield new and more effective ways of looking at the client's situation. The professional may misconstrue the meanings the client constructs for the professional's advice or treatment, with the result that he misses an opportunity for effective intervention.

These games of control and evasion acquire additional importance when the client's situation is uncertain, unique, or unstable; for the reflection-in-action which is essential to appropriate action in situations such as these may take on the meaning of "weakness." To admit uncertainty, to make it apparent that one needs to conduct experiments, may look and feel like a loss of control when the basic theme of professional-client interaction is a game of control and evasion.

Thus the familiar Model I world of professional-client relations tends to inhibit the professional's capacity to reflect-in-action. This is true when merely private reflection-in-action is called for, and is all the more true of reciprocal reflection-in-action; when, for example, the professional may wish to test his assumptions about the client's understandings or intentions.

This type of interaction is a special case of what Argyris and I have called a "primary inhibitory loop."[7] Here, conditions of uncorrectable error reinforce, and are reinforced by, Model

I theories-in-use. When the situation is uncertain, vague, or ambiguous, when the inquirer's understandings are internally inconsistent or incongruent, then it is difficult and may be impossible to detect and correct one's errors. When the situation is uncertain, for example, it is not clear what expectations one ought to have, and therefore it is not clear what would constitute an outcome mismatched to expectation. When one's description of the situation is vague or ambiguous, it is not directly testable. When one's system of understandings is internally inconsistent, the very same outcome may seem an error and not an error. And when espoused theory is incongruent with theory-in-use, then an outcome may be an error in relation to the first and a match in relation to the second.

In order to make it possible to detect and correct errors in the situation, it is necessary to remove or reduce such conditions as these. For example, if the situation is uncertain, it is necessary to construct and test a model of it. If one's descriptions or rules are vague, it is necessary to make them precise enough to test. But in the primary inhibitory loop uncertainty does not lead to theory building, nor does vagueness lead to clarification and precision. On the contrary, an experienced uncertainty may trigger a defensive reaction in which the professional or the client denies his uncertainty. Vagueness may be used as a vehicle for the exercise of control or for the evasion of control. For example, a patient may deliberately keep his description of his symptoms vague in order to foil his physician's efforts to control his behavior. A lawyer may present his understanding of the situation in a vague way in order to increase his client's dependence on him and make the client easier to control. A professional may use vagueness in a strategy of mystery and mastery by which he seeks to control his client, and the client may respond in kind with a passive, apparently compliant version of the same strategy. Thus conditions of uncorrectable error stimulate Model I responses, and these, in turn, tend to reinforce conditions of uncorrectable error.

Breaking into a self-reinforcing system such as this means working at the Model I behavioral world. It is not enough for one party to decide, unilaterally, that he will no longer be a party to such win/lose games. He must also work toward creation of conditions in the behavioral world which will increase the likelihood that the other party will make a similar decision. Either the client or the professional may initiate this work, though the professional is in some ways better positioned to do so. Whichever one begins, however, he will need to bring to the interaction a theory-in-use which enables him to be free of causal responsibility for the other's defensiveness. For it is defensiveness which makes it hard to surface and inquire into the dilemmas inherent in the initial shift toward the reflective contract.

The professional, for example, may go beyond private assessments of his client's readiness for such a shift. He may try to frame choices for his client. How much does the client wish to know? To what extent does he wish to become a participant in the professional's inquiry?

In conjunction with this, the professional may voice the dilemma he feels, stating, for example, that he wants, on the one hand, to convey to the client his evolving understanding of the situation, but that, on the other hand, he is concerned about the risk of frightening or confusing the client. In doing this, he may achieve two effects. First, he may make it easier for the client to admit that he might well be frightened or confused by such an initiative; and second, he may model a way of acting that will help the client to surface dilemmas or negative feelings which he experiences in the situation.

A client's initiative might take the form of offering his picture of the meaning of something the professional has done or said, asking then whether the professional had intended to convey this meaning. Or the client may ask whether the professional would be willing to admit him into his private reflections on the case.

There is no reason to believe that it is possible to leap from old to new contract. Expectations are not easily transformed, especially in the situations of stress and anxiety that characterize many professional-client interactions, and the competences for reflective conversation are not acquired simply as a result of deciding to do so. It is very likely that the shift, where it occurs, will proceed gradually and with difficulty as professionals and clients increase their willingness to experiment with new modes of interaction, increase their confidence in their capacity to deliver the new sorts of behavior, and begin to experience the satisfactions which flow from the new contract.

On the other hand, some of the conditions favorable to the reflective contract are already present. There are clients ready to enter into such a contract, frustrated at the unwillingness of professionals to abandon the traditional relationships. And there are professionals equally frustrated at being unable to find clients who do not expect and demand the old mystique. In these sorts of cases, it may take very little to set the process of change in motion.

Research and Practice

The traditional model of the proper relation of research and practice is still very much alive. For example, it underlies Glazer's explanation of the dilemmas of the schools of the minor professions and Schein's schema of professional knowledge. It is embedded in the tendency of many professional schools to conceive of themselves as schools of applied science, reserving the highest status for the scientists whose theories the more practice-oriented faculty members are supposed to apply. It is epitomized in medicine by the dictum that "those who study whole organs bow down to those who study sections, and those who study sections bow down to those who study cells."

In some parts of some practices—medicine, agronomy, engineering, dentistry, management, for example—practitioners can and do make use of knowledge generated by university-based researchers. But even in these professions, and certainly in Glazer's "minor" ones, large zones of practice present problematic situations which do not lend themselves to applied science. What is more, there is a disturbing tendency for research and practice to follow divergent paths.[8] Practitioners and researchers tend increasingly to live in different worlds, pursue different enterprises, and have little to say to one another. Teachers have gained relatively little from cognitive psychology; political and administrative practice has gained little from the policy sciences; and management science has contributed relatively little to the practice of management. The divergence of research and practice exacerbates the practitioner's dilemma which I have called "rigor or relevance," and tempts the practitioner to force practice situations into molds derived from research.

Clearly, then, when we reject the traditional view of professional knowledge, recognizing that practitioners may *become* reflective researchers in situations of uncertainty, instability, uniqueness, and conflict, we have recast the relationship between research and practice. For on this perspective, research is an activity of practitioners. It is triggered by features of the practice situation, undertaken on the spot, and immediately linked to action. There is no question of an "exchange" between research and practice or of the "implementation" of research results, when the frame- or theory-testing experiments of the practitioner at the same time transform the practice situation. Here the exchange between research and practice is immediate, and reflection-in-action is its own implementation.

Nevertheless, there are kinds of research which can be undertaken outside the immediate context of practice in order to enhance the practitioner's capacity for reflection-in-action. "Reflective research," as I shall call it, may be of four types, each of which already exists at least in embryo. Frame analysis, the study of the ways in which practitioners frame problems and roles, can help practitioners to become aware of and criticize their tacit frames. Description and analysis of images, category schemes, cases, precedents, and exemplars can help to build the repertoires which practitioners bring to unique situations. A most important kind of research has to do with the methods of inquiry and the overarching theories of phenomena, from which practitioners may develop on-the-spot variations. And practitioners can benefit from research on the process of reflection-in-action itself.

I shall consider each of these briefly, noting existing instances of each, suggesting in each case the outline of an agenda for further inquiry.

Frame analysis. At any given time in the life of a profession, certain ways of framing problems and roles come into good currency. When Quist frames the problem of the design of the school as one of "imposing a discipline on the screwy site," and when Dean Wilson frames the problem of malnourishment as one of "gaps in a process of nutrient flow," they bound the phenomena to which they will pay attention. Their frames determine their strategies of attention and thereby set the directions in which they will try to change the situation, the values which will shape their practice.

When the town planner, in our earlier example, frames his

intermediate role in terms of a balancing act, he determines the kinds of problems he will set in the various contexts of his practice. The construction of a role frame is superordinate to and longer lasting than the setting of particular problems.

When practitioners are unaware of their frames for roles or problems, they do not experience the need to choose among them. They do not attend to the ways in which they *construct* the reality in which they function; for them, it is simply the given reality. Thus, for example, a planner may take for granted that the housing problem is one of preserving and increasing the stock of decent housing; what else could it be? A development economist may assume without question that the problem in a developing country is that of increasing the rate of industrialization, the growth of gross national product, and the pool of foreign currency available for exchange.

When a practitioner becomes aware of his frames, he also becomes aware of the possibility of alternative ways of framing the reality of his practice. He takes note of the values and norms to which he has given priority, and those he has given less importance, or left out of account altogether. Frame awareness tends to entrain awareness of dilemmas.

When a professional community embodies multiple and conflicting ideas in good currency about the frames appropriate to the construction of problems and roles, then practitioners, educators, and students of the profession confront such dilemmas. One cannot be a member of the community without taking account of them. In the field of psychotherapy, as I have noted earlier, practitioners have to deal with a bewildering variety of "schools." Leston Havens has proposed that these can be grouped into the broad categories of objective-descriptive, interpersonal, psychoanalytic, and existential psychiatry.[9] Architects face a similar predicament. They may choose, for example, to be "historicists," focussing on the development of variations on historical precedents. They may identify with the "modern movement," which has sought to free itself from historical precedent but has now become something of a tradition in its own right. They may concentrate on building as a craft which utilizes and gives prominence to the unique properties of materials. They may see building as an industrial process which calls for new technologies and for building-systems. Or they may give primary importance to the idea of architecture as a social process in which the users of buildings should participate in design.

Social workers may approach their tasks as clinical caseworkers, monitors and controllers of social behavior, deliverers of social services, advocates of the rights of their clients, or as community organizers. Indeed, in the heady days of the 1960s, some social workers moved sequentially through all of these ways of framing practice roles.[10] Planners, as I have mentioned, construct variations on the roles of policy analysis, design, advocacy, regulation, management, or mediation. In a science-based profession like medicine, a practitioner may see himself as a clinician devoted to the diagnosis and treatment of the diseases of individual patients, as a practitioner of preventive medicine concerned with the larger life situations of whole communities, or as an advocate for the rights and needs of groups of people deprived of decent medical care.

Frame analysis may help practitioners to become aware of their tacit frames and thereby lead them to experience the dilemmas inherent in professional pluralism. Once practitioners notice that they actively construct the reality of their practice and become aware of the variety of frames available to them, they begin to see the need to reflect-in-action on their previously tacit frames. So Quist and the Supervisor reflect with their students on the framing of the design or therapeutic situation; so the town planner might reflect on his balancing act.

Traditionally, the discussion of alternative frames, values, and approaches to practice tends to appear in professional communities in the mode of debate among representatives of the contending schools of thought. There is a great deal of polemical writing, in this vein, in the literatures of such fields as architecture, psychiatry, planning, social work, and divinity. There is also a literature of debate in such fields as law, engineering, and medicine between practitioners of the establishment and their radical critics. In this sort of writing, the style of communication is primarily ideological. The protagonists of the various points of view do not reflect *on* their frames but act *from* them, seeking to defend their own positions and attack the positions of their opponents. The readers of these literatures may be helped to become aware of alternative points of view, but they are not much helped to reflect on the different frames that underlie them.

Systematic, scholarly reflection on the frames implicit in multiple approaches to reality originates in the sociology of knowledge, and especially in the groundbreaking work of Karl Mannheim.[11] Mannheim and his followers have attempted to analyze how particular views of reality evolve out of the concrete situations of particular social groups, bearing the stamp of the perceived interests of those groups. The sociologists of knowledge have emphasized, for example, how class interests and values are manifested in the ostensibly "objective" findings of philosophers, scientists, and scholars. But at least in its early embodiments, the sociology of knowledge has been less concerned with the realities framed within particular professions than with the frames implicit in the ideologies of politics and political economy. And even when sociologists of knowledge have more recently concerned themselves with the professions, as in the growing sociology of science, their perspective is apt to be rather distant from the concerns of the practitioner.[12] They seem to be less interested in helping practitioners to reflect-in-action than in pursuing the self-initiated research agenda of their own scholarly community.

When analysts influenced by the sociology of knowledge attempt to study the professions in a way that will be useful to the practitioners themselves, they encounter several unavoidable questions. What sorts of frame analysis will be useful to practitioners who wish to reflect on their own frames? What message, beyond mere relativism, does the sociology of knowledge offer to practitioners of a profession?

The work of Leston Havens is of particular interest in this connection. He is a psychiatrist writing for other psychiatrists, with the expressed aim of helping them make sense of the "babble of voices" which bedevils their profession, and in his *Approaches to the Mind,* he advocates systematic eclecticism.[13] He sees the contending schools of psychiatric thought as a reservoir of available theories, techniques, and approaches to practice, from which the practitioner should choose elements according to the special features of the case before him. Havens proposes that the psychiatrist master an art of psychotherapy rather like the art of teaching described by Tolstoy in the passage I have quoted earlier. The psychotherapist should derive from the various schools of psychiatric thought a range of techniques from which he can select at will those that will help him solve the problems presented by the particular patient.

The difficulty I find in this approach is its implicit reliance on an unexamined idea of effectiveness. The various schools of psychiatric thought represent different ways of framing the therapist's role. The existential psychiatrist differs from the psychoanalyst not only in the techniques he employs but in his way of conceiving what it means to be a therapist, his stance toward the patient, and what he defines as a successful outcome of therapy. When Havens speaks of selecting the approach best suited to a particular patient, he makes implicit reference to an idea of effectiveness which is constant for all patients. But with change of frame, the idea of effectiveness also changes.

It may be that the schools of psychiatric thought are sources of techniques from which practitioners of various persuasions may benefit. On the other hand, to adopt an eclectic stance toward psychiatric pluralism is to assume that the differences among the schools can be dissolved, eventually, in a superordinate science of psychotherapy; and for this, Havens can offer little or no evidence. Indeed, he takes a more promising approach to the matter in a later book, *Participant Observation*. [14] Here he offers the reader an account of the "interpersonal psychiatry" of Harry Stack Sullivan. He does not merely describe Sullivan's techniques but provides a systematic picture of Sullivan's way of aligning himself with the patient over against the patient's material, which patient and therapist will observe and analyze together. He portrays Sullivan's efforts to engage with his patient in "research projects" which help the patient to "raise his sights" above the narrow channel through which he normally sees. Havens gives us an inside view of Sullivan's world of practice, conveying what it would be like to be this sort of therapist. But from time to time, he shifts perspective so as to allow us to compare Sullivan's way of seeing and practicing with the ways of other schools.

Havens's study of participant observation is less a compendium of techniques and principles than an exercise in literary or art criticism, one that helps the reader to walk for a while in the writer's or artist's world, sharing his enterprises and methods, seeing as he sees. It is a kind of frame-analysis which would be very useful, indeed, not only within the special field of psychiatry, but for all professional practitioners who wish to engage in frame reflection.

In its more general form, this sort of frame analysis would help practitioners to experience the world they would create for themselves if they adopted a particular way of framing the practice role. It would convey the experience of problem setting and solving, the self-definitions and the definitions of success and failure, that would be inherent in a particular choice of role-frame. It would not furnish criteria for choice among approaches to the profession, but it would help the practitioner to "try on" a way of framing the practice role, getting a feeling for it and for the consequences and implications of its adoption. It would help the practitioner to understand the competences he would need, and the kind of person he would become, if he framed his role in a particular way; and it would thereby support the practitioner's efforts at frame reflection.

Repertoire-building research. We have seen earlier that when practice situations do not fit available theories of action, models of phenomena, or techniques of control, they may nevertheless be *seen as* familiar situations, cases, or precedents. Repertoire-building research serves the function of accumulating and describing such exemplars in ways useful to reflection-in-action, and it varies from profession to profession.

Lawyers are familiar with studies of legal cases and judicial precedents in which the researcher asks what laws, regulations, or precepts were considered relevant to the case? By what lines of reasoning did the judge determine which of several contending interpretations of precedents was to be used to link the present case to the relevant law? Such cases may serve as exemplars in a double sense. They describe precedents to which judges and lawyers can have access as they deal with new cases, and they also exemplify ways of thinking about the problem of linking knowledge of rules to particular problems of judicial decision. It is important to note, however, that existing studies of legal precedents and cases have tended to overlook the practice of negotiations with which many lawyers are mostly concerned, the problems of client relationships, and the ethics of legal behavior. With the recent attention to "lawyering," such case studies are beginning to make their appearance.[15]

In architecture, the idea of precedent has been associated with particular buildings like the Duomo, with collections of buildings like the Italian hill towns, or with the devices peculiar to a particular architect ("an artifice, the sort of thing Aalto might invent"). Beyond the mere naming or showing of precedents, repertoire-building research in architecture may go on to analyze how an architect thought about the problem he posed, the solution he found, the domains from which he drew his language of designing. Quist's case, as we have described and analyzed it, might be seen as a contribution to such research.

Historically, the use of case method in business education followed its introduction into the curriculum of the Harvard Law School; but in such institutions as the Harvard School of Business Administration, the development of case method has had a life of its own. Cases are developed, for example, to depict the full problematic situation of a business firm, as it might present itself to a manager. Or cases may be used to raise a particular kind of business problem, such as a problem of estimating market size. A skillful case teacher draws out critical facts, and by a sequence of astutely chosen questions leads students through a process of inquiry which serves both to structure the "solution space" of the situation at hand and to demonstrate a mode of thinking about business problems.

In medicine, the case histories are frequently delivered in a conventional format which describes the patient's complaint and presenting symptoms, the physician's diagnosis, including the clinical evidence on which he based it, the treatment given, the clinical outcomes, and the resulting prognosis. Case histories of this sort, even if less formally presented, may serve as exemplars. A physician may be helped to arrive at a diagnosis in a new case by seeing it as a case history with which he is familiar. But again, case histories may also be used to reveal the physician's process of inquiry—the way in which he perceives and describes the patient, his manner of listening to the patient's descriptions of his complaints, the process by which he identifies possible explanations, conceives of strategies of diagnosis or treatment, and tests them.

Repertoire-building research is widely practiced, but tends to focus on the starting situation, the actions taken, and the results achieved. Such cases may usefully display linkages between features of action, outcome, and context, but they do not reveal the path of inquiry which leads from an initial framing of the situation to the eventual outcome. Often they involve a kind of historical revisionism in which the case writer acts as though a view of the case which arose only at the end of inquiry had been available to him from the very beginning. When a case study more nearly represents the evolution of inquiry, it may provide the reader with exemplars in the double sense I have described.

Research on fundamental methods of inquiry and overarching theories. This kind of research has connections to both of those described above. A practitioner's fundamental principles, in the sense I have in mind, are closely connected both to his frames and to his repertoire of exemplars. Nevertheless, it is important to give this kind of research a place of its own. It has to do with method and theory in a sense different from the sense usually given to these terms under the perspective of technical rationality.

By methods and theories fundamental to a practice, I mean those that some practitioners have learned to use as springboards for making sense of new situations which seem, at first glance, not to fit them. In this sense, an overarching theory and a generic method of inquiry which is inseparable from it are used to *restructure* a situation so that, eventually, one can validly say that the theory fits the situation.

Dean Wilson's use of process-flow models and the Supervisor's use of psychoanalytic theory are cases in point. Wilson's process-flow model consists of a set of ideas about *processes*, a belief that any situation can be understood in terms of process, and a family of methods for the measurement, description, and quantitative analysis of processes. To understand malnourishment in children in terms of process flow required a feat of imaginative restructuring. It was necessary to invent and test methods of measurement so that processes resulting in malnourishment could be described in terms of successive operations performed on nutrients and the losses incurred with each such operation. Similarly, the Supervisor could use his understanding of psychoanalytic theory to describe the patient's material, as recounted by the Resident, in terms of an underlying psychodynamic model of inner conflicts that give rise to self-defeating behavior.

In both cases, the theory and its associated method are used to restructure what is going on so that the practitioners can explain it. Indeed, this kind of restructuring is what he means by explanation. Moreover, the restructured material lends itself to the kind of intervention that the practitioner is good at undertaking.

Research on such fundamental theories and methods may be of two kinds. Researchers may try to discover how this process of recognition and restructuring works by examining episodes of practice, as we have examined the practices of Wilson and the Supervisor. This sort of research may help other practitioners to enter into a way of seeing, restructuring, and intervening which they may wish to make their own.

In the second sense, research on fundamental theories and methods would take the form of an "action science." An action science would concern itself with situations of uniqueness, uncertainty, and instability which do not lend themselves to the application of theories and techniques derived from science in the mode of technical rationality. It would aim at the development of *themes* from which, in these sorts of situations, practitioners may construct theories and methods of their own.

The idea of an action science has a precursor in the work of Kurt Lewin, much of which has the thematic character which enables practitioners to use it in their own reflection-in-action. Such notions as "gatekeeper roles," "democratic and authoritarian group climates," and "unfreezing" are metaphors from which managers, for example, can build and test their own on-the-spot theories of action. In his *Inner Contradictions of Rigorous Research,* [16] Chris Argyris speaks of the "optimal fuzziness" of ideas such as these, and contrasts their useful imprecision with the unusable precision of the research of certain students of Lewin who have attempted to convert his metaphors to their image of social science. When "democratic climate" is translated into multiple factors, variously correlated with other factors, it ceases to be an idea useful for action.

Argyris and William Torbert,[17] among others, have advanced the idea of an action science in the domain of social psychology. But in very different domains the idea has also had its protagonists. Britt Harris, a well-known developer of computer simulations for urban planning, has recently proposed that such models should no longer be considered as theories which predict or explain urban phenomena (functions they have generally failed to fulfill) but as metaphors from which urban planners and policy makers may construct their own accounts of unique and changing situations.[18] Harris's proposed shift from model to metaphor reflects his awareness of the complexity, instability, and uniqueness of the urban phenomena with which formal modellers have concerned themselves since World War II. It reflects the sense that, although formal modellers may have failed to produce precise and generalizable representations of such phenomena as patterns of urban growth, their models may serve, nevertheless, as ways of seeing useful to planners and policy makers confronted with concrete situations of action.

Some urban planners already use models in the way Harris proposes, just as Wilson uses the idea of process flow, the Supervisor uses the idea of "inner conflicts," and some managers and consultants use the Lewinian ideas of "gatekeeper," "democratic group climate," and "unfreezing." In its further development action science would explore, in as many different domains as are of interest to practitioners, such questions as these: What are the features of the themes, metaphors, and fuzzy propositions of action science which make them usable in reflection-in-action? What kinds of evidence are appropriate to their development prior to their use in action, and how ought we to relate such evidence of on-the-spot experiment? What are the norms of rigor appropriate to action science?

The development of action science cannot be achieved by researchers who keep themselves removed from contexts of action, nor by practitioners who have limited time, inclination, or competence for systematic reflection. Its development will require new ways of integrating reflective research and practice.

Research on the process of reflection-in-action. In the Piagetian block-balancing experiments which I have described, the authors studied the conditions under which some children were able to respond to the surprising behavior of the offweighted blocks by restructuring their theories-in-action. The shift from geometric-center to center-of-gravity theories was found, for example, to depend on the children's apprehension of patterns of error and on a subtle shift of attention from success in block balancing to exploration of the properties of the blocks.

In the MIT Teachers' Project, which I have also mentioned, the project leaders wanted to encourage the teachers to reflect-in-action. They hypothesized that as teachers began to get in touch with their own intuitive understandings of such phenomena as tune building and the apparent movements of the moon, they would also learn to attend to their students' intuitive understandings and would begin to think in new ways about the collision of those understandings with the privileged knowledge of the school.

As they tried to promote the teachers' reflection-in-action, they became aware of things that fostered or impeded it. They noted the fixed, stereo-typical categories ("he doesn't know his number facts," "he hasn't learned to think abstractly") with which some teachers first explained the students' behavior. They found that the teachers were inhibited in their efforts to conduct experiments by their feelings of shame and vulnerability over what they saw as poor performance. They noted that certain powerful ideas, such as the idea of "giving the child reason," enabled the teachers to become curious about behavior which might be otherwise dismissed with peremptory judgments. They observed that by the very act of describing their understanding of a task, the teachers could sometimes restructure it.

In work Chris Argyris and I have done with students attempting to reflect on their interpersonal theories of action, we have been struck by phenomena similar to these, including especially the role played by fear of failure.[19] Individuals who want to experiment with the theory of action we have called Model II are sometimes able to invent strategies consistent with it. Nevertheless, between their invention of a new strategy of action and their attempt to produce it, they are often derailed by the intrusion of familiar, patterned responses. These "automatic intercepts" seem to serve the function of protecting the individual from exposure to failure, but they also assure his continued performance according to familiar routines.

These vignettes of research on the process of reflection-in-action suggest that researchers must take account of the interweaving of cognitive, affective, and group dynamic effects. As we try to understand the nature of reflection-in-action and the conditions that encourage or inhibit it, we study a cognitive process greatly influenced by "cognitive emotions"[20] and by the social context of inquiry. In order to study reflection-in-action, we must observe someone engaged in action. We may set a task for performance, as in the block-balancing experiments, or may try to learn how someone is thinking and acting as he carries out a task he has set for himself. In some cases, we may interview a subject or ask him to think out loud as he works on the task. In other cases, we may combine research and intervention, seeking, for example, to help the subject think his way through a situation of cognitive failure. Often, merely by asking a question like, "How are you thinking about it now?" we produce an intended or unintended intervention which changes the subject's understanding and shifts the direction of action.

In all such cases, the subject's feelings about the task, about his own performance, and about his relation to the researcher are essential parts of the process under study. "Hawthorne effects" are unavoidable. The researcher cannot exempt himself and ignores at his peril his own contribution to the social context of the experiment. He is, in Geoffrey Vickers's phrase, an agent-experient who must try to become aware of his own influences on the phenomena he is trying to understand. The authors of the block-balancing experiments comment, for example, on their attempts to make on-the-spot tests of their own theories-in-action. When the researcher adopts a strategy of combined observation and intervention (and in the last analysis he may be capable of no other strategy), he may find that he can help his subject to reflect-in-action by allowing himself to experience and reveal his own confusion.

In order to study reflection-in-action, the researcher must learn an art of experiment in which reflection-in-action plays a central part.

Researchers and practitioners. In the kinds of reflective research I have outlined, researchers and practitioners enter into modes of collaboration very different from the forms of exchange envisaged under the model of applied science. The practitioner does not function here as a mere user of the researcher's product. He reveals to the reflective researcher the ways of thinking that he brings to his practice, and draws on reflective research as an aid to his own reflection-in-action. Moreover, the reflective researcher cannot maintain distance from, much less superiority to, the experience of practice. Whether he is engaged in frame analysis, repertoire building, action science, or the study of reflection-in-action, he must somehow gain an inside view of the experience of practice. Reflective research requires a partnership of practitioner-researchers and researcher-practitioners.

This partnership may take a variety of forms. Groups of practitioners may support one another in reflective research, as Parlett suggests in his study of teachers and counselors of the hearing-impaired.[21] The reflective researcher may take on the role of consultant to the practitioner. Reflective research may become a part of continuing education for practitioners, as in the work of Barry Jentz and William Ronco.[22] The researcher may stand to the practitioner in a relationship of participant observation. The practitioner may take time out to become a reflective researcher, moving in and out of research and practice careers.

To the extent that such partnerships grow in importance and begin to occupy an important place in the research enterprises of the professional schools, universities and practice institutions will enter into new relationships. University faculty will become interested in professional practice, not only as a source of problems for study or internships for students, but as a source of access to reflective practice. As a consequence, a new meaning will be given to activities usually considered peripheral to the conduct of the research university. Field work, consultation, and continuing education, often considered as second-class activities or as necessary evils, will rise to first-class status as vehicles for research, the main business of the university.

Conversely, practice institutions may come to see themselves increasingly as centers of research and education. As the teaching hospital has long functioned, under a model of applied science, as a research and educational institution, so business firms, law offices, social welfare agencies, engineering groups, and architectural offices, may recognize the reflection-in-action of their members and make a place for the reflective research which will support it.

The agenda of reflective research will be generated out of dialogue between reflective researchers and practitioner-researchers, and will be constrained by the requirement that the research be of the kind that practitioners can also undertake.[23] In consequence, there will be a new approach to the sometimes vexing question of the implementation of research. Implementation will be built into the process of reflective research, for practitioners will gain and use insights derived from it as they participate in it.

The roles of practitioner and researcher will have permeable boundaries, and research and practice careers will intertwine as a matter of course. While the relative weight given to reflective research or to practice might vary considerably in the course of a career, one would normally expect practitioners to function on occasion as reflective researchers, and vice versa.

Within the universities, the professional schools, in so far as they become centers of reflective research, may become increasingly independent of the disciplinary departments and increasingly autonomous in their evolution of their own standards of rigor and relevance in research. One might then expect a reduction of the status differential between the research disciplines and the professional schools and with this, a reduction in the dilemmas of the schools of the minor professions which Glazer has so well described.

Nevertheless, it is unlikely that the new roles and relationships of practice and research will wholly displace the old. In such fields as medicine, dentistry, agronomy, and engineering, where relatively stable zones of practice lend themselves to the model of applied science, it is more likely that the two systems of relationship will coexist. But how? If the universities allow them to compartmentalize, there will be a major loss of opportunity which could contribute to the university's decline. If the universities seek new integrations of research and practice, of reflective research and applied science, then they will have to make the epistemology of practice a focus not only for intellectual attention but for institutional redesign.

Institutions for Reflective Practice

Increasingly, the lives of professionals in our society are bound up with the lives of the formal bureaucratic organizations through which most work is done. For engineers, physicians, lawyers, architects, teachers, and social workers, bureaucracies are the institutional settings of professional practice. And for such institutions as industrial firms, public agencies, schools, research institutes, law firms, and architectural offices, professional practitioners are necessary to the performance of organizational work. As society becomes increasingly subject to professional management, professionals tend increasingly to play out their roles within bureaucracies that depend upon the exercise of professional knowledge.

Max Weber, the prophet of bureaucracy, saw very clearly that bureaucracy would require and foster the professionalization of its members. He saw moreover that bureaucracy demanded and reinforced a particular model of professional knowledge, that of technical expertise.

> The management of the office follows general rules, which are more or less stable, more or less exhaustive, and which can be learned. Knowledge of these rules represents a special technical learning which the officials possess. It involves jurisprudence, or administrative or business management.[24]

> Bureaucratization offers above all the optimum possibility for carrying through the principle of specializing administrative functions according to purely objective considerations. Individual performances are allocated to functionaries who have specialized training and who by constant practice learn more and more.[25]

And in his vision of the coming dominance of the bureaucratic form of organization, Weber also foresaw, at least dimly, the widespread professionalization of occupations which would accompany the bureaucratization of social life.

From the earliest intellectual awareness of the bureaucratic phenomenon, then, it has been clear that bureaucracy is bound up with technical expertise. It is only a small step from this to the observation that a shift in our view of professional knowledge, away from technical expertise, portends a significant change in the idea and reality of bureaucratic organization.

We can get a sense of the meaning of this shift by considering the idea of organizational learning.

Formal organizations are task-systems, systems of roles and rules, within which individuals serve as agents for the realization of organizational values, missions, policies, and strategies of action. Individual members contribute to the accumulation of organizational reservoirs of knowledge about the environment, strategies of action, and experiences which sometimes become exemplars for future action. Individuals' contributions enter into organizational memories, maps, and programs, on which other individuals draw as they enact their roles. So, for example, members of the consumer products firm described in chapter 8 contribute to and draw on organizational learning about product development.

In general, the more an organization depends for its survival on innovation and adaptation to a changing environment, the more essential its interest in organizational learning. On the other hand, formal organizations also have a powerful interest in the stability and predictability of organizational life. An organization is a cooperative system in which individuals depend on the predictability of one another's responses. Managers must rely on the predictable behavior of their subordinates. Surprise, which is essential to learning, is inimical to smooth organizational functioning. Thus organizations evolve systems of error detection and correction whose function is to maintain the constancy of variables critical to organizational life. They are "dynamically conservative."[26]

Significant organizational learning—learning which involves significant change in underlying values and knowledge structure—is always the subject of an *organizational predicament*. It is necessary to effective organizational adaptation, but it disrupts the constancies on which manageable organizational life depends.

In addition, as I have noted earlier, the individual agents of organizational learning operate within a social system which shapes their behavior. They have individual interests and theories of action which they bring to the creation of the behavioral world in which they live, a behavioral world which may be more or less conducive to the public testing of private assumptions, the surfacing of dilemmas, and the public discussions of sensitive issues. They belong to subgroups which often enter into win/lose games of attack and defense, deception, and collusion. In so far as these social systems determine the boundaries and directions of organizational inquiry, they are "learning systems"; and in organizations like the consumer products firm they may severely constrain organizational learning.

In the light of these observations, we can more usefully explore the meaning of reflective practice within a bureaucracy. Reflection-in-action is both a consequence and cause of surprise. When a member of a bureaucracy embarks on a course of reflective practice, allowing himself to experience confusion and uncertainty, subjecting his frames and theories to conscious criticism and change, he may increase his capacity to contribute to significant organizational learning, but he also becomes, by the same token, a danger to the stable system of rules and procedures within which he is expected to deliver his technical expertise.

Thus ordinary bureaucracies tend to resist a professional's

attempt to move from technical expertise to reflective practice. And conversely, an organization suited to reflective practice would have features very different from those of familiar bureaucratic settings.

Let us consider the case of a public school. The teachers who participated in the MIT Teachers' Project were employed in urban public schools. As they began to learn to value and engage in reflective teaching practice, they continued to work in these schools. Thus their experience can throw some light on the question of reflective practice in a bureaucracy.

I shall describe a school typical of the ones in which they taught. Such a school is built, in a very special sense, around a theory of knowledge. There is a concept of privileged knowledge which it is the business of teachers to teach, and students to learn. This concept of knowledge is embodied in texts, curriculum, lesson plans, examinations; indeed, it is institutionalized in every aspect of the school. Teachers are seen as technical experts who impart priviledged knowledge to students in a system built, in Israel Scheffler's phrase, on the metaphor of "nutrition."[27] Children are fed portions of knowledge, in measured doses. They are expected to digest it and to give evidence, in class response and examinations, that they have done so. The curriculum is conceived as a menu of information and skills, each lesson plan is a serving, and the entire process is treated as a cumulative, progressive development.

Within the school, the order of space and the order of time conform to this basic image. The school building is divided into classrooms, each of which contains a teacher and a group of twenty or thirty students clustered together according to grade level. Each classroom is self-contained and the teacher is for the most part isolated within it. Temporally, the school day is divided into periods an hour or so in length, each of which is supposed to be dedicated to covering the knowledge content contained in a lesson plan. Days of the week, months, and school year are similarly divided, according to the curricular map of privileged knowledge.

The efficient transmission of knowledge requires a system of controls. The teacher is supposed to convey standard units of knowledge to large numbers of students and must employ measures, in the form of quizzes and examinations, in order to determine what the students have learned or failed to learn. Through the use of marks, grade promotions, and more informal means, students are rewarded for their ability to demonstrate that they have digested the appropriate knowledge and skill, and they are punished for their failure to do so. Special programs are available for those whose failure to pass appropriate tests is attributed to learning disability.

Teachers are also subject to a similar system of controls. They are monitored, and rewarded or punished, according to the measures of their students' progress. And just as teachers function as centers of instruction and control in relation to students who are peripheral to them, so teachers occupy peripheral roles in relation to their supervisors. Curriculum and lesson plans, as well as measures of performance and rewards and punishments, emanate from a center and are imposed on teachers at the periphery. The function of the supervisor is that of assuring that teachers do carry out the functions expected of them, providing them with resources for doing so, allocating rewards and punishments to them according to their measured performance.

In the control of both students and teachers, a high priority is placed on *objectivity*. It is considered important to achieve quantitative measures of proficiency and progress which are independent of individual judgments. These are much preferred to qualitative, narrative accounts of the experience of learning or teaching. Quantitative measures permit the system of control, and the other systems that depend on it, to take on an appearance of consistency, uniformity, precision, and detachment.

The scope of the teacher's attention to her students is supposed to be largely determined by the boundaries of the curriculum. She is to be concerned with students from the point of view of their relative success or failure in assimilating the materials of the lesson plan. Their lives outside of school—what they do there and what knowledge or skill they display there—fall outside the limits of her proper concern. Similarly, when new technology enters the school, its function is to extend the teacher's capacity to transmit the elements of the curriculum. Computers, films, and audiovisual devices are designed to supplement the teacher's work of communication and testing, drill and practice.

These are some of the main features of an urban public school. They are built around a special view of privileged knowledge, its communication and its acquisition. But they also conform to the outlines of a bureaucratic system. The school presents itself as governed by a system of objectively determinable formal rules and procedures which are administered through a hierarchy. The school contains a knowledge structure which includes not only the content of the curriculum but technologies of measurement, communication, control, and maintenance, which are essential both to teaching and administration. Officials of the school are specialists, presumed to have technical expertise. They place a high value on objectivity and on procedural refinement.

Of course, the school as an institution of technical rationality and bureaucratic efficiency has an underside, frequently noted by its members, its constituents, and its critics. Students may respond to the school by "turning off," diverting their real energies and creativity to the world outside the school. Or they learn to beat the system by optimizing to the measures of performance, discovering how to pass tests, get grades, and move through the levels of the system, without thinking very much about the knowledge they are supposed to be acquiring. Similarly, teachers often learn to optimize to the measure of control on *their* performance, striving to meet the letter of the standards imposed on them without worrying very much about whether, or how, their students are learning; or they may think about these things but reserve such thoughts for the world outside the school. Students learn to evade their supervisors' control, giving nothing more than lip service to the formal system. Such games of control and evasion are often embedded in political networks, as individuals form alliances for the purpose of gaining or protecting territory, security, and status.

What happens in such an educational bureaucracy when a teacher begins to think and act not as technical expert but as reflective practitioner? Her reflection-in-action poses a potential threat to the dynamically conservative system in which she lives.

She tries to listen to her students. She asks herself, for example, How is he thinking about this? What is the meaning of his confusion? What is it that he already knows how to do? But if she really listens to a student, she entertains ideas for action that transcend the lesson plan. She may wish, for example, to concentrate for a time on the nature of a student's error or confusion. Why does he write, "$36 + 36 = 312$"? As she begins to understand how he thinks about the task, she may invent new questions, new activities for the student to try, and new ways of helping him learn addition. The lesson plan must be put aside then, or else it must become a rough ground plan for action, a skeleton around which the teacher develops variations according to her on-the-spot understanding of the problems of particular students. Curriculum becomes an inventory of *themes* of understanding and skill to be addressed rather than a set of materials to be learned. Different students present different phenomena for understanding and action. Each student makes up a universe of one, whose potentials, problems, and pace of work must be appreciated as the teacher reflects-in-action on the design of her work.

The freedom to reflect, invent, and differentiate would disrupt the institutional order of space and time. If the teacher must somehow manage the work of thirty students in a classroom, how can she really listen to any one of them? If she is held rigorously accountable to a sequence of hour-long periods in which specified units of subject matter are to be covered, then she cannot follow the logic of her reflection-in-action. Classes must be small or readily divisible into smaller units, and each teacher must be free to introduce variations in the institutional schedule.

The teacher's isolation in her classroom works against reflection-in-action. She needs to communicate her private puzzles and insights, to test them against the views of her peers.

She must expand the scope of her interest in students. What they know how to do in the world outside the school becomes deeply interesting to her, for it suggests the intuitive competences on which she can build.

A reflective teacher needs a kind of educational technology which does more than extend her capacity to administer drill and practice. Most interesting to her is an educational technology which helps students to become aware of their own intuitive understandings, to fall into cognitive confusions and explore new directions of understanding and action.[28]

Accountability, evaluation, and supervision would acquire new meanings. There would be a shift from the search for centrally administered, objective measures of student progress, toward independent, qualitative judgments and narrative accounts of experience and performance in learning and teaching. Supervision would concern itself less with monitoring the teacher's coverage of curriculum content than with assessment and support of the teacher's reflection-in-action.

As teachers attempted to become reflective practitioners, they would feel constrained by and would push against the rule-governed system of the school, and in doing so they would be pushing against the theory of knowledge which underlies the school. Not only would they struggle against the rigid order of lesson plans, schedules, isolated classrooms, and objective measures of performance; they would also question and criticize the fundamental idea of the school as a place for the progressive transmission of measured doses of privileged knowledge.

In fact, the participants in the Teachers' Project had a variety of kinds of experiences as they attempted to live out in their classrooms the new understandings and attitudes they were acquiring. Their schools were in varying degrees approximations to the stereotyped picture I have just drawn. A few teachers had a great deal of discretionary freedom, and were able to make their classrooms into enclaves of nontraditional teaching. Some were frustrated by the traditional patterns and expectations built into the institutional routines of the school. A few felt that the new approach to teaching was "too good for that school."

What is clear is that, in a real-world school which tried to encourage reflective teaching (as in the reflective contract between professional and client), conflicts and dilemmas would surface which are absent, hidden, or of minor importance in an ordinary school. In order to engage the learning capacities and difficulties of particular students, a school would have to manage student/teacher ratios much smaller than twenty-five to one. In the face of resource constraints, how would appropriate differentiations of curriculum and teaching attention be determined? Where teachers were encouraged to reflect-in-action, the meaning of "good teaching" and "a good classroom" would become topics of urgent institutional concern. Such questions could no longer be dismissed by reference to objective measures of performance. Indeed, a major question would hinge on the relationship between such measures and the qualitative judgments of individual teachers. Principals would have to ask, in framing their own roles, whether to "let a thousand flowers bloom" or to advocate their own standards of excellence. If they chose the former, in the name of the teacher's freedom of action or in the spirit of participatory democracy, would the school fall into the kind of permissiveness and intellectual sloppiness which characterized some of the alternative schools of the 1960s?[29] And if principals chose the latter course, what would happen to the teacher's freedom to reflect-in-action? In a school supportive of reflective teaching, a supervisor would advocate his own standards of educational quality while at the same time inquiring into teachers' understandings, confronting what he sees as poor teaching while at the same time inviting teachers to confront his own behavior. Yet in the Model I worlds of most schools, it is far more likely that supervisors would oscillate between centralized control and "a thousand flowers."

In a school supportive of reflective teaching, teachers would challenge the prevailing knowledge structure. Their on-the-spot experiments would affect not only the routines of teaching practice but the central values and principles of the institution. Conflicts and dilemmas would surface and move to center stage. In the organizational learning system with which we are most familiar, conflicts and dilemmas tend to be suppressed or to result in polarization and political warfare. An institution congenial to reflective practice would require a learning system within which individuals could surface conflicts and dilemmas and subject them to productive public inquiry, a learning system conducive to the continual criticism and restructuring of organizational principles and values.

I have dwelt on the case of a public school because of the illuminating experience of the Teachers' Project, but schools are fundamentally similar to the other bureaucratic settings of professional practice.

Wherever professionals operate within the context of an established bureaucracy, they are embedded in an organizational knowledge structure and a related network of institutional systems of control, authority, information, maintenance, and reward, all of which are tied to prevailing images of technical expertise. In industry, engineers and managers occupy specialized technical roles, function according to highly articulated procedures, and tend to be precisely located within a hierarchical system of authority. Not only production and engineering, but marketing, sales, personnel, finance, and general management are increasingly defined as technical specialties. Indeed, industry is often seen as the prototype of technical, bureaucratic rationality. Critics of the schools speak disparagingly, for example, of the "industrialization" of education.[30]

Large-scale social service agencies, hospitals, and architectural offices have also come to function in the technical, bureaucratic world. Here too professional work tends to be channeled within a specialized task system and subjected to objective measures of performance and control. Within these systems, practitioners are increasingly constrained by technical advances in the measurement and proceduralization of work. In the name of cost reduction, for example, welfare workers have now become objects of the sort of time and motion study and efficiency expertise which originated in industry in the early decades of the twentieth century. Computerized information systems are used increasingly to monitor and control the performance of individual workers. At the lower and middle levels of the professional work force, computerized systems are beginning to replace human beings.

The technological extension of bureaucracy, which reinforces the confinement of professional work to precisely defined channels of technical expertise, exacerbates the inherent conflict between bureaucracy and professional indentity. Within highly specialized, technically administered systems of bureaucratic control, how can professionals think of themselves as autonomous practitioners? How can they strive to achieve standards of professional excellence, cultivate artistry, and concern themselves with the unique features of a particular case? An industrial technologist chafes at general management's subordination of product safety to short-term return on investment. A welfare worker feels deprofessionalized because control systems aimed at increasing his efficiency prevent him from attending to the interests of individual clients. These professionals bear a more than superficial resemblance to blue collar workers deskilled by the numbing monotony of the assembly line.

The tensions inherent in the bureaucratization of professional work tend to amplify when professionals seek to become reflective practitioners. A practitioner who reflects-in-action tends to question the definition of his task, the theories-in-action that he brings to it, and the measures of performance by which he is controlled. And as he questions these things, he also questions elements of the organizational knowledge structure in which his functions are embedded. Thus a human service worker who thinks critically about his practice may also criticize an agency-wide pattern of selective inattention to the most needy members of the client population. An engineer who reflects-in-action may perceive a pattern of error which he attributes to an excessive reliance on routinized systems of quality control. Reflection-in-action tends to surface not only the assumptions and techniques but the values and purposes embedded in organizational knowledge.

To the extent that an institution seeks to accommodate to the reflection-in-action of its professional members, it must meet several extraordinary conditions. In contrast to the normal bureaucratic emphasis on uniform procedures, objective measures of performance, and center/periphery systems of control, a reflective institution must place a high priority on flexible procedures, differentiated responses, qualitative appreciation of complex processes, and decentralized responsibility for judgment and action. In contrast to the normal bureaucratic emphasis on technical rationality, a reflective institution must make a place for attention to conflicting values and purposes. But these extraordinary conditions are also necessary for significant organizational learning.

The predicament of the reflective practitioner in a bureaucracy is another face of the predicament of organizational learning. Reflection-in-action is essential to the process by which individuals function as agents of significant organizational learning, and it is at the same time a threat to organizational stability. An organization capable of examining and restructuring its central principles and values demands a learning system capable of sustaining this tension and converting it to productive public inquiry. An organization conducive to reflective practice makes the same revolutionary demand.

The Place of the Professions in the Larger Society

According to the tradition of technical rationality, the professions mediate between science and society and translate scientific research into social progress. The model of professional knowledge as technical expertise, based on the application of science, underlies the traditional contract between the autonomous professional expert and his client, the traditional exchange relationship between practitioner and researcher, and the rather paradoxical incorporation of ostensibly autonomous professionals within the highly specialized structures of bureaucratic systems. In all of these ways, which I have described earlier in this chapter, the tradition of technical rationality contributes to the place of the professions in the larger society.

The tradition of Technical Rationality has an additional impact, however, which we have not yet discussed. It has given rise to our dominant model of the formation of public policy. On this view, policy making is a process of social choice. Rational policy choices derive from policy analyses which select from among available courses of action those which maximize social benefits and minimize social costs.[31] Policy analysis is conceived as a technical process which occurs within a political context. The analyst employs sophisticated techniques in order to measure and compare the impacts of alternative policies, but he depends in several ways on the political process. The political process supplies the definitions of policy objectives, social benefits, and social costs. Sometimes policy analyses are conceived as inputs to elected officials who make the final policy choices. And more recently, proponents of the dominant model of policy making have recognized that policies are converted to programs of action through processes of implementation which may be guided or distorted by politics.[32]

According to this model, the key roles in public policy are performed by professionals. Professionals supply technical expertise in substantive fields of policy such as health care and housing. They meet the technical demands of policy analysis. They design, implement, and evaluate government programs, and as experts in the techniques of legislation and vote getting, they manage the political process. The technical complexity of rational social choice demands professional expertise.

To the radical critics of the Technological Program, however, the professionalization of public policy is a technocratic distortion of democratic values. Professionals are a self-serving elite who put science-based technique at the service of the business class and under a facade of objectivity and value neutrality feather their own and their masters' nests. Just as professionals use their special status to control and coerce their clients, so, in technocratic government, they use technical expertise to suppress the powerless and the dispossessed. Moreover, their claim to extraordinary knowledge is an empty one. Beneath the mystery of professional expertise lies ignorance and manipulation.

The radical critique carries a utopian vision of social reform. It is necessary to demystify the professions, exposing class interest masquerading as Technical Rationality, so that society can achieve democracy, equality, and social justice. It is necessary to demonstrate the coerciveness of the professions, to show how they have misappropriated knowledge, so as to pave the way for a new breed of citizen-professionals committed to social justice. In the meantime, there is a need for counterprofessional advocates and adversaries who can effectively resist professionally engineered subversion of the public interest and the rights of clients. The people must be educated to their rights and disabused of their traditional respect for self-proclaimed experts. Counterprofessionals, who can fight the experts on their own ground, should defend the poor against urban renewal and gentrification, protect patients from the callous intrusions of the medical profession, and help the dispossessed turn the legal system to their own advantage. In the same vein, the supposedly objective findings of scientific research must be exposed as rationalizations for class interests. Counterresearchers are needed to point out the establishment bias of neoclassical economics, the business and middle-class bias of the urban planners, and the pretensions of industrial engineers who propose "technological fixes" for the social problems of energy and environmental quality.

In the field of public policy, demystification of the professions takes the form of debunking the myth of rational social choice. Policy analysis is not rational choice but a rationalization of political interests. The task of social reform is to empower the relatively powerless—blacks, women, ethnic minority groups, the aged, the disabled, prisoners—to organize for an effective voice in the politics of policy making. Citizens must be organized around such public issues as disarmament, nuclear safety, and environmental quality. Not only the legal system but propaganda, strikes, protests, and the full repertoire of social action must be used to stop the power plays of the establishment or to make sure that the dispossessed get "a piece of the action." All of this requires expertise. So in the course of the past twenty years counterprofessionals have emerged to play critical roles in advocating the rights of the dispossessed and organizing citizens' groups around issues of public interest. Like the professionals who serve government and industry, counterprofessionals contribute substantive expertise, provide alternative rationales for public action, and put their techniques of negotiation and infighting at the service of those who strive for a voice in the political process.

With the help of the counterprofessionals, militant minorities and citizens' groups have succeeded in transforming public policy. "Special interest politics" has become the order of the day. In field after field, special interest groups have succeeded in bringing about laws and regulations aimed at curbing the excesses of established institutions. More recently, as these successes have triggered reactions from the Right, public policy has become a field of visible political contention in which all sides—established institutions, adversaries of the establishment, and counteragents of the Right—have armed themselves with professional expertise.

It does not follow, of course, that professionalization of political disputes leads to public consensus. Often, on the contrary, the addition of professional expertise serves to extend political conflict. But there is a well-known theory of democracy which explains and justifies this process, a theory which appeals to radical critics as well as to their traditional opponents. On this view, democracy consists in a play of countervailing powers which tends, when it is effective, to prevent any one group from establishing permanent domination over the others.[33] Conflicts among groups are kept within manageable bounds by institutional mechanisms for the resolution of political disputes, that is, by the courts, the voting booth, and the bargaining table. Increasingly these institutions have become arenas for the activities of professional advocates and adversaries.

But the social reforms of the radical critics are also vulnerable to criticism.

There is something inconsistent about a demystification of professional expertise which leads to the establishment of a breed of counterprofessional experts. Apparently even in a world liberated from the dominance of established interests there is a need for special knowledge; and in a world of established interests armed with professional expertise there is a need for counterexpertise. But experts tend to behave like experts. Citizen-professionals and professional advocates may also show themselves to be disposed to unilateral control of their clients and interested in the preservation of their own special status. In socialist countries, citizen-professionals have become a "new class," an elite group operating from bureaucracies that display both the insensitivity and the sluggishness we have learned to associate with the bureaucratic phenomenon.[34] Counterprofessionals may succeed in containing the free movement of established interests, but their success is often accompanied by unwanted side effects. When environmentalists succeed in blocking land development, for example, they may also contribute to the shortage of low- and middle-class housing.[35] The regulatory mechanisms brought into being by the protest movements of the 1960s and early 1970s have frequently turned out to be ineffective in solving the social problems for which they were designed.[36] And the traditional institutions for dispute settlement are often incapable of converting political contention to acceptable social action.

The courts, which have taken on an enormously expanded role in such fields as urban education, environmental regulation, and public housing, have shown a very limited capacity to arbitrate among the claims of contending professionals. Caught in the crossfire of conflicting technical positions, judges have often resorted to the technicalities of the law without deeply understanding the substantive problems of policy at stake in their decisions. And when judges have taken responsibility for the management of urban schools or public housing, they have had recourse to professionals who reintroduce, under the auspices of the courts, whatever biases accompany their expertise. The electoral process often fails to produce stable solutions to public problems. When conflicting professional judgments about policy are put to a vote, the results often reflect nothing more substantial than the winds of political change. And when elected officials deliberate over policy conflicts, their legislative compromises are often so vague as to allow those conflicts to reemerge when administrators try to convert policies to programs.

As the limits of judicial and electoral mechanisms have become manifest, the bargaining table has gained prominence. Professional mediation, which originated in the field of labor-management negotiation, has begun to spread to the fields of land use, hazardous-waste disposal, and environmental quality. These extensions of the mediating role are still in their infancy, and it remains to be seen how they will evolve. Already, however, a danger has become apparent. Given the nature of their task, mediators tend in practice to define success in terms of keeping the peace. When new information threatens emerging agreement, it tends to be dismissed as "dangerous knowledge."[37] Thus mediators may pursue agreement at the expense of understanding.

When the professional representatives of contending social factions cannot agree about issues of policy, society has recourse to the courts, the electoral process, and the bargaining table. But when the disputed issues are technically and evaluatively complex, it is small wonder that institutions for dispute settlement yield results perceived as arbitrary or merely expedient, or that they reintroduce a disturbing element of professional judgment. When they dispense with expertise, they suffer from its absence; and when they rely on it, they reintroduce its dangers.

There is a similar contradiction in the social reforms of the radical critics. They seek to demystify professional expertise in order to eliminate or contain the professionals who serve the interests of the dominant class. But they cannot dispense with professionals, either to conduct the technically complex business of society or to counter the excesses of the established professions. So they reintroduce the evils of expertise.

So long as the conduct of society depends upon special knowledge and competence, there will be an essential place for the professions. And so long as the professions are shaped by traditional models of knowledge and practice, neither the ideology nor the institutional reforms of the radical critics will eliminate the evils of expertise.

The idea of reflective practice is an alternative to the traditional epistemology of practice. It leads, as we have seen, to new conceptions of the professional-client contract, the partnership of research and practice, and the learning systems of professional institutions. Now I would like to suggest how it might also lead us to think differently about the roles of professionals in public policy and about the place of the professions in the larger society.

The idea of reflective practice leads, in a sense both similar to and different from the radical criticism, to a demystification of professional expertise. It leads us to recognize that for both the professional and the counterprofessional, special knowledge is embedded in evaluative frames which bear the stamp of human values and interests. It also leads us to recognize that the scope of technical expertise is limited by situations of uncertainty, instability, uniqueness, and conflict. When research-based theories and techniques are inapplicable, the professional cannot legitimately claim to be expert, but only to be especially well prepared to reflect-in-action.

From this perspective, it is not difficult to see how the traditional epistemology of practice holds a potential for coercion. We need not make the (possibly valid) attribution that professionals are motivated by the wish to serve class interests or protect their special status. Whenever a professional claims to "know," in the sense of the technical expert, he imposes his categories, theories, and techniques on the situation before him. He ignores, explains away, or controls those features of the situation, including the human beings within it, which do not fit his knowledge-in-practice. When he works in an institution whose knowledge structure reinforces his image of expertise, then he tends to see himself as accountable for nothing more than the delivery of his stock of techniques according to the measures of performance imposed on him. He does not see himself as free, or obliged, to participate in setting objectives and framing problems. The institutional system reinforces his image of expertise in inducing a pattern of unilateral control.

If we accept these criticisms of Technical Rationality, we will no longer uncritically accept the professional's claim to mandate, autonomy, and license. If there are important limits to the scope of technical expertise, we will want to make sure that professionals do not overstep those limits in their claims to authority based on merely technical competence. If technical expertise is value-laden, and technical experts have interests of their own which shape their understandings and judgments, then we will recognize the need for social constraints on professional freedom. On the other hand, we will also respect the professional's claim to extraordinary knowledge in the areas susceptible to technical expertise, and we will place a special value on practitioners who reflect-in-action both on their own evaluative frames and in situations which transcend the limits of their expertise.

These considerations complicate the task of describing the appropriate place of the professions in the larger society. Under the perspective of reflective practice, professionals are neither the heroic avant-garde of the Technological Program nor a villainous elite who prevent the people from taking control of their lives. Professionals are more appropriately seen, I think, as participants in a larger societal conversation; when they play their parts well, they help that conversation to become a reflective one.

In the processes by which ideas of social problems and solutions come into good currency, descriptions of reality are socially constructed. Through our public institutions, through the media, through the actions of intellectuals, and through the processes of public debate, we construct ideas powerful for action concerning the issues and crises of our society, the problems to be solved, the policies to be adopted. When we act from these ideas, we change social reality. Sometimes we make our ideas real, but also thereby create new problems and dilemmas. The "we" who act in this way are agents of the society. We are agents-experient, in Geoffrey Vickers's sense, who are at once the subjects and the objects of action. We are *in* the problematic situation that we seek to describe and change, and when we act on it, we act on ourselves. We engage in a continuing conversation with the larger societal situation of which we are a part, rather as a designer (Quist, for example) converses with his design situation. Like him, we construct a view of the situation; we act from it, thereby changing the situation; but we also elicit "back-talk" which takes the form of unanticipated meanings, problems, and dilemmas.

In the web of such societal conversations, policy formation—the description of social problems, the passage of legislation, the design and implementation of government programs—constitutes a single strand. The process of social problem setting, for example, is far more comprehensive and complex than the process by which public policy problems are set.[38] But public policy represents an aspect, sometimes the formalization, of the more comprehensive process. And public policy, when it has been designed and converted to public action, enters into the larger societal process, changing it once again. Thus for example over the past thirty years ideas about "urban crime" have come into good currency. The setting of the social problem of urban crime has been a complex process of describing an aspect of urban reality, a process in which the police, judges, correctional officials, citizens' groups, social researchers, novelists, filmmakers, and mass media have played their various parts. The many different voices involved in this process have brought multiple, often conflicting, frames to the description of the phenomenon. Urban crime has been seen, for example, as a consequence of the form of the city, which leaves concentrations of poor minority groups in a center surrounded by affluent (and vulnerable) suburbs. It has been seen as failure of the police and the courts to provide swift and sure punishment. It has been seen as a by-product of the culture of poverty. And it has been seen as a manifestation of a streak of ineradicable evil in human nature. Through processes about which we understand relatively little, I believe, particular descriptions of the phenomenon of urban crime have at various times become powerful for action. In the late 1960s, for example, urban crime came to be seen as an expression of a "racist society." The Kerner Commission gave this view of the status of formal public policy, and the urban programs of Lyndon Johnson's Great Society were, in some measure, a response to it. Later, in partial reaction to the effects of those programs and partially in response to other currents in the society, a "law and order" view of urban crime became powerful and new policies of criminal justice, emphasizing the swift and sure apprehension and punishment of criminals, came into effect. In the past twenty years or so, both of these views of the phenomenon have been alive in the society and have at various times predominated.

The struggle to define the situation, and thereby to determine the direction of public policy, is always both intellectual and political. Views of reality are both cognitive constructs, which make the situation understandable in a certain way, and instruments of political power. In the larger societal conversation with the situation, problem setting, policy definition, and interpretation of the situation's "back-talk" are always marked by intellectual inquiry and by political contention.

Implications for the Professions and Their Place in Society

In these processes the leading roles are often played by professionals. It is the social critics, the policy analysts, the advocates, the researchers, the elected officials, and the administrators who function as agents of inquiry. But their contributions to the description of social reality are always embedded in a process of political contention. Professionals represent the views and values of established interests, and other professionals advocate the interests of the dissident and the dispossessed. It is one group of correctional officials, judges, police chiefs, social researchers, and policy analysts who have championed the "law and order" perspective on urban crime, and another such group which has championed a view of the criminal justice system as a social evil which criminalizes and makes victims of the poor and dispossessed. As professionals play their roles in the process of public policy—and in the more comprehensive societal conversation in which that process is embedded—they are voices of institutionalized contention, actors in an essentially adversarial process.

The uses of institutionalized contention are undeniable. The radical critics of the professions are right in their claim that professional expertise can be used, wittingly or unwittingly, to mask the biases of established interests. There is no reason to suppose that professionals can be trusted to perceive the coerciveness of the institutions they represent; and even when they perceive it, there is no reason to suppose that professionals alone can act effectively to change the directions of institutional behavior. There is undeniable social utility in counterinstitutions which criticize and resist the excesses of established institutions, and advocate the rights and interests of the relatively powerless. But increasingly, as we have seen, the professionally instrumented play of countervailing powers has led to the polarization of society, to pendulum swings from one extreme position to its opposite, to stalemate, and to frustration at our inability to manage a vital, cumulative process of societal inquiry.

Apparently the social issues at the center of the play of countervailing powers are not problems to be solved but complex predicaments.[39] When such predicaments, or dilemmas, become the focus of political contention, and when professionals are enlisted in the service of the contending parties, we get polarization, pendulum swings, and stalemate. We do not get new views of social reality which take account of the perceptions of those locked in combat. We do not get public inquiry into the dilemmas which underlie our swings from one policy extreme to another. And we do not get reflective listening to the situation's "back-talk," the kind of listening which leads policy makers to criticize and restructure their views of policy problems.

In order to achieve such outcomes as these, professionals engaged in the political contention of the policy-making process would have to be capable of inquiry within an adversarial setting. They would have to be capable of advocating and acting on their own views of reality while at the same time subjecting them to reflection, of taking an adversarial stance toward their opponent's views while at the same time striving to understand them. Professionals in conflict with one another would also have to be capable of reciprocal reflection-in-action.

When societal predicaments are grasped only through institutionalized contention, where each contending party sees a piece of the reality and embodies his perception in a view which he treats as a battle-cry, then it is unlikely that a fuller and deeper understanding of the predicament will become powerful for public policy. In order for society's conversation with its situation to become reflective, individuals involved in adversarial processes must undertake reflective inquiry. The question is, are they likely to do so? Is the idea of reciprocal reflection in an adversarial setting any less utopian than the Technological Program or the radical ideal of liberation?

I have had two recent experiences that seem to me to bear on this question.

Recently I attended a conference of activists from the consumer movement. The conference was especially interesting because several generations of the movement were in attendance. The older ones had devoted their lives to the enterprise of constraining the freedom of industrial firms to merchandise products that are unsafe or inferior. The youngest had been inspired by the muckraking and organizing methods of Ralph Nader. The middle-aged had labored in the vineyards of the established consumer organizations. All groups were agreed, however, that the consumer movement had reached a turning point. Victories had been achieved but the victories had begun to seem Pyrrhic. Through advertising and public relations, industrial firms had begun to turn consumerism to their own benefit. Hard-won regulatory reforms had proved difficult or impossible to implement. The future directions of the consumer movement seemed far from clear. Toward the end of the conference, I suggested with some trepidation that the future of the movement might lie in the development of a new strategy which combined adversarial process with cooperative inquiry. The responses to this idea fell along generational lines. The oldest participants found the suggestion unthinkable: how could they cooperate with their traditional enemy? The middle-aged participants were intrigued but skeptical. The youngest asserted that the idea was a familiar one, which some of them were already pursuing. They were helping consumer products manufacturers to develop programs of product safety, reliability, and quality assurance in order to comply with the regulations which the consumer movement had helped to put in place.

Not long after this experience, I had a visit from an industrial manager who was director of product safety for a large chemical company. He wanted my help in thinking through a problem of organizational learning. In one division of his company, people had learned a way of working with federal regulators that they had found extraordinarily effective. As they developed new chemical products and gathered data on their environmental effects, they made full and immediate disclosures to the federal regulators. They had discovered that when regulators had early access to data and were able to participate in its interpretation, they were inclined to work cooperatively with the industry's representatives. Sometimes, it was true, early disclosure led to a negative regulatory judgment; but over the long run this approach had significantly reduced the delays and difficulties usually experienced in the process of gaining federal approval. Surprisingly, the policy of full and immediate disclosure seemed to have produced a climate in which regulators and industry scientists were disposed to explore and understand one another's point of view. But in other divisions of the firm, the approach to regulation was very different. Here regulators were considered as adversaries who should be fed tailored information packaged in carefully prepared cases submitted for approval. My visitor wanted help in thinking how to get the other divisions to learn what one division already knew.

These two examples do not, of course, establish the presence of a widespread interest in, much less a capacity for, cooperative inquiry within an adversarial context. At best, they constitute an "existence proof." Some professionals are interested in this process and have manifested some capacity for it. I cannot say how widespread the interest is, or how broadly distributed the capacity may be. Professionals in the field of environmental and energy policy have begun to talk and write in this vein. In Europe, proponents of a "new social contract" have argued that dilemmas of national economic policy are rooted in issues of political economy which can be effectively managed only when the traditional adversaries—government, labor, and business—work out processes of cooperative inquiry into economic policy. In some communities threatened with economic dislocation, representatives of the industrial democracy movement have instituted "search conferences" in which traditionally adversarial sectors—business, labor, and local government—have participated in long-term cooperative inquiry aimed at community development. Eric Trist's work in Jamestown, New York, is a notable case in point.[40]

There seems, then, to be some growing recognition of the need for cooperative inquiry within adversarial contexts. The idea of reflective practice leads to a vision of professionals as agents of society's reflective conversation with its situation, agents who engage in cooperative inquiry within a framework of institutionalized contention. The question remains, however, whether it is utopian, in the pejorative sense, to suppose that professionals who occupy key roles in the public policy process can learn on a broad basis to engage in reciprocal reflection-in-action.

In earlier chapters, I have offered evidence that some professional practitioners do have a capacity for reflection-in-action on their own frames and theories of action. I have also noted limits to reflection-in-action which result from the behavioral worlds and organizational learning systems that individuals are skilled at creating. I have argued that in order to broaden and deepen their capacity for reflection-in-action, professional practitioners must discover and restructure the interpersonal theories of action which they bring to their professional lives.

What kind of a question are we posing when we ask whether such a vision is merely utopian? The existence of a widespread capacity for reciprocal reflection-in-action is unlikely to be discovered by an ordinary social science which tends to detect, and treat as reality, the patterns of institutionalized contention and limited learning which individuals transcend, if at all, only on rare occasions. The extent of our capacity for reciprocal reflection-in-action can be discovered only through an action science which seeks to make what some of us do on rare occasions into a dominant pattern of practice.

Notes

Chapter 1

1. Everett Hughes, "The Study of Occupations," in Robert K. Merton, Leonard Broom and Leonard S. Cottrell, Jr., eds., *Sociology Today* (New York: Basic Books, 1959).

2. H.L. Wilensky, "The Professionalization of Everyone?", *American Journal of Sociology* 70 (September 1964): 137–158.

3. For example, Scott Throw, *One L: An Inside Account of Life in the First Year at Harvard Law School* (New York: G.P. Putnam's Sons, 1977).

4. Ivan Illich, *A Celebration of Awareness: A Call for Institutional Revolution* (Garden City, N.Y.: Doubleday, 1970).

5. See, for example, *The New Professionals*, Gross and Osterman, eds. (New York: Simon and Schuster, 1972).

6. Kenneth Lynn, Introduction to "The Professions," Fall 1963 issue of *Daedalus*, Journal of the American Academy of Arts and Sciences, p. 649.

7. Richard Hofstadter, *Anti-Intellectualism in American Life*, quoted in Jethro Lieberman, *The Tyranny of Expertise* (New York: Walker and Company, 1970), p. 1.

8. John F. Kennedy, quoted in Lieberman, *Tyranny of Expertise* p. 5.

9. R.E. Lane, "The Decline of Politics and Ideology in a Knowledgeable Society," *American Sociological Review*, 31, (October 1966).

10. Amitai Etzioni, *The Active Society* (New York: The Free Press, 1968). Daniel Bell, "Notes on the Post-Industrial Society," *The Public Interest*, 6 and 7, (Winter and Spring 1967).

11. Lane, "Decline of Politics," p. 653.

12. Daniel Bell, "Labor in the Post-Industrial Society," *Dissent*, 19, 1 (Winter 1972): 70–80.

13. Ibid.

14. Wilbert Moore, *The Professions* (New York: Russell Sage Foundation, 1970), pp. 15–16.

15. Lieberman, *Tyranny of Expertise*, p. 54.

16. Paul Freund, "The Legal Professions," *Daedalus* (Fall 1963): 696.

17. Ibid., p. 697.

18. Lynn, *Daedalus* (Fall 1963): 651.

19. Bernard Barber, "Some Problems in the Sociology of the Professions," *Daedalus* (Fall 1963): 686.

20. James Gustafson, "The Clergy in the United States," *Daedalus* (Fall, 1963): 743.

21. William Alonso, "Cities and City Planners," in *Daedalus* (Fall 1963): 838.

22. See my *Beyond the Stable State* (New York: Random House, 1971), for a discussion of these.

23. For example, Peter Marris and Martin Rein, *Dilemmas of Social Reform* (New York: Atherton Press, 1967).

24. See Osterman and Gross, *New Professionals;* Lieberman, *Tyranny of Expertise;* and *Professionalism and Social Change,* Paul Halmos, ed., *The Sociological Review Monograph* 20 University of Keele, (December 1973).

25. Arlene K. Daniels, "How Free Should Professions Be?" in Eliot Freidson, ed., *The Professions and Their Prospects* (Beverly Hills: Sage Publications, 1971), p. 56.

26. Alan Gartner, *The Preparation of Human Service Professionals* (New York: Human Sciences Press, 1976), p. 121.

27. Robert Perucci, "In the Service of Man: Radical Movements in the Professions," in Halmos, *Professionalism and Social Change,* pp. 179–194.

28. See, for example, David Halberstam, *The Best and the Brightest* (New York: Random House, 1972) and Charles R. Morris, *The Cost of Good Intentions* (New York: W.W. Norton, 1980).

29. Charles Reich, *The Law of the Planned Society,* quoted in Lieberman, *Tyranny of Expertise,* p. 268.

30. David Rutstein, *The Coming Revolution in Medicine* (Cambridge, Mass.: MIT Press, 1967).

31. For example, Marie Haug, "Deprofessionalization: An Alternate Hypothesis for the Future," and Martin Oppenheimer, "The Proletarianization of the Professions", in Halmos, *Professionalism and Social Change.*

32. Halmos, in his introduction to the volume he has edited (Halmos, 1973), observes that the "contemporary climate of opinion is radically and bitterly antiprofessional." (p. 6) Antiprofessional critics wish to "deprofessionalize the professions . . . by creating a para-professional or subprofessional constituency and endowing it with power increasingly to match the power of the fully licensed professionals." (p. 7) But he goes on to say that "the very radical denunciatory campaigns are coupled with political demands for more generously provided, and more equitably distributed, competent, and therefore presumably professional personal services." (p. 7)

33. Dr. Ephraim Friedman, Dean of the Albert Einstein School of Medicine, private communication to the author.

34. Dr. William Pownes, former Dean of the Sloan School of Management, private communication to the author.

35. Dr. Harvey Brooks, former Dean of the Harvard University School of Applied Physics, private communication to the author.

36. Harvey Brooks, "The Dilemmas of Engineering Education," *IEEE Spectrum* (February 1967): 89.

37. Ibid., p. 90.

38. The language here is borrowed from John Dewey. In his *Logic: the Theory of Inquiry*, Dewey proposed that problems are constructed from situations of indeterminacy, problematic situations, that we apprehend through the experience of worry, trouble, or doubt.

39. Russell Ackoff, "The Future of Operational Research is Past," *Journal of Operational Research Society*, 30, 2 (Pergamon Press, Ltd., 1979): 93–104.

40. Ibid., pp. 90–100.

41. Ibid., p. 94.

42. Ibid., p. 100.

43. Erik Erikson, "The Nature of Clinical Evidence," in Daniel Learner, ed., *Evidence and Inference* (Glencoe, Ill.: The Free Press of Glencoe, 1958), p. 72.

44. Dr. Ephraim Friedman, private communication to the author.

45. The case of the John Hancock Building, in Boston, Massachusetts, is an interesting example. When the glass windows in this towering and beautiful skyscraper began to shatter, it was impossible for skilled engineers to arrive at a confident analysis of the problem. In the building itself, the phenomena were too complex to analyze; and experiments that might clarify matters were either prohibitively expensive or dangerous. In the wind tunnel, models were developed and experiments were performed, but there was little confidence that the wind tunnel was a good representation of the actual conditions in the building. In the end, all windows were fitted with new, heavier, tougher, and more expensive panes of glass. Every once in a while, one still shatters.

46. Harvey Brooks, private communication to the author.

47. Leston Havens, *Approaches to the Mind* (Boston: Little, Brown, Inc., 1973).

48. Nathan Glazer, "The Schools of the Minor Professions," *Minerva*, (1974).

Chapter 2

1. A.M. Carr-Saunders, *Professions: Their Organization and Place in Society* (Oxford: The Clarendon Press, 1928). Quoted in Vollmer and Mills, eds., *Professionalization* (Englewood Cliffs, N.J.: Prentice-Hall, 1966), p. 3.

2. Wilbert Moore, *The Professions* (New York: Russell Sage Foundation, 1970), p. 56.

3. Ibid.

4. Ibid., p. 141.

5. Jethro Lieberman, *Tyranny of Expertise* (New York: Walker and Company), p. 55.

6. Nathan Glazer, "Schools of the Minor Professions," *Minerva*, (1974): 346.

7. Ibid., p. 363.

8. Ibid., p. 348.

9. Ibid., p. 349.

10. Moore, *The Professions*, p. 56.

11. Edgar Schein, *Professional Education* (New York: McGraw-Hill, 1973), p. 43.

12. Ibid., p. 39.

13. William Goode, "The Librarian: From Occupation to Profession," reprinted in Vollmer and Mills, *Professionalization*, p. 39.

14. Ibid.

15. Ibid.

16. Ernest Greenwood, "Attributes of a Profession," reprinted in Vollmer and Mills, *Professionalization*, p. 11.

17. Ibid., p. 19.

18. Ibid., p. 12.

19. Harvey, Brooks, "Dilemmas of Engineering Education," *IEEE Spectrum* (February 1967): 89.

20. Schein, *Professional Education*, p. 44.

21. Barry Thorne, "Professional Education in Medicine," in *Education for the Professions of Medicine, Law, Theology and Social Welfare* (New York: McGraw-Hill, 1973), p. 30.

22. Ibid., p. 31.

23. Ibid.

24. Alan Gartner, *Preparation of Human Service Professionals* (New York: Human Sciences Press, 1976), p. 80.

25. Ibid., p. 93.

26. Derek Bok, "The President's Report," reprinted in *The Harvard Magazine*, (May–June 1979): 83.

27. Ibid., p. 84.

28. Ibid.

29. From private conversations with three Harvard Business School faculty members.

30. See, for example, Richard J. Bernstein, *The Restructuring of Social and Political Theory* (New York: Harcourt Brace Jovanovich, 1976).

31. I first used this term in *Technology and Change* (New York: Delacorte Press, 1966).

32. Auguste Comte, quoted in Jurgan Habermas, *Knowledge and Human Interests* (Boston: Beacon Press, 1968), p. 77.

33. Of course, the problem of the lack of agreement about ends has engaged the attention of many of the protagonists of the positivist epistemology of practice. Approaches to this problem have ranged from the search for an ultimate end, to which all others could be subordinated; to a "universal solvent" for ends, as in the utility functions of the welfare economists; to the "piecemeal social engineering" proposed by Karl Popper. For a discussion of these, their defects and merits, see Charles Frankel, "The Relation of Theory to Practice: Some Standard Views," in *Social Theory and Social Intervention,* Frankel et al., eds. (Cleveland: Case Western Reserve University Press, 1968).

34. Edward Shils, "The Order of Learning in the United States from 1865 to 1920: the Ascendancy of the Universities," *Minerva*, XVI, 2 (Summer 1978): 171.

35. Ibid., p. 173.

36. Thorsten Veblen, *The Higher Learning in America,* reprint of 1918 edition, (New York, Hill and Wang, 1962).

37. Ibid., p. 15.

38. Ibid., p. 23.

39. Bernard Barber, in "Some Problems in the Sociology of the Professions," *Daedalus* (Fall, 1963): 674.

40. Everett Hughes, "Higher Education and the Professions," in *Content and Context: Essays on College Education,* Carl Kaysen, ed. (New York: McGraw-Hill, 1973), p. 660.

41. The term is taken from Clifford Geertz, "Thick Description: Toward an Interpretive Theory of Culture," in Clifford Geertz, *The Interpretation of Cultures* (New York: Basic Books, 1973).

42. Schein, *Professional Education*, p. 44.

43. Ibid., p. 45.

44. Herbert Simon, *The Sciences of the Artificial* (Cambridge, Mass.: MIT Press, 1972), p. 55.

45. Ibid., p. 56.

46. Ibid.

47. Ibid., p. 57.

48. Ibid., p. 61.

49. Bernstein, *Restructuring*, p. 207.

50. Gilbert Ryle, "On Knowing How and Knowing That," in *The Concept of Mind* (London: Hutcheson, 1949), p. 32.

51. Andrew Harrison, *Making and Thinking* (Indianapolis: Hackett, 1978).

52. Chester Barnard, in *The Functions of the Executive* (Cambridge, Mass.: Harvard University Press, 1968, first published 1938), p. 302.

53. Ibid., p. 305.

54. Ibid., p. 302.

55. Ibid., p. 306.

56. Michael Polanyi, *The Tacit Dimension*, (New York: Doubleday and Co., 1967), p. 4.

57. Ibid., p. 12.

58. Chris Alexander, *Notes Toward a Synthesis of Form*, (Cambridge, Mass.: Harvard University Press, 1968).

59. Ibid., p. 53.

60. Ibid., p. 55.

61. Geoffrey Vickers, unpublished memorandum, MIT, 1978.

62. The whole of contemporary linguistics and psycholinguistics is relevant here—for example, the work of Chomsky, Halle, and Sinclair.

63. Alfred Schutz, *Collected Papers* (The Hague: Nijhoff, 1962).

64. Ray L. Birdwhistell, *Kinesics and Context* (Philadelphia: University of Pennsylvania Press, 1970).

65. Jonathan Evan Maslow, "Grooving on a Baseball Afternoon," in *Mainliner* (May 1981): 34.

66. Barbel Inhelder and Annette Karmiloff-Smith, "If you want to get ahead, get a theory," *Cognition* 3,3: 195–212.

67. Ibid., p. 195.

68. Ibid., p. 202.

69. Ibid., p. 203.

70. Ibid.

71. Ibid., p. 205.

72. Ibid.

73. Ibid.

74. Ibid., p. 203.

75. Ibid., p. 199.

76. Leo Tolstoy, "On Teaching the Rudiments," in *Tolstoy on Education*, Leo Wiener, ed. (Chicago and London: University of Chicago Press, 1967).

77. The staff of the Teachers' Project consisted of Jeanne Bamberger, Eleanor Duckworth, and Margaret Lampert. My description of the incident of "giving the child reason" is adapted from a project memorandum by Lampert.

Chapter 3

1. The origins of this case study are in a review of architectural education in which I participated during the late 1970s. The study, supported by the Andrew Mellon Foundation, was directed by Dean William Porter of the MIT School of Architecture and Planning and Dean Maurice Kilbridge of the Harvard Graduate School of Design. Several participant/observation studies were conducted in design studios at universities at several locations in the United States. It is from one of these that I have drawn the protocol which follows. It was recorded by Roger Simmonds, then a graduate student of mine. I am grateful to Simmonds for his help in this, as well as to William Porter, Julian Beinart, Imre Halasz, and Florian Buttlar, with all of whom I had illuminating conversations. Dean Porter, especially, helped to initiate me into the world of architectural thinking.

2. Quist and Petra are fictitious names which Simmonds assigned to the participants in the design review.

3. The term "language game" is taken from Ludwig Wittgenstein's *Philosophical Investigations* (New York: Macmillan Company, 1953).

4. Jeanne Bamberger and I invented this notion, and used it in our "The Figural-Formal Transaction", Division for Study in Research in Education, Working Paper, MIT, 1978.

Chapter 4

1. Norman Zinberg, "Psychiatry—A Professional Dilemma", in *Daedalus* (Fall, 1963).

2. Leston Havens, *Approaches to the Mind*, (Boston: Little, Brown, Inc., 1973).

3. The protocol discussed in this section was first recorded by two student researchers, in the course of a seminar on professional education which I conducted in 1978. The two students—Bari Stauber and Mike Corbett—worked together with the psychiatric resident to collect the protocol and the interview material. Each of them wrote a term paper on the protocol. Although my analysis departs from theirs in many respects, I am indebted to them for the protocol and for their ideas.

4. Erik Erikson, "The Nature of Clinical Evidence," in Daniel Lerner, ed., *Evidence and Inference* (Glencoe, Ill.: The Free Press of Glencoe, 1958), p. 74.

5. Ibid., p. 75.

6. Ibid., p. 76.

7. Ibid., p. 89.

8. Ibid., p. 83.

9. Ibid., p. 87.

10. Ibid., p. 79.

11. Ibid., p. 80.

12. This term, first introduced by David Bakan, has been developed in *Theory in Practice*, by Chris Argyris and Donald A. Schön (San Francisco: Jossey-Bass, 1974).

Notes

Chapter 5

1. I am thinking here of Wittgenstein's use of "seeing-as" (see Ludwig Wittgenstein, *Philosophical Investigations* (New York: Macmillan Company, 1953). In reference to examples such as "seeing the figure as a box" and "seeing the duck/rabbit picture as a rabbit," Wittgenstein points out that seeing-as is at once, and ambiguously, a process of seeing and thinking.

2. Thomas Kuhn, "Second Thoughts on Paradigms," in *The Essential Tension* (Chicago and London: University of Chicago Press, 1977).

3. Ibid., p. 307.

4. This account of the logic of theory-testing experiment follows the lines set forth by Karl Popper in his *Conjectures and Refutations* (New York: Harper & Row, 1968).

5. I have drawn this example from an article by J. C. Jones, "Feeding Behavior of Mosquitoes," *Scientific American* 238 (June, 1978): 138–40.

6. Popper, *Conjectures*.

7. In *Experience and Reflection* (Philadelphia: University of Pennsylvania Press, 1959), E.A. Singer has propounded the thesis that scientific hypothesis ought to be understood "in the imperative mood."

8. See Elton Mayo, *The Human Problems of an Industrial Civilization* (New York: MacMillan, 1933).

9. The idea of the relation of knower to known as a "transaction" derives from the work of John Dewey. See A. F. Bentley and John Dewey, *Knowing the Known* (Boston: Beacon Press, 1949).

10. The phrase is from Geoffrey Vickers, unpublished memorandum, MIT, 1978.

11. Lisa Peattie introduced me to this term.

12. See Michael Polanyi, *Personal Knowledge* (Chicago: University of Chicago Press, 1958).

Chapter 6

1. Nathan Glazer, "Schools of the Minor Professions," *Minerva*, (1974): 348.

2. See William Schwartz and Stephen Pauker et. al., "Toward the Simulation of Clinical Cognition: Taking a Present Illness by Computer," *The American Journal of Medicine*, 60 (June 1976): 991–996.

3. Harvey Brooks, "Dilemmas of Engineering Education," in *IEEE Spectrum*, (February 1967).

4. W.I.B. Beveridge, *The Art of Scientific Investigation* (New York: Random House, 1957).

5. Richard Nelson, "The Link Between Science and Invention: The Case of the Transistor," in *The Rate and Direction of Inventive Activity Economic and Social Factors*, Universities-National Bureau Conference Series, No.13 (Princeton: Princeton University Press, 1962).

6. Ibid., p. 557.

7. Ibid., p. 562.

8. Ibid.

9. Ibid., p. 563.

10. Ibid., p. 567.

11. Thomas Kuhn, "Second Thoughts on Paradigms," *The Essential Tension* (Chicago and London: University of Chicago Press, 1977), p. 305.

12. Ibid.

13. Robert Oppenheimer, "Analogy in Science," *American Psychologist*, 11, 3 (1956): 127–135.

14. Kuhn, "Second Thoughts," p. 306 ("both an appropriate formalism and a new way of attaching its consequences to nature").

15. See my "Generative Metaphors in the Setting of Social Policy Problems," in *Metaphor and Thought*, Andrew Ortony, ed., (Cambridge: Cambridge University Press, 1979).

16. Ibid. The example of the paintbrush, originally described in my *Displacement of Concepts* (New York: Humanities Press, 1963), originally occurred during my tenure at Arthur D. Little, Inc., in Cambridge, Mass.

17. Dean Wilson, unpublished project report, 1977.

18. From a report of the Community Systems Foundation, Cali, Colombia, 1978.

Chapter 7

1. This summary of the history of the city planning profession is taken in large part from Mel Scott, *American City Planning Since 1890* (Berkeley, Cal.: University of California Press, 1969).

2. See, for example, Herbert Gans, *Urban Villagers* (New York: The Free Press, 1965).

3. The case study presented here is derived from videotapes and interview notes originally collected by William Ronco, then a graduate student in the Department of Urban Studies and Planning at MIT. I am grateful to Dr. Ronco for his help in generating this material and for his contributions to earlier versions of its analysis. The material presented in this article is substantially different from earlier treatments of it, however, and the responsibility for it is entirely my own.

4. See Chris Argyris and Donald A. Schön, *Theory in Practice* (San Francisco: Jossey-Bass, 1974).

Chapter 8

1. Frederick Taylor, *Principles of Scientific Management* (New York: Norton and Co., 1967, first published 1911).

2. Henry Mintzberg, *The Nature of Managerial Work* (New York: Harper & Row, 1973).

Notes

Chapter 9

1. Thomas Kuhn has begun to explore the issue of translation across appreciative systems of frames—he discusses it in terms of the predicament of translation across scientific paradigms—in his "Postscript" to *The Structure of Scientific Revolutions*, (Chicago: University of Chicago Press, 1962), Kuhn distinguishes between the "persuasion" by which parties to a dispute may arrive at agreement, within a shared paradigm, and the "conversion" by which scientists sometimes shift from one paradigm to another.

2. Hannah Arendt, *Thinking*, Volume I of *The Life of the Mind* (New York: Harcourt Brace Jovanovich, 1971).

3. Reported by George Ball and Charles Bohlen, in David Halberstam, *The Best and the Brightest* (New York: Random House, 1972).

Chapter 10

1. Ivan Illich, *Deschooling Society*, Vol. XLIV of the World Perspectives series, Perennial Library, (New York: Harper & Row, 1970). But for a more scholarly version of a similar argument, see Magali Larson, "Professionalism: Rise and Fall," in *International Journal of Health Services*, 9, 4 1979.

2. A view summarized in Paul Halmos, *Professionalism and Social Change*, The *Sociological Review* Monograph 20, University of Keele, December 1973.

3. See, for example, John Van Maanan, "Observations on the Making of Policemen," *Human Organization*, 32, 4 (Winter 1973): 407–418.

4. Marie Haug, "Deprofessionalization: An Alternate Hypothesis for the Future," in Halmos, *Professionalism and Social Change*.

5. Everett Hughes, "The Professions in Society," in *The Canadian Journal of Economics and Political Science*, 26, 1 (February 1960): 54–61.

6. This term, first introduced by Samuel Taylor Coleridge to describe the stance appropriate to the reading of poetry, has become commonplace in contemporary discussions of education.

7. Chris Argyris and Donald A. Schön, *Organizational Learning* (Reading, Mass.: Addison-Wesley, 1978).

8. See Martin Rein and Sheldon White, "Knowledge for Practice," DSRE Working Paper, MIT, Cambridge, Mass., October 1980.

9. Leston Havens, *Approaches to the Mind* (Boston: Little, Brown, 1973).

10. See Nathan Glazer, "Schools of the Minor Professions," *Minerva*, (1974).

11. Karl Mannheim, *Ideology and Utopia* (New York: Harvest Books, 1936).

12. See, for example, David Bloor, *Knowledge and Social Imagery*, (London: Routledge & Kegan Paul, 1976).

13. Havens, *Approaches to the Mind*.

14. Leston Havens, *Participant Observation* (New York: Jason Aronson, Inc., 1976).

15. See, for example, Gary Bellow, *The Lawyering Process* (Mineola, N.Y.: The Foundation Press, 1978).

16. Chris Argyris, *The Inner Contradictions of Rigorous Research* (New York: Academic Press, 1980).

17. William Torbert, *Creating a Community of Inquiry* (New York: John Wiley & Sons, 1976).

18. Britton Harris argues that formal optimization models are best treated as metaphors for planning decisions, in *A Paradigm for Planning*, forthcoming.

19. Chris Argyris and Donald A. Schön, "The Role of Failure in Double-Loop Learning," unpublished memorandum, 1979.

20. Israel Scheffler, "The Cognitive Emotions," *The Teachers College Record*, 79, 2 (Dec. 1977): 171–186.

21. Malcolm Parlett, "Reflecting on Practice," manuscript, London, England, 1981.

22. See Barry Jentz and Joan Wofford, *Leadership and Learning* (New York: McGraw-Hill, 1979).

23. Kevin Lynch has made this point in his recent proposals for an agenda of research in urban design.

24. Max Weber, "Bureaucracy," in Oscar Grusky and George A. Miller, eds., *The Sociology of Organizations* (New York: Free Press, 1940), p. 7.

25. Ibid., p. 13.

26. This view, which has shaped most thinking about democracy in contemporary political science, is presented, for example, in Seymour Lipset, Martin Trow, and James Coleman, *Union Democracy*, (New York: Doubleday Anchor, 1956).

27. Israel Scheffler, *The Language of Education* (Springfield, Ill.: C.C Thomas, 1960).

28. An example of such an educational technology is described at length in Seymour Papert, *Mindstorms: Children, Computers and Powerful Ideas* (New York: Basic Books, 1981).

29. See Chris Argyris, "Alternative Schools: A Behavioral Analysis," *Teachers College Record*, 75, 4 (May 1974): 424–452.

30. See, for example, Samuel Bowles and Herbert Gintis, *Schooling in Capitalist America* (New York: Basic Books, 1976).

31. This view of public policy formation as a process of rational choice has been set forth, for example, in Richard Zeckhauser and Edith Stokey, *A Primer for Policy Analysis*, (New York: Norton, 1978).

32. See, for example, Jeffrey Pressman and Aaron Wildavsky, *Implementation* (Berkeley: University of California Press, 1979).

33. Lipset et al, *Union Democracy*.

34. Milovan Djilas, *The New Class* (New York: Holt, Rinehart & Winston, 1974).

35. See Bernard Frieden, *The Environmental Hustle*, (Cambridge, Mass.: MIT Press, 1980).

36. There have been many studies in the 1970s which have observed and criticized the ineffectiveness of the regulatory mechanisms set up in response to the advocacy and protest movements of the 1960s. See, for example, Lawrence Bacow, *Bargaining for Job Safety and Health*, (Cambridge, Mass.: MIT Press, 1980).

37. Mario Cuomo uses this phrase, and illustrates its application, in his *Forest Hills Diary* (New York: Random House, 1974).

38. Martin Rein and I have argued this point in "Problem-Setting in Policy Research," in Carol Weiss, ed., *Using Social Research in Public Policy Making* (Lexington, Mass: D.C. Heath, 1977).

39. See, for example, Peter Marris and Martin Rein, *Dilemmas of Social Reform* (New York: Atherton Press, 1967).

40. Eric Trist, "New Directions of Hope," *Regional Studies*, 13 (Elmsford, N.Y.: Pergamon Press, 1979): 439–451.

Index

Index

doctor/patient relationship, 293, 294, 295–96

doing-as, 139, 140, 166

eclecticism, systematic, 313–14

education, 17, 23, 38–39; *see also* professional education

Ekroad, Kip, 196, 199, 200–201

electoral process, 343–44

Eliot, Charles William, 29

ends, *see* means/ends

engineering, 14, 23, 42, 308, 312, 325; as applied science, 171–72; design professions in, 76–77; as model of instrumental practice, 34, 38–39; as model of technical practice, 31; problem setting and implementation in, 187–88; as science-based profession, 168, 169

engineering design: art of, 171–76; development of transistor example, 177–82; gun-metal color process example, 172–76, 182, 268, 271, 273

Enlightenment (the), 31

Erikson, Erik, 16, 108, 116–18, 136

error, uncorrectable, 304–6

exemplar(s), 138–39, 183–84, 269, 315–17

experiment(s), 177; bounds of, in practice situation, 151–52; controlled, 143–44, 149–50, 151, 165; explanatory, 145; move-testing, 146 (*see also* move[s]); reflection-in-action in, 322–23; in Technical Rationality model, 141–45; in theory building, 181; *see also* on-the-spot experiment

expertise, 326, 327, 337; move from, to reflective practice, 329–36, 345–54; mystique of, 288–89, 304; professional knowledge as, 339; in reflective practice, 295–96, 298; required by counterprofessionals, 341; supplied by professionals in policy-making, 339–40, 342, 349; *see also* knowledge

exploration, 153, 156, 166

failure, fear of, 321–22

Flexner Report, 28

forestry, 168

form (norm), 97

frame analysis, 309–15, 323

frame experiment(s) (frame-testing), 40, 41–42, 63, 165–66, 269, 309; *see also* on-the-spot experiment

Fried, Mark, 208

Galileo, 183

Gans, Herbert, 208

Glazer, Nathan, 168, 172; major/minor professions, 23, 26–27, 45, 46, 47–48, 204, 293–94, 307, 308, 325

Great Society program, 348

Gustafson, James, 8

Harris, Britt, 319–20

Harrison, Andrew, 51

Havens, Leston, 17, 106, 108, 310; *Approaches to the Mind*, 313–14; *Participant Observation*, 314

Harvard University: Law School, 316; School of Business Administration, 29, 316

Hawthorne Effect, 149, 322

Higher Learning in America, The (Veblen), 35

Hobbes, Thomas, 31

Hofstadter, Richard, 6

Hughes, Everett, 4

Huyghens, Christian, 183

hypotheses, new, 181–82, 269

hypothesis testing, 146–47, 157, 166, 177, 269; in architecture and psychotherapeutic examples, 149–56; confirmed/disconfirmed, 146–47, 150, 166, 181; leads to invention, 181–82

"If you want to get ahead, get a theory" (Inhelder and Karmiloff-Smith), 56–59

Illich, Ivan, 5, 288

industrial engineers, 77

industrialism, 32

Index

Massachusetts Institute of Technology, Teacher Project, 66–68, 299, 321, 329, 334, 336

means/ends, 40, 41; in Positivism, 33–34, 165; in problem setting, 46, 47; in reflection-in-action, 68

media, 270–72, 275; of architecture, 128, 157–59; of psychotherapy, 128; repertoire of, 158–59

mediation, professional, 344

Medicaid, 10

Medicare, 10

medicine, 7, 13, 14, 31, 41–42, 312, 325, 340; exemplars in, 316–17; as model of instrumental practice, 34; as model of science-based technology, 38–39; prototype of profession, 23, 28; research/-practice status in, 308; role frames, 311; as science-based profession, 168–70

Mental Health Act of 1964, 107

metaphor(s), 138, 279; generative, 184–87, 269, 319

meteorology, 168

Method of Agreement (experimental method), 142, 143

Method of Concomitant Variations (experimental method), 142–44

Method of Difference (experimental method), 142–43

Mies van der Rohe, Ludwig, 78

Mill, John Stuart, 142, 143

ministry, see divinity (profession)

Mintzberg, Henry, 240

modelling, 43–44, 186–87, 203; example, 272

Moore, Wilbert, 22, 24

move(s), 131, 151, 152, 164, 166, 269; affirmed, negated, 146, 181; as experiments, 157, 158, 160; and termination of reflection, 280

move testing, 146, 153–55, 177

mystery/mastery, 126, 227, 229, 230, 233, 262, 304, 305

Nader, Ralph, 351

National Research and Development Corporation, 37

Nelson, Richard, 177, 179, 180

New York City, 12

norms: in managing, 266; in professional/client relationship, 292, 294, 303

Notes Toward a Synthesis of Form (Alexander), 52–53

nursing, 168

objectivity (norm), 133, 166, 273, 312; in public schools, 330–31, 335; violated in hypothesis testing, 149–50

"On Teaching the Rudiments" (Tolstoy), 65–66

on-the-spot experiment, 63, 66, 166, 308–9, 320; in architecture and psychotherapy examples, 94, 122, 124–25, 131, 132; and constancy of appreciative system, 272; evaluation of, 133–36; in managing, 265, 266; rigor in, 133, 141–56; in teaching, 335

operations research, 16, 37, 43, 238

Oppenheimer, Robert: "The Role of Analogies in Science," 183

optometry, 168

organizations, formal, 327–29; interpretation of troubles in (example), 246–50; restructuring of principles and values in, 335–36, 338; school as, 331–32; stability and predictability in, 327–29, 332, 338; see also learning systems, organizational

overlearning, 61

overload, 7–8

Papert, Seymour, 279

Parlett, Malcolm, 323

Participant Observation (Havens), 314

philosophy of science, 48–49

Piven, Francis, 208

planning, 38–39, 268, 273, 311, 312; evolving context of, 204–10

pluralism, professional, 17, 18–19, 41–42, 129–30, 273, 310–11; in architecture, 77–78, 102, 272–73, 310–11; discussion of, 312–15; dilemmas inherent in, 311–12; in management, 236–41, 243, 266; in planning, 204–5; in psychotherapy, 106–8

Index

autonomy, and license, 11–12, 13, 288, 289–90, 291, 296–97, 298, 299, 340, 345–46; conflicts of values, goals, interests, 17–19; loss of faith in, 4–5, 9, 11–13, 39; in public policymaking, 339–42, 349, 350; self-criticism by, 12–13, 18; self-serving, 340; as technical experts, 288

professional schools, 31, 35–36, 46–47, 307–8, 324, 325; curriculum of, 27–30; see also architecture, schools of (pluralism)

professions: critique of, 5, 12–13, 14, 287–88, 290, 293, 294, 296–97, 298, 312, 340–42, 344–46, 349, 356n32; defined, 22; demystification of, 288, 289, 290, 340–41, 342, 344–45; essential to society, 3–7, 8, 13, 39 (see also professional knowledge); implications of reflection-in-action for, 287–354; institutional context of, 274–75, 343–46; major/minor, 23, 24–26, 42, 46, 48, 204, 293–94, 307–8, 325; patterns and limits of reflection-in-action across, 267–83; place of, in society, 338–54; scholarly literature on, 22; science-based, 168–203

psychiatry, 105–6, 312; schools of, 106–7

psychoanalysis, 106, 107

psychotherapy, 128–30, 268; example, 105–27, 273, 311; multiple schools of, 17, 310, 313, 314; storytelling as virtual world in, 160–62

public interest: planning and, 206–7, 208

public policy, 39; demystification of professions in, 341–42; political contention in, 342, 348–51, 353, 354; professionalization of, 339–42, 345–54; in reflective societal conversation, 347–48; Technical Rationality model of, 339–40

public testing of private assumptions, 328; see also town planning, example

reality: construction of, 310, 311; descriptions of, 346–47, 349; views of, 312–13, 348, 350

reflecting-in-practice, 59–69

reflection: interferes with action, 275,

276–81; on knowing-in-practice, 61, 62; leading to experiment and theory, 181; on reflection-in-action, 126, 127, 243, 263–64, 282; seeing-as, 182–87

reflection-in-action, 49–69, 141; architecture design example, 77–104; cause and consequence of surprise, 328; compared with Technical Rationality (model), 164–67; as ethic for inquiry, 164; examples of, 63–65; implications of, as epistemology of practice, 287–354; limits to, 267, 275–83, 353; limits to, in management, 242, 244, 254–55, 264–66; limits to, in town planning example, 210, 228–34; in managing, 241–44, 263–66; within organizational learning system, 236–66; patterns and limits of, across professions, 267–83; and professional/client relationship, 295–307; in psychotherapeutic example, 105–27; reciprocal, 304–5, 306, 350–51, 353–57; relation with technical problem solving: engineering design example, 171–76; research on process of, 309, 320–23; stance toward inquiry in, 163–64; structure of, 128–67; underlying process of, 102–4; when needed, 153, 156

reflection-on-action, 276, 277, 278

reflective conversation with situation, 151, 163, 164, 165, 167, 170; across professions, 268, 272, 273, 274, 280, 281; in architecture and psychotherapy examples, 130–32, 135, 136, 141, 148; engineering design as, 76–104, 172, 175–76, 188; in management, 242, 245, 265; in professional/client relationship, 295–307; in psychotherapy example, 124–27; in public policy, 346–47, 348, 349, 350, 353; reflective practice takes form of, 295

reflective practice, 295–307, 353; as alternative to traditional epistemology of practice, 345–54; and bureaucratization of professional work, 337–38; institutions for, 326–38; in science-based professions, 168–203; see also reflection

regional planning, 76

Reich, Charles, 12

repertoire(s): of cases, maxims, materials:

Index